D1708331

THE CARE AND EDUCATION OF AMERICA'S YOUNG CHILDREN: OBSTACLES AND OPPORTUNITIES

THE CARE AND EDUCATION OF AMERICA'S YOUNG CHILDREN: OBSTACLES AND OPPORTUNITIES

Ninetieth Yearbook of the
National Society for the Study of Education

PART I

Edited by
SHARON LYNN KAGAN

Editor for the Society
KENNETH J. REHAGE

Distributed by THE UNIVERSITY OF CHICAGO PRESS ● CHICAGO, ILLINOIS

The National Society for the Study of Education

Founded in 1901 as successor to the National Herbart Society, the National Society for the Study of Education has provided a means by which the results of serious study of educational issues could become a basis for informed discussion of those issues. The Society's two-volume yearbooks, now in their ninetieth year of publication, reflect the thoughtful attention given to a wide range of educational problems during those years. In 1971 the Society inaugurated a series of substantial publications on Contemporary Educational Issues to supplement the yearbooks. Each year the Society's publications contain contributions to the literature of education from more than a hundred scholars and practitioners who are doing significant work in their respective fields.

An elected Board of Directors selects the subjects with which volumes in the yearbook series are to deal and appoints committees to oversee the preparation of manuscripts. A special committee created by the Board performs similar functions for the series on Contemporary Educational Issues.

The Society's publications are distributed each year without charge to members in the United States, Canada, and elsewhere throughout the world. The Society welcomes as members all individuals who desire to receive its publications. Information about current dues may be found in the back pages of this volume.

This volume, *The Care and Education of America's Young Children: Obstacles and Opportunities*, is Part I of the Ninetieth Yearbook of the Society. Part II, which is published at the same time, is entitled *Evaluation and Education: At Quarter Century*.

A listing of the Society's publications still available for purchase may be found in the back pages of this volume.

Library of Congress Catalog Number: 90-063417
ISSN: 0077-5762

Published 1991 by
THE NATIONAL SOCIETY FOR THE STUDY OF EDUCATION

5835 Kimbark Avenue, Chicago, Illinois 60637
© 1991 by the National Society for the Study of Education

First Printing, 5,000 Copies

Printed in the United States of America

Contributors to the Yearbook

Editor, SHARON LYNN KAGAN, Associate Director, Bush Center in Child Development and Social Policy, Yale University

BARBARA BOWMAN, Director of Graduate Studies, Erikson Institute, Chicago

BETTYE CALDWELL, Donaghey Distinguished Professor of Education, Center for Research on Teaching and Learning, University of Arkansas, Little Rock

DAVID ELKIND, Professor of Child Study, Lincoln Filene Center for Citizenship, Tufts University

LILY WONG FILLMORE, Associate Professor of Education, University of California, Berkeley

ELLEN GALINSKY, Co-director, Families and Work Institute, New York City

W. NORTON GRUBB, Professor of Education, University of California, Berkeley

ASA G. HILLIARD III, Fuller E. Callaway Professor of Urban Education, Georgia State University

LILLIAN KATZ, Director, ERIC Clearinghouse on Elementary and Early Childhood Education, University of Illinois at Champaign-Urbana

GWEN MORGAN, Senior Policy Consultant, Work/Family Directions, Inc. and Academic Director, Centers for Child Care Policy and Training, Wheelock College

DOUGLAS R. POWELL, Professor of Early Childhood Education, Purdue University

BERNARD SPODEK, Professor of Early Childhood Education, University of Illinois at Champaign-Urbana

EDWARD ZIGLER, Sterling Professor of Psychology and Director, Bush Center in Child Development and Social Policy, Yale University

Acknowledgment

The National Society for the Study of Education is deeply appreciative of the work of the contributors to this timely volume. Their analyses of the challenges and opportunities confronting all who are concerned about the early care and education of young children provide perspectives that will help the general reader as well as the specialist think critically about this important area of education.

The Society is especially grateful to the editor, Sharon Lynn Kagan, for the wisdom she displayed in planning the volume, for the time and effort she devoted to working with contributors, and for her competent assistance at every stage in the long process of bringing the book to completion.

Editor's Preface

This Ninetieth Yearbook of the National Society for the Study of Education marks the sixth time the Society has devoted a landmark yearbook to issues related to early childhood education. Such emphasis simultaneously reveals the commitment of the Society to the early years and the tenacity of the issues surrounding this domain of education. A cursory review of the contents of the Society's past early childhood volumes affirms the presence of certain pedagogical themes: discerning the relationship between child development theory and educational practice; confirming the appropriate content and method of teacher preparation; defining early childhood education comprehensively and holistically; and using research to improve pedagogy. These fundamental issues transcend time and place, bespeaking a generational continuity of enduring challenges that confront the field.

While wrestling with similar philosophical and pedagogical issues, the volumes vary considerably in tone and intent. Some were clearly written to spark action. For example, the Sixth Yearbook (1907), while containing its fair share of philosophy and pedagogy, was published with the hope of stirring change. In exposing the "bald" truth regarding the relation of kindergarten education to the first years of school education, the volume was optimistically offered as a "contribution to the solution of one of the most urgent problems in American education." Through it, kindergarten and primary teachers and supervisors would renew thought and study and thus "become better able to co-operate intelligently and effectively in their great work." Others, such as the Twenty-eighth Yearbook (1929), were written to chronicle a "new and different conception of the educational significance of the first half-dozen years of life." And still others, like the Seventy-first (1972), sought to reflect upon necessary changes mandated by growth in knowledge and recognition of past mistakes.

In addition to implicit differences in intent, the volumes vary because of their explicit attention to changes in context. Each reflects the sociopolitical ethos of its time, and, in doing so, firmly establishes early childhood education as a social and educational enterprise. For example, N. Searle Light, writing in the preface to the Forty-sixth Yearbook (1947), suggests that early childhood endured the "tests of depression and war." Advocating social adequacy and individual competence and deeming choice the essential prerequisite for responsibility and freedom, Light saw society's new needs as "singularly identical with the ends toward which early childhood education has been slowly moving." No less optimistic about the value of early childhood, but tempered by the events of their era, authors of the Seventy-first Yearbook bravely addressed extant sociopolitical challenges. Sociolinguistic and cultural differences were explored, as was the expanding role of the media and other institutions. In retrospect, much like our own images observed in mirrors over time, the field of early childhood—reflected through NSSE volumes—has been a beacon of both continuity and change.

Those who find comfort in this pattern will, hopefully, not be disappointed by this volume. It, too, addresses continuity and change. Like its predecessors, the Ninetieth Yearbook discusses many of the persistent issues of the field, but it does so within the context of dramatic changes that have characterized the field in the late 1980s and early 1990s.

Predicated on research popularized during the 1980s that attested to the benefits of high-quality early intervention for low-income children and dramatic increases in the paid labor force participation of mothers, child care and early education crescendoed to national prominence in the late 1980s and early 1990s. Long regarded as an issue of the poor or working poor, child care became important to new constituencies, including corporate America, media, and policymakers. Concerned about recruiting and maintaining an adequate employee pool presently, corporations instituted family-related policies and services, including care and family support. Moreover, corporate America, concerned about global competition and the diminished competence of its present and future workforce, invested in education with growing emphasis on the early years.

Such concern did not escape policymakers' attention. Inundated by media and school accounts of escalating high school drop-out, teen pregnancy, and welfare dependence rates, policymakers began to listen. Motivated by the concerns of parents, professionals, unions, and corporate America, policymakers at the local, state, and federal levels enacted record numbers of early intervention programs. The 101st Congress closed with, among other major accomplishments, increases in Head Start and a momentous Child Care and Development Block Grant.

The backdrop of events that led to such dramatic policy initiatives also precipitated difficult challenges for the field. Though armed with a new definition of quality that transcended child care and early education, the field was also besieged by challenges that accompanied the new attention. Never known for its internal cohesion, child care and early education experienced new acrimony as burgeoning new programs competed for space, staff, and children. The call for more child care was often equated with appeals for early schooling, signaling a national debate regarding the structure and governance of early education. While new data affirmed the benefits and costs of early intervention, practitioners were forced to operate programs with considerably fewer dollars than those allocated for exemplary efforts, thereby compromising quality for the children who needed and benefited most from early intervention. Funding shortages led to rapid staff turnover in most sectors of the industry, exacerbating the difficulty of recruiting qualified personnel to an already "low-status" field. Moreover, while acutely aware of the correlates of quality early education and the negative consequences of cognitive pressure, early childhood programs, irrespective of setting, were becoming more academic and pressured.

Never before has the profession had such opportunity, yet been so divided on how to capitalize on the attention and support accorded it. Never has the nation been so torn in coming to grips with its definitions of social responsibility versus private rights. Never have partnerships and collaboration been more necessary and contention more prevalent. Never have issues, lying dormant for so long, demanded such fresh assessment and re-evaluation. This is the context of and the rationale for the Ninetieth NSSE Yearbook, *The Care and Education of America's Young Children: Obstacles and Opportunities.*

Though impossible to contain chapters on all the issues germane to the field, the volume focuses on three areas: (1) issues of pedagogy; (2) issues of partnerships and linkages; and (3) issues of policy. Pedagogical challenges, cast in a 1990s context, are addressed by noted scholars—Elkind, Bowman, Fillmore, and Katz. Not dodging difficult issues, Elkind defines quality in light of current and intensified family and school pressures, while Katz addresses the changing nature of pedagogy. With minorities becoming the majority of the school population in many states during the 1990s, Bowman and Fillmore press us to reexamine our thinking about and services to culturally and linguistically diverse young children.

The issues of partnerships included in this volume are not substantively new. Yet, placed within the 1990s context, they take on

new urgency. Public school sponsorship is being debated as is the
need for better articulation between schools and preschool programs.
Caldwell's discussion illuminates the difficult challenges associated
with both. While partnerships with parents have been the sine qua non
of early care and education, they, too, are taking on a new patina as
parental expectations for their children increase while the amount of
time many spend with their children decreases. The challenges of
1990s parent partnerships are discussed by Powell. Furthermore,
given increased personnel demands occasioned by new programs
coupled with the comparatively diminished financial incentives to
enter the field, training needs are escalating. Spodek discusses training
within the 1990s context, examining how traditional partnerships
between practice and theory can be articulated in light of 1990s
pressures. As suggested earlier, the 1990s have ushered in robust
partnerships between corporations and early childhood programs,
discussed in this volume by Galinsky.

The final section of the volume focuses on issues of policy,
highlighting the factors that shape it and that it shapes. Zigler discusses
the application of research to policy, illuminating the challenges and
benefits of this linkage. Blatant manifestations of policy, evidenced in
the regulations that govern early care and education services, are
discussed by Morgan. Hilliard illuminates some clear policy pitfalls in
his chapter on equity, access, and segregation. In considering
governance and funding of early care and education, Grubb addresses
tenacious federalist issues. In the final chapter, the editor posits a new
definition of excellence and suggests strategies that may help move
early care and education from a series of isolated fragmented programs
to a cohesive delivery system.

Though very reminiscent of the continuity and change themes
presented in past NSSE Yearbooks, this volume is distinguished in
two important ways. First, as its title suggests, it is concerned not
solely about the education of young children, but about their care *and*
education. It takes this stance premised on the knowledge that,
pedagogically, quality care for young children is the same as quality
education. While child care and education settings may be
distinguished by many variables including their names, funding
sources, histories, regulations, and even the length and range of
services, pedagogically, quality in a Head Start, child care, or public
preschool classes is isomorphic. Consequently, this volume addresses
issues faced by the combined field of early childhood education and
child care.

Second, unlike its predecessors, this NSSE early childhood volume has an explicit policy thrust. This construction reflects the growing recognition that early care and education practice is not only a pedagogical issue. This is not to diminish the importance of pedagogy, but to suggest that if pedagogy is to be maximized it must be accompanied by supportive policy. Indeed, pedagogy, partnerships, and policy represent the infrastructure upon which the future of quality early care and education practice rests. Because each represents a mainstay of the early childhood profession, it is only appropriate that pedagogy, partnerships, and policy should have each become a mainstay of this volume.

To Ann Lieberman, Kenneth Rehage, and the Board of Directors of the National Society for the Study of Education, and to Edward Zigler, I owe thanks for support, and early care and education owes thanks for ongoing commitment.

To the mainstays and men in my life—Louis, Gerald, and Peter— I dedicate my work on this volume. Though of different generations and lands, your principles and values, like those of this wonderful profession, transcend time and place. For all you are and for all you have given and enabled, I thank you.

SHARON L. KAGAN
New Haven, Connecticut
December, 1990

Table of Contents

Section One
Issues of Pedagogy

Section Two
Issues of Partnerships and Linkages

Section One
ISSUES OF PEDAGOGY

CHAPTER I

Developmentally Appropriate Practice: A Case Study of Educational Inertia

DAVID ELKIND

American education is heavily institutionalized. It is closely tied to colleges and universities that engage in teacher training and to various research-oriented graduate schools of education. Education in this country has equally strong ties to the multibillion dollar educational publishing industry. In addition, education is dependent upon local, state, and federal government for funding. In the last few decades, the federal government has become much more involved in education through various titled programs for the disadvantaged and the handicapped. Moreover, in many communities, local school boards dictate educational policy with little or no educational expertise to back them up. Finally, educational systems, particularly in large cities, are heavily bureaucratized.

Because education is so closely intermeshed with other social institutions, true educational reform can only come about when there is a systemic change that simultaneously alters all of the intertwined components of the educational establishment. Such a systemic change, however, has to begin at the philosophical and conceptual level. This is true because all of the various components of the educational institution share an implicit educational philosophy. This philosophy might be called *psychometric* and looks at education from a quantitative perspective that will be described in more detail below. It is this shared underlying philosophy that welds the various components of the educational system together and is the true barrier to authentic educational reform.

1

This philosophical and conceptual barrier is the real reason why contemporary classroom innovations and curricular reforms have little or no chance of effecting any significant and lasting change in education. If the educational innovation is in keeping with the underlying philosophy, then it is not truly innovative and will change nothing. On the other hand, if the innovation is at variance with the underlying philosophy it will never be properly implemented and will eventually be rejected as unworkable.

A current example of an educational innovation at variance with the underlying educational philosophy is the concept of "developmentally appropriate practice." A comparison of the philosophy underlying this conception and the philosophy that dictates extant educational practice makes it easy to predict that developmentally appropriate practice has little if any chance of being implemented in our schools. The comparison thus provides an interesting case study of how underlying philosophies can determine the acceptance or rejection of a particular educational innovation.

The principle of developmentally appropriate educational practice, that the curriculum should be matched to the child's level of developmental ability,[1] has been favorably received in educational circles. This positive reception is, however, quite extraordinary. In fact, developmentally appropriate practice represents a philosophy of education in total opposition to the "psychometric" educational philosophy that dictates educational practice in the majority of our public schools. Perhaps that is why developmental appropriateness has been honored more in word than in deed.

The first aim of this chapter is to highlight some of the differences between these two educational philosophies. A second aim is to contrast a few of the practical educational implications of the two philosophies. A final aim is to argue that true educational reform in this country will only come about when we have a paradigm shift away from the reigning psychometric educational psychology.

Two Philosophies of Education

Any philosophy of education must include a conception of the learner, the learning process, the information to be acquired, and finally the goals or aims of education. The developmental philosophy differs from the psychometric philosophy on all four counts. Before proceeding, I should say that the developmental approach to be presented here derives from the research and theory of Jean Piaget.[2]

THE CONCEPTION OF THE LEARNER

Within a developmental philosophy of education, the learner is viewed as having *developing* mental abilities. All individuals are assumed to attain these abilities (with the exception of the retarded) although they may not all attain them at the same pace. For example, we expect that all children will attain the concrete operations which Piaget described as emerging at about the age of six or seven.[3] These operations, which function much like the group of arithmetic operations, enable children who have attained them to learn rules and to apply them. At the same time, not all children will attain these operations at the same age. Accordingly, from this perspective, individual differences in ability have to be seen as differences in *rates* of intellectual growth.

This conception of mental ability contrasts with that of a psychometric philosophy of education. According to this philosophy, the learner is seen as having *measurable* abilities. The psychometric position assumes that any ability that exists must exist in some amount and is, therefore, quantifiable. For example, intelligence tests—the flagship of the psychometric philosophy—are designed to assess individual differences in the ability to learn and to adapt to new situations. From the psychometric perspective, individual differences in performance are regarded as reflecting differences in *amount* of ability.

These opposed conceptions of human ability, both of which contain some truth, nonetheless have far different pedagogical implications. From a developmental perspective, which views abilities as growing, the important task is to *match curricula* to the level of children's emerging mental abilities. Hence the principle of developmental appropriateness. Curricular materials should only be introduced after the child has attained the level of mental ability needed to master those materials. This in turn means that curricula have to be studied and analyzed to determine the level of mental ability required to comprehend them.

A case in point is the concept of number. Piaget's work demonstrates clearly that children acquire the concept of number in a sequence of stages that are related to age.[4] The young child has a concept of nominal number in which number is equivalent to a name on a baseball or the numerals on a football jersey. At the second stage, the child arrives at ordinal number and grasps that one number means more than another, but not by how much. Number is a rank without units. Only by the age of six or seven do children attain a true or unit conception of number wherein a number stands for a fixed unit or number of units. The practical implications of this understanding of the development of number have been nicely described by Constance Kamii.[5]

From a psychometric point of view, however, the most important thing is to *match children* of equal amounts of ability. Bright children are assumed to be able to learn more per unit of time than is true for less bright children. In practice this results in so-called "ability grouping," which in effect allows bright children to go through the material more quickly than slower children. This psychometric orientation also underlies the provision of special classes for both the gifted and the retarded. These are critical issues that warrant much more detailed treatment than can be given here. It can be said, however, that from a developmental point of view, in the majority of cases, ability grouping is a strategy for avoiding developmentally appropriate practice.

THE CONCEPTION OF THE LEARNING PROCESS

Within the developmental philosophy of education, learning is always a *creative* activity. Whenever we learn anything we engage the world in such a way as to create something new that reflects both our own mental activity and the material with which we have dealt. We never simply copy content but always stamp it with our own unique way of viewing the world. The child from Connecticut who heard the Lord's Prayer as "Our Father in art in New Haven, Harold be thy name," is not the exception but the rule. Everything we learn has a subjective as well as an objective component.

The conception of learning as a creative or constructive process has a very important practical implication. In effect it means that we cannot talk of learning independently of the content to be learned. The material to be learned will always interact with the learning process in some special way. Long after Piaget discovered the successive stages and organizations of mental operations he continued to study how children attained different concepts such as space,[6] geometry,[7] time,[8] and movement and speed.[9] In so doing he emphasized that knowing the stages of mental development does not provide any special insight into how children use these operations in the attainment of any particular concept. The only way to discover how children go about learning a particular subject matter is to study how in fact they utilize their mental abilities to master it.

From the psychometric point of view, in contrast, learning

consists of a set of principles (such as intermittent reinforcement) or a set of skills (e.g., decoding) which are independent of the content to be learned. Early workers in this tradition enunciated principles such as "mass" vs. "distributed" or "whole" vs. "part" learning which were presumed to operate independently of the content to be learned. Indeed, early studies of memory employed nonsense syllables specifically to eliminate the effect of content on the study of the memory process.[10]

The limitations of this approach were dramatically demonstrated by Bruner, Goodnow, and Austin in their seminal work on problem solving.[11] Until this publication, problem solving had been talked about in terms of "trial and error"[12] or sudden "insight"[13] and much of the work on problem solving was done with animals. What Bruner and his colleagues demonstrated was that when you presented human subjects with complex problems they employed complex problem-solving activities, namely, "strategies." Put differently, the content of the problem determined the level of problem-solving activities the subjects employed.

Nonetheless, this insight seems to have been lost. The current interest in teaching children thinking skills,[14] learning strategies,[15] or computer programming[16] is a regression to the idea that thought and content can be treated separately. It is assumed that once children learn thinking skills, or learning strategies, or computer programming, these skills will automatically be transferred to new contents. To be sure, there is transfer of training but it is far from automatic. Transfer works when students are active, not passive, learners.[17] But what does activity mean if not that the student is consciously aware of the contents about which he or she is thinking, or to which he or she is applying strategies. Mental process is always content oriented.

The developmental approach thus argues that there is little or no automatic transfer from one subject matter to another. This lack of transfer is not because there are no general abilities but rather because each subject matter is different and requires a *novel utilization* of general abilities to be fully assimilated. To be sure, the developmental approach recognizes that children no less than adults can learn general strategies for dealing with similar subject matters. Writers learn general strategies for dealing with plots, characters, and so on, and researchers learn general strategies for dealing with their chosen matters of investigation. But these general strategies are nonetheless limited to a particular realm of problems and usually do not work outside that realm.

In contrast, the psychometric approach assumes automatic transfer of learned strategies and skills across subject matter areas because it assumes that the common elements which all subject matters share are more salient than their individual variations.

This difference between the developmental and psychometric approaches contains a certain irony. The developmental approach is generally regarded as a "nature" approach because of its emphasis upon development; the stages and the limits are set by growth and maturation. The psychometric approach is, on the other hand, regarded as a "nurture" approach because of its heavy emphasis on environmental influences. Yet when it comes to transfer, it is the developmental approach that places emphasis on the uniqueness of content (the environment) while the psychometric approach dismisses the variability of content (nurture) and emphasizes the generalizability of general mental processes (an essentially nature position).

THE CONCEPT OF KNOWLEDGE

From a developmental perspective, as I have indicated above, knowledge is always a construction and the result is inevitably a joint product representing contributions of the subject and the object. This is far from a new idea and harks back to the Kantian resolution of idealist (all knowledge is a mental construction) and the empiricist (all knowledge is a copy of an externally existing world) interpretations of how we come to know the world.[18] Kant argued that the mind provides the "categories" of knowing while the real world provides the content. Knowledge is thus always a construction of the mind interacting with the world and cannot be reduced to either one.

What Piaget added to the Kantian solution—and what makes Piaget a neo-Kantian—was his demonstration that the categories of knowing (the mental operations of intelligence) are not constant, as Kant supposed, but rather change with age.[19] This adds a developmental dimension to the Kantian version of the construction of knowledge. As their mental operations develop, children are required to reconstruct the realities they elaborated at the previous developmental level. In effect, the child creates reality, and recreates it, out of his or her experiences with the environment.

The reality of the young child, his or her knowledge of the world, is thus different than the reality of the older child and adult. Young children, for example, believe that a quantity changes in amount when it changes in appearance—say that the amount of liquid in a low flat container becomes more when it is poured into a tall narrow one.

Older children have a different reality and appreciate the fact that a quantity remains the same in amount across any change in its appearance—that quantity is conserved. Looked at in this way, the young child's conception of quantity is not "wrong" but is, in fact, as developmentally appropriate as the older child's grasp of conservation.

From the psychometric point of view, on the other hand, knowledge is something which the subject acquires and that can be measured independently from the processes of acquisition. This separation is reflected in the distinction between intelligence (ability) and achievement (content) tests. One consequence of the separation between learning and content is that knowledge can be measured against an external standard and independently of the learner. When compared to this external standard the child's responses can be assessed as being either "right" or "wrong."

To be sure, there is a right and wrong with respect to some types of knowledge. The Bastille was stormed in 1789 not 1650 and two plus two equals four not five. We have to distinguish here between what I have called *fundamental* knowledge,[20] which we construct on our own, and *derived* knowledge, which is constructed by others and which we acquire secondhand. The terms "right" and "wrong" are useful only in connection with derived knowledge, but not with regard to fundamental knowledge. (But even here we have to recognize that there is a subjective component even to derived knowledge. Derived knowledge is always encrusted with personal associations. We may remember dates by associating them with particular images and math facts with the aid of rhymes and so on.)

The developmental approach introduces the idea that there can be differences in knowledge without these being "right" or "wrong." The idea of difference, rather than right or wrong, is important not only with respect to fundamental knowledge but also with respect to creative thinking. Many bright children, for example, come up with ideas that are different from those of their peers or teachers but these are often treated as "wrong" rather than as different and original. One bright child, when asked to write something about the color blue, talked about Picasso's blue period and was teased and jeered. A greater respect for appreciating difference, as well as right or wrong, would reduce the stress experienced by so many of the bright children in our schools.

And, in general, teaching children that there are knowledge, qualities, and traits that are neither right nor wrong, but simply different, is important from many perspectives. For example, a nonjudgmental approach to social traits is essential in teaching children about different cultures, religions, and languages. It is also useful in teaching children about the arts. Young people need to learn that different people can have contrasting tastes in music, in literature, and in art and that these are not really right or wrong, simply different.

THE AIMS OF EDUCATION

Given the above description of the developmental philosophy of education, the aims of developmental education are straightforward. That is to say, if the learner is seen as a growing individual with developing abilities, if learning is regarded as a creative activity, and if knowledge is seen as a construction, then the aim of education must surely be to facilitate this growth, this creative activity, and this construction of knowledge. Piaget put the aims of education from a developmental perspective this way:

The principle goal of education is to create men who are capable of doing new things, not simply repeating what other generations have done—men who are creative, inventive, and discoverers. The second goal of education is to form minds which can be critical, can verify, and not accept everything that is offered. The great danger today is of slogans, collective opinions, ready made trends of thought. We have to be able to resist them individually, to criticize, to distinguish between what is proven and what is not. So we need pupils who are active, who learn early to find out by themselves, partly by their own spontaneous activity and partly through material we set up for them; who learn early to tell what is verifiable and what is simply the first idea to come to them.[21]

The aim of developmental education is then to produce creative, critical thinkers. This is not achieved by teaching children and adolescents thinking skills, but rather by creating developmentally appropriate learning environments that will encourage and challenge the child's emerging mental abilities. Creative and critical thinking are not skills to be taught and learned but rather reflect basic orientations toward self and the world that can only be acquired when children are actively engaged in constructing and reconstructing their physical, social, and moral worlds.

In contrast, the aims of psychometric education are to produce children who will score high on tests of achievement. In other words, the aim of education is to maximize the acquisition of quantifiable knowledge and skills. Perhaps former Secretary of Education William J. Bennett put this view of the aims of education as well as anyone:

We should want every student to know how mountains are made, and that for most reactions there is an equal and opposite reaction. They should know who said "I am the state" and who said "I have a dream." They should know about subjects and predicates, about isosceles triangles and ellipses. They should know where the Amazon flows and what the First Amendment means. They should know about the Donner party and about slavery, and Shylock, Hercules, and Abigail Adams, where Ethiopia is, and why there is a Berlin Wall.[22]

In this statement, Bennett echoes a theme that was also sounded in the influential monograph *A Nation at Risk*, which was published five years earlier[23] and which decried the poor performance of American students on achievement tests compared to the performance of children from other countries, particularly Japan. And Bennett's remarks also foreshadowed the best-selling critiques of education by Bloom and by Hirsch, who also see American education as failing to educate children with the basic knowledge of Western civilization.[24]

To be sure, young people should be exposed to Shakespeare, know the basics of geography, and be familiar with current events. A developmental approach does not deny the value and importance of such knowledge. It is rather a question of what comes first. From a developmental perspective, children who are curious, active learners will acquire much of the knowledge that writers like Bennett, Bloom, and Hirsch advocate and many other things as well. But creating curious, active learners *has to precede* the acquisition of particular information and therein lies the difference between the two philosophies of education.

To put the difference more succinctly, the developmental approach tries to create students who *want to know* whereas the psychometric approach seeks to produce students who *know what we want*.

Practical Implications of the Developmental Philosophy

Now that we have looked at these two contrasting educational philosophies, we can review a few of the implications of a developmental perspective for the practice of education. Again, my interpretation will be largely based upon the Piagetian conception of the development of intelligence.

TEACHER TRAINING: THE TEACHER AS A CHILD DEVELOPMENT SPECIALIST

In most disciplines, students have to learn the basic material of their discipline. A physics student has to learn about the rules that govern the physical world. Likewise a chemistry major must learn the basic chemical elements and how they interact. Biology students learn first about plants and animals. The only discipline wherein students do not learn the basic material of their discipline is education. Students take courses in curriculum, in methods, in educational philosophy, in assessment and in classroom management. They take only one or at most two courses in child or educational psychology.

But the basic material of education is not curriculum, not assessment, and not methods. The basic material of education is children and youth. A teacher training program that was truly developmentally appropriate would have students major in child development. Trained in this way, a teacher would be, first and foremost, a child development specialist. Students with a strong foundation in child development can then integrate what they learn about curriculum, assessment, and management with what they know about how children think and learn at successive age levels. Without knowing about human development, there is no central core upon which the student can build an integrated sense of educational practice.

From a developmental point of view, the recommendation of the Holmes Group[25] (a group of Deans of Schools of Education from all parts of the country) to do away with the undergraduate major in education and substitute a year or two of graduate training and internship will not produce better teachers. This is true because the Holmes group sees the problem of teacher training as one of educational *organization* whereas from a developmental point of view it is not the organization of teacher training that is the problem but rather the *content* of that training.

There *is* a need for undergraduate teacher training, not in traditional education courses, but in child development. What we need are undergraduate departments of child development where students can get an integrated sequence of courses that cover the social, intellectual, and emotional development of children and youth. This course of instruction combined with a variety of laboratory experiences that involve the student in observing and working with children, is really the only way to prepare teachers for working in classrooms.

CURRICULUM: AN EXPERIMENTAL APPROACH

From a developmental point of view, there are several principles that should guide curriculum construction.

First, a curriculum must be constructed empirically and not a priori. There is no way to figure out how children learn a subject matter without studying how they actually go about learning it. In this connection it is truly a scandal that many curriculum publishers not only fail to do research on the materials they produce; they do not even field test them! In no other profession would we allow a product to be placed on the market without extensive field testing. And the felony is compounded when, after teachers have learned to cope with the problems in the curricula, they are confronted with a new equally untested edition.

In a truly developmental educational system there would be many opportunities for teachers to construct and test out their own materials. They could see what works and what doesn't and try out different sequences and methods. The way the material works will also depend upon the group of children who are in the classroom that year as well. So a curriculum should never be final but always open, flexible, and innovative. That sort of curriculum is exciting for the teacher as well as for the pupils and makes the learning and curriculum innovation a cooperative venture.

Second, and consistent with the appropriateness theme, I believe that a curriculum should be localized, particularly for elementary school children. I know that this is contrary to trends in other countries that have uniform curricula for all children. Japan and France are but two of the countries with such uniform national curricula. England too is initiating a uniform national curriculum in 1990. But such a national curriculum can eliminate the possibility of individualizing curricular materials to include particulars from the local environment where the children actually live and learn. Such localized curricula have a great deal of intrinsic interest for children.

For example, in learning mathematics, children living in Hawaii might be presented with matching coconuts and palm trees whereas children in the Northeast might be asked to match acorns and oaks. Likewise, it would add to children's enjoyment if the stories they read took place in their own community or one like it. In social studies, too, children are more delighted to find a picture of a building in which they have actually been than one they have never seen. To be sure, children like stories about places and events different from their own. Nonetheless, they also enjoy reading stories that relate directly to the world they live in. Children, no less than adults, appreciate *both* fantasy and the realism of local reference.

The idea of a localized curriculum does not, of course, preclude regional or national general curricular goals. There is no problem with setting regional and national levels of achievement in different subject matter areas so long as the local schools can individualize their materials to make them more accessible and interesting to the children of that locale. The danger of a national curriculum is that it often comes to utilize uniform content for all children. It is the uniform content, not the general goals of a national curriculum, which can be so deadly dull for children.

A recent Gallup poll (September, 1989) indicates that some 70 percent of educators want national, uniform goals. The danger is that if such goals are adopted, they will be translated into specific contents to be taught at specific grade levels. Given the ethnic, racial, cultural, and economic diversity of our society, demands for curricular uniformity are in direct contradiction to the needs for curriculum flexibility and innovation that the developmental approach prescribes.

Finally, curricula need to be studied to determine their level of developmental difficulty. Developmental difficulty is quite different from psychometric difficulty.[26] The psychometric difficulty of a curriculum or a test item is determined by the number of children at a particular age level who get that item correct. A curriculum or test item is generally assigned to the grade or age level where 75 percent of the children at that age level pass the item.

Developmental difficulty, in contrast, has to be determined by examining the "errors" children make in attempting to master a problem or task. For example, when young children who have been taught the short *a* sound are asked to attach the long *a* sound to it, they have great difficulty. The problem is that they are being asked to grasp that one and the same letter has two different sounds. The understanding that one and the same symbol can have two different meanings or sounds, however, requires the attainment of the mental abilities Piaget calls concrete operations.[27] A developmental teacher would thus avoid teaching phonics until he or she was quite sure that most of the children had attained concrete operations.

Again, the developmental difficulty of any particular curriculum material cannot be determined a priori but only by active investigation. Part of the experimental work of teaching would be to explore the developmental difficulty of the available curricular materials and to try out new materials that might work differently or better.

INSTRUCTION: AUTHENTIC TEACHING

Developmentally speaking, it is as impossible to separate the learning process from the material to be learned as it is to separate learning from instruction. From this point of view, the teacher is always a learner as well as a teacher and the children are teachers as well as learners. The teacher who experiments with curricula is learning both about the curricula and about the children he or she teaches. And children who work cooperatively with one another and who experiment with curriculum materials are teaching as well as learning.

One way to highlight the difference between authentic teaching and psychometrically oriented teaching is to look at the way question asking is handled in the two types of instruction. The teacher coming from a psychometric orientation often asks questions to determine whether or not the child has the right answer. The authentic teacher often asks questions to get information, not to test what the student knows or understands. It is the difference between Piaget's semiclinical interview aimed at eliciting the child's original and spontaneous convictions as opposed to intelligence or achievement tests which seek to determine what the child knows or has learned.

Questioning children to discover what they think reflects the fact that the authentic teacher is first and foremost an enthusiastic learner. It also reflects the fact that he or she truly believes that we have something to learn from children. To be sure, we all ask rhetorical questions at times to stimulate discussion, but that type of question asking should be the exception rather than the rule.

ASSESSMENT: DOCUMENTATION

Developmental assessment involves documenting the work a child has done over a given time period. Most usually this is done by having a child keep a portfolio that includes some of his or her writing, drawing, mathematics explorations, and so on. In looking through such a portfolio we get a good idea of the quality of work the child is capable of doing and his or her progress over the given time period.

Such portfolios have many fringe benefits. Not only do they inform parents of what children are doing but they provide a very concrete record of a child's educational progress for the child as well. Once they are grown, many young people take great pleasure in looking over the work they have done as children. This gives them a sense of how far they have progressed and also a sense of the continuity of their development. It is very nourishing to their growing sense of personal identity.

Psychometric assessment involves measuring the child's achievement by means of published or teacher-made tests. The child's progress is evaluated on the basis of his or her performance on the tests. In contrast to a portfolio of work, the psychometric approach provides a number or a *grade* that symbolizes both the quantity and quality of the work the child has done over a given time period. Numbers and grades can be a useful shorthand method for symbolizing a student's progress, but it lacks the richness of the portfolio and its historical value for the young person.

Although psychometric testing is useful, it has many risks that are currently being realized. For example, testing is often done without regard to what goes on in the classroom. Kindergarten screening tests are a case in point. Although such tests purport to measure whether or not the child is "ready" for kindergarten, they do no such thing. The tests make it appear that readiness is in the child's head rather than existing as a relation between the child and the curriculum. How a child will do in a particular classroom depends more upon what goes on in that classroom than upon the score the child received on the test.

We return here to the issue of transfer. The psychometric approach assumes that performance on a test automatically translates into performance in a classroom situation. But the developmental approach insists that no such transfer takes place and that to know how a child is going to perform in a particular classroom, you have to assess that child on the challenges he or she will meet in the classroom. Even at the college level, SATs are not good predictors of college performance. Why should we expect tests to predict better at an age when children are much more variable and much less sophisticated test takers?

Conclusion

In this chapter I have tried to demonstrate that although developmentally appropriate practice as an idea is being rhetorically well received in educational circles, it really has little chance of being implemented. Without a change in underlying philosophy, changes in educational practice will be superficial at best. And that is true for the adoption of developmentally appropriate practice. No classroom or school can be genuinely developmentally appropriate when its underlying philosophy is psychometric. It is this psychometric philosophy that explains contemporary educational inertia.

Is there any way to get education moving in the right direction? Kuhn argues that in science inertia is overcome when one scientific paradigm replaces another.[28] As I indicated in my introduction, however, educational institutions are too imbedded in the society to change in the manner of science. Yet some indices of movement are visible and they are coming from the means of changing social institutions inherent within the society. One of these is the legal system. In two states, Kentucky and Texas, the legislatures have declared the educational systems unconstitutional because the amount spent per pupil varies from community to community. These rulings will force educational reorganization.

Industry is another institution within the society that may help to move education in the direction of true reorganization. In some parts of the country (e.g., Beaverton, Oregon), each school has been adopted by a local company that takes some responsibility for the educational program. Finally, coalitions of educators and parents have begun to move the state boards of education. In North Carolina, such a coalition has gotten the legislature to remove testing from the first three grades. In Boston, the citizens have just voted to have the school board appointed rather than elected. Hopefully this will bring educators onto that ruling body.

Certainly education is an enormous and enormously encrusted institution but it can move and is being moved, slowly to be sure, but moved all the same.

FOOTNOTES

1. Sue Bredekamp, *Developmentally Appropriate Practice in Early Childhood Programs Serving Children from Birth through Age 8* (Washington, DC: National Association for the Education of Young Children, 1987).

2. See, for example, Jean Piaget, *The Psychology of Intelligence* (London: Routledge and Kegan Paul, 1950).

3. Ibid.

4. Jean Piaget, *The Child's Conception of Number* (London: Routledge and Kegan Paul, 1952).

5. Constance Kamii, *Number in Preschool and Kindergarten* (Washington, DC: National Association for the Education of Young Children, 1982).

6. Jean Piaget and Barbel Inhelder, *The Child's Conception of Space* (London: Routledge and Kegan Paul, 1956).

7. Jean Piaget, Barbel Inhelder, and Alina Szeminska, *The Child's Conception of Geometry* (New York: Basic Books, 1960).

8. Jean Piaget, *The Child's Conception of Time* (London: Routledge and Kegan Paul, 1967).

9. Jean Piaget, *The Child's Conception of Movement and Speed* (London: Routledge and Kegan Paul, 1970).

10. D. J. Murray, "Research on Human Memory in the Nineteenth Century," in *Human Memory*, ed. J. G. Seamon (New York: Oxford University Press, 1980).

11. Jerome S. Bruner, Jacqueline J. Goodnow, and George A. Austin, *A Study of Thinking* (New York: Wiley, 1956).

12. Edward L. Thorndike, *Human Learning* (New York: Century Co., 1921).

13. Wolfgang Kohler, *The Mentality of Apes* (New York: Harcourt Brace, 1927); Karl Duncker, "On Problem Solving," *Psychological Monographs* 58, no. 5 (1945): 1-113.

14. Joan Boykoff Baron and Robert J. Sternberg, *Teaching Thinking Skills: Theory and Practice* (New York: W. H. Freeman, 1987).

15. Claire E. Weinstein and Richard E. Mayer, "The Teaching of Learning Strategies," in *Handbook of Research on Teaching*, 3d ed., ed. Merlin C. Wittrock (New York: Macmillan, 1986).

16. Seymour Papert, *Mindstorms* (New York: Basic Books, 1980).

17. D. N. Perkins and Gavriel Salomon, "Teaching for Transfer," *Educational Leadership* 46, no. 1 (1988): 22-32.

18. Immanuel Kant, *Critique of Pure Reason* (New York: Wiley, 1943).

19. Jean Piaget, *The Principles of Genetic Epistemology* (New York: Basic Books, 1972).

20. David Elkind, *Miseducation: Preschoolers at Risk* (New York: Knopf, 1987).

21. Richard E. Ripple and Verne N. Rockcastle, eds., *Piaget Rediscovered: A Report of the Conference on Cognitive Studies and Curriculum Development* (Ithaca, NY: School of Education, Cornell University, 1964).

22. William J. Bennett, *First Lessons: A Report on Elementary Education in America* (Washington, DC: U.S. Department of Education, 1986).

23. National Commission on Excellence in Education, *A Nation at Risk: The Imperative for Educational Reform* (Washington, DC: U.S. Department of Education, 1983).

24. Allan Bloom, *The Closing of the American Mind* (New York: Simon and Schuster, 1987); E. D. Hirsch, Jr., *Cultural Literacy: What Every American Needs to Know* (Boston: Houghton Mifflin, 1987).

25. Holmes Group, *Work in Progress: The Holmes Group One Year On* (East Lansing, MI: Holmes Group, 1989).

26. David Elkind, "Forms and Traits in the Conception of Human Intelligence," *Intelligence* 3 (1982): 101-120.

27. David Elkind, "Stages in the Development of Reading," in *New Directions in Piagetian Theory and Practice*, ed. Irving E. Sigel, David M. Brodzinsky, and Roberta M. Golinkoff (Hillsdale, NJ: Erlbaum, 1981).

28. Thomas S. Kuhn, *The Structure of Scientific Revolutions*, 2d ed. (Chicago: University of Chicago Press, 1970).

CHAPTER II

Educating Language Minority Children: Challenges and Opportunities

BARBARA BOWMAN

"Why can't all Americans speak standard English?" This plaintive cry reflects the distress many citizens feel as linguistic diversity becomes an increasing source of social divisiveness and school failure. In many school districts, the number of languages and dialects spoken by children and their families is staggering: the languages of Central and South America, Africa, and Asia mix with the various American dialects to create classrooms in which communication is problematic. Many children enter school unable to understand or express themselves clearly in standard English and in school they do not learn to speak and write it correctly, or to use it to learn other subjects. Across America, these children are failing to learn the academic skills necessary to share in the economic, social, and political life of the country. A serious problem today, language diversity will soon become even more serious. Assuming that current population trends continue, over the next decade in many schools the number of children speaking foreign languages and nonstandard dialects will become the majority, challenging the ability of schools to educate them or their standard-English-speaking peers.

In a nation that is increasingly composed of people who speak different languages and dialects, the old notion of melting them together through a common language is attractive. English literacy is essential to school success. A high level of proficiency facilitates communication and simplifies the educational task. Unfortunately, what seems desirable as a theoretical construct is difficult to apply in practice. Children who come from language minority communities often do not become proficient in standard English or master the academic skills schools try to teach.

Why is it so difficult to establish a national language in which all teachers can teach and children can learn? The answer rests in the confound among development, culture, and language. Simply

17

instructing young, linguistically different children in the vocabulary and syntax of standard English can not guarantee a homogeneous language community. Language is deeply social; it is learned against a background of emotionally charged relationships and shared experience; and it stems from perceptions of group membership. The tie of young children to their family language and community values is so strong they are often unwilling or unable to make the cultural shift necessary to learn to speak and write in standard English. If schools are to be effective helping linguistically different children become bilingual (become literate in standard English as well as their home language), teachers must appreciate the importance of language and culture to the development of young children.

Development, Culture, and Language

Cultures are universal in the sense that they all address similar human concerns, but they have different ways of accomplishing these human purposes. Evans-Pritchard pointed out that Christian men show respect for their religion by taking off their hats but keeping on their shoes, while Muslims will show similar respect by keeping on their hats and removing their shoes.[1] The two groups have equivalent but different cultural beliefs and practices.

At another level, differences in how groups think and act are more than a matter of using different words for the same purposes. Anyone who believes that the only or primary difference between Arabs and Christians is how they behave in a house of worship will be seriously misled. Sapir said, "The worlds in which different societies live are distinct, not merely the same world with different labels attached."[2] Differences in culture are more than whether members of the community eat white bread, corn pone, or tortillas. The behavior of people varies under similar conditions, and the beliefs, values, and assumptions that underlie their behavior also differ.

Culture influences the psychological processes on which behavior rests, affecting how people perceive the world, how they understand the physical environment, events, and other people. Culture forms a prism through which members of a group see and create "shared meanings" for experience. These meanings are often implicit and represent unconscious definitions of what is right and, therefore, normal human behavior. The assumption that the sense one's own group has made of experience is the only reasonable perspective leads to cultural blind spots, making it difficult for people to understand and communicate with those from other groups.

Development is similar. While the major developmental changes in children are remarkably alike across culture groups, the specific knowledge and skills learned may look quite different. It is useful to make a distinction between the structure of development and forms of behavior. Structure refers to the changes that occur in children's minds as a result of the interaction of their biological potential with experience, reflected in achievements like learning language, categorizing systems, and interpersonal relationships. Children also acquire forms of behavior from family and community, including learning a specific language, a specific way of categorizing things, and particular relationships with others. Both structure and form are responsive to the social experiences made available to children through their interaction with people and things.

Learning a primary language is a developmental milestone for young children. Linguistic interactions act as triggers for developmental change (language learning), but they also shape its expression. Some children learn Spanish, some standard English, and some nonstandard dialects, such as black English. They all learn a language with equal linguistic potential,[3] but what they learn is, of course, different. The language children learn reflects not just a grammar, but the deeper cultural ideas of family and community.

CONTEXT AND LANGUAGE

The messages carried by language are embedded in the contexts in which language is used. Children learn to derive and create meaning for language from the "contexts" in which speech and meaning are coordinated. In order to communicate, children require a knowledge of grammar, but they must learn much more. As the ideas of the social world are brought to bear through the language of the older members of the community, children come to know, to expect, and to attribute meanings to words. Children acquire "scripts" for the various interactions they have with people and things in which language and meanings are integrated. These scripts may vary even among people who speak the same language, as is evident when people within the same language community but of different social class use their common language quite differently.

Adults structure scripts (action and verbal sequences) for children, helping them both to understand and to make themselves understood. It is not unusual for adult speakers to "translate" the speech of toddlers, thus helping the child to "make meaning." By knowing about the child's past experience, the helping adult assists in the expression of the child's ideas. But not just the child's ideas. How the adult restates the child's communication is deeply affected by the adult's interpretation of the meaning of the experience itself. Thus, when the toddler comments unintelligibly when going too close to the hot stove, the adult may linguistically interpret the experience as "no, no," or as "hot," or as not worthy of comment. Gradually children internalize the adult rules for "making meaning" as they participate together in activities.

Rogoff wrote, "to understand children's actions, it is essential to place these actions in the context of the children's interpretation of the task to be accomplished, the goal in performing the activity, and the broader social context of such activities in the children's experience."[4] Therefore, linguistic expression must be interpreted against a backdrop of prior social experience as it shapes children's responses to new situations. An example of this was given by Lawson,[5] who noted that the pattern of answering questions characteristic of African-American children leads them to different answers to test questions than white children. The study described how African-American children's answers to test questions were analogical (answers that related objects or events to themselves or their experience), rather than referential (answers that name the object or event). While all the children gave answers of both types, the frequency with which children from each group used each response type was different. This suggests that both types of response (analogic and referential) were in the children's repertoire; however, the children used the type that in their past experience was appropriate to question-asking scripts. What was different was their assessment of the question-answering strategy called for in the test situation.

When adults come from different cultures, and use different languages and dialects than children use, they may be unaware of the difference between their understanding of a "context" and the children's, between their expectations for behavior in various contexts and the children's. When children and adults do not share common experiences and common beliefs about the meaning of experiences, adults are less able to help children encode their thoughts into language.

LANGUAGE AND IDENTITY

Erik Erikson said "No ego can develop outside of social processes which offer workable prototypes and roles."[6] Children learn to act, believe, and feel in ways that are consistent with those of their community. The goals and objectives presented, the relationships available, and the behavior and practices recommended by family and friends are gradually internalized and contribute to a child's definition of "self." In the United States, ethnicity is one of the most powerful aspects of a person's identity. Giordano wrote that identification with an ethnic group "involves conscious and unconscious processes that fulfill a deep psychological need for identity and historical continuity."[7]

Ethnicity affects behavior in rather obvious ways, from table manners to ritual celebrations, but it also affects linguistic expression. Language is an integral part of a group's joint experience. Speaking the same language unites individuals with bonds of common meaning and also serves as a marker of group membership; it is the cement for group members' relationships with one another. The shared past and current allegiance of the group are the bedrock for the "common meanings" they teach their children through their language. Group membership determines which language or dialect members speak and also when, how, to whom, and in what way they talk to each other and to those outside their group. Language, then, is both a form for expressing meaning and a way of declaring membership in a particular group. Both of these functions of language make it an essential component of identity.

It is easy to underestimate how subtly ethnicity affects linguistic expression. The broad spectrum of behaviors that owe their meaning to the unique beliefs and practices of particular communities is illustrated here by several examples.

According to Shade, the African-American's *Weltanschauung* is one of caution, wariness, and a sense of distrust."[8] Such a perspective may deter children from talking and sharing their feelings, views, and opinions in places where they feel unsure of their reception. And indeed, researchers have described African-American children who were reluctant to speak in school, even though they had a full and rich command of language in informal settings where black English was spoken.[9]

Studies of child abuse and neglect in various communities show considerable differences in their definitions and ratings of abusive and neglectful behaviors.[10] Children who come from communities where spanking is common may feel little embarrassment in discussing physical punishment in school, while children from communities where spanking is considered abusive may refuse to disclose even a minor slap.[11]

McGoldrick noted that ethnic groups vary in their response to and communications about pain, their symptomologies, and their beliefs about the causes of illness.[12] Such differences lead, for instance, to different treatment preferences for psychological complaints in German and Iranian communities, with Germans willing participants in talk therapy and Iranians preferring medicine to relieve their psychological discomfort.[13]

Wise reported the plight of an Ottawa Indian girl whose teacher believed she had low self-esteem and referred her for psychological testing and counseling.[14] The teacher's belief was based on the fact that the child seldom made eye contact when she spoke to her. The teacher didn't know that for Ottawa Indians (and some other Native American tribes) it is a "sign of disrespect" to look an older person in the eye.[15]

Groups have been found to vary in a number of perceptual, cognitive, and linguistic characteristics.[16] One such characteristic is field sensitivity as opposed to field independence. Field-dependent people are said to prefer a more global view of the world, rather than focusing on the parts or pieces of a visual field. African-American and Mexican-American children have been found to "prefer the field-dependent approach while Euro-Americans demonstrated a field-independent preference."[17] The assumption is that children belonging to each group will respond to what they consider the more salient aspects of the environment. Schools tend to reward those children who are more field independent and prone to breaking down problems rather than to those responding more intuitively and holistically.

Racial identity is a particular form of ethnicity, made more meaningful because of the negative beliefs and expectations of the majority group about people of color. Katz contends that by the age of three many children already exhibit awareness of racial cues and are well able to differentiate on the basis of skin color or other racial features when such differences are important in their community.[18]

In the United States, while all ethnics are minorities, all minority groups do not share a similar national environment. Some ethnic communities, particularly African-American, Hispanic (Mexican-American, Central American, and Puerto Rican) and Native American, are the butt of prejudice and discrimination. Although most members of these groups are of mixed racial heritage, people with African-American or Native American ancestry are usually described as racially colored and are often subject to personal and institutional racist practices.

The meaning of experience (and therefore their language) is substantially different for these minorities than for children who belong to "white ethnic" groups. Ogbu noted that "caste-like minorities" (African-Americans, Hispanics, and Native Americans) may·reject academic achievement and standard English because the goals and skills of school have not traditionally benefited their community.[19] He attributes the poorer performance of black children in school to their community's experience of prejudice and discrimination rather than to intellectual differences of individuals. Caste-like groups do not have equal access to and rewards from the various roles and institutions in the society, thus they have developed different goals and different behavior. The behavior that makes sense if one expects fair treatment in school, a job equal to one's educational competence, housing wherever one wishes to live, respect from one's peers, and other rewards taken for granted by whites, seems foolish to those who have no such expectations. Racial minorities in the United States have developed parallel cultures and languages to cope with their discrimination and isolation. These often seem inexplicable and counterproductive to members of white groups; however, the ways of talking and behaving of these groups are deeply embedded in past and present realities and will not be easily altered unless the future offers new and less painful alternatives.

Learning a language, and the cultural values and beliefs that underlie its usage, is a normal developmental step in the lives of young children. What children learn is dependent on the meanings their caregivers and intimates ascribe to experience. These meanings are often hidden in subtle differences in the uses of oral and written speech, the construction of grammars, and the selection and definitions of vocabulary. All of these aspects of language are tied to the child's emerging sense of self, of which group identity is a significant factor.

While children are deeply rooted in their own family and community—their own culture—all children who live in the same community and share a culture are not identical. Group markers, whether of ethnicity, social class, gender, or race do not describe any one individual belonging to that group. Children's behavior results from the integration of group mores with their own individual (genetic/temperamental) characteristics, the adaptation of cultural expectations with their developmental (age/stage) capabilities, and from the syntheses of the conflicting roles, beliefs, and attitudes of the various members of the child-rearing community. Culture is learned, and different children within each community learn to be somewhat different.

Teaching Culturally Different Children

It should be clear from the above discussion that teaching linguistically different children is complicated and difficult and not amenable to a quick and easy strategy like "make them all speak English." As Douglas Barnes has said, "the actual (as opposed to the intended) curriculum consists in the meanings enacted or realized by a particular teacher and a particular class."[20] No matter what language is spoken in the classroom, sensitive teachers of linguistically different children must create common meanings; since speech can not stand alone, both children and teachers must understand what is meant by what is said.

CLASSROOM COMMUNICATION

Classroom discourse presents a challenge to most young children as they learn new rules for communication. The use of formal language, teacher leadership, and control of verbal interchange, question/answer formats, and reference to increasingly abstract ideas are characteristic of classroom environments with which many children are unfamiliar. To the extent that the rules governing these interactions overlap with ones children have already learned, teacher/child communication is easier. Children whose past experience is most similar to that of teachers and whose social knowledge and expectations fit easily into mainstream institutions will have an easier time understanding classroom instruction. Children whose past experience is not congruent will have to learn new ways of "making meaning" before they can use language to learn. Incongruities can be as obvious as when children speak a foreign language, or as subtle as when they use "home grown" expressions to indicate body functions ("I want to water the grass" meaning "I need to go to the toilet").

Contextual misfits in children's and teacher's communications can be exemplified in the following scenario. The teacher, having worked hard to design a curriculum for kindergartners on fruit (one that included seeing and tasting as well as pictures and labeling), wants to check that her students have absorbed her lesson. It is easy to imagine her disappointment when she asks, "what is a banana" and an African-American child answers, "My grandmother ate one." The teacher may assume the child has not been listening to her lesson, is unable to grasp the distinction between fruit and not-fruit, or is unable to categorize at that level of abstraction. Yet, an African-American child may know a great deal about bananas—including that they belong to a category called "fruit"—and still make a person-referenced response because in her experience it is an appropriate way to respond to questions.

DEVELOPMENTALLY APPROPRIATE CURRICULUM

"Developmentally appropriate" is an expression currently used to describe high-quality curriculum for young children.[21] The term evokes a vision of classroom experiences synchronized with each child's maturational/experiential status so that what is presented to be learned is consistent with the child's capacity to learn, thereby insuring school success. The concept appeals both as educational philosophy and as common sense.

But teachers faced with the challenge of teaching children from different cultural communities are hard pressed to decide what is "developmentally appropriate." If the children speak different languages and dialects, if they have different ways of expressing themselves, how can teachers know what children mean by what they say? Or what children think teachers mean by what they say? If children from some groups are hesitant to talk in school, how can teachers organize group expressive language experiences? If children from some groups are dependent on nonverbal clues for meaning, how can teachers stress word meaning? How can teachers test mastery of the curriculum if children do not speak a standard language or use the same styles of communication? How can teachers inspire a child to speak their language if the child has learned to see the school language and institutional practices as irrelevant or hostile to him and his family? Cultural diversity makes it hard for teachers to assess each child's current developmental status, to find common educational experiences that promote further development, and to measure the achievement of educational objectives.

Given the complexity of the interaction between culture, language, and development, is it possible to design a developmentally appropriate curriculum that is culturally sensitive? The answer is "no" if by that we mean that we can use the same curriculum for all children. Children who have been socialized in different worlds will not understand the language of curriculum in the same way. On the other hand, recognition of a few developmental principles can provide a framework of thinking about curriculum for the culturally sensitive teacher. The following list of principles is not meant to be exhaustive but to provide a beginning for teachers trying to bridge the gap between children's cultural/linguistic backgrounds and school objectives for achievement.

First, teachers need to learn to recognize developmental equivalences in patterns of behavior. All children have learned many of the same things—language, category systems, interpersonal communication styles—before they come to school. Although these accomplishments may look quite different, their developmental adequacy should not be questioned; there are a number of "equally good" ways to shape development. When children do not respond to the social and cognitive expectations of school, the teacher should look first for a developmentally equivalent task that the child does know. For instance, children who do not talk in the classroom can be observed on the playground or at home. Children who do not separate attribute cards correctly may be asked to do so with car logos, beads, buttons, or other culturally relevant objects. Children who do not listen to stories about the seasons may be spellbound by one about a basketball player, or a pow wow. If in doubt, teachers should assume that culturally different children are normal and look again, recognizing that their vision may be clouded by their own cultural myopia. It is by assuming developmental equivalence that adults can begin the search for the fit between their and the child's understanding of a situation or of a task to be performed.

Second, it is essential not to value some ways of achieving developmental milestones over others, since young children are particularly sensitive to how adults value them. Hilliard points out that because the behavior of African-American children is so different, they are often judged to be deficient in their development rather than just different. The result is that healthy and normal children are diagnosed as sick or retarded.[22]

Speaking a common language is the cement that binds individuals to a group. Thus young children who speak nonstandard dialects and different languages are reluctant to give up this bond to their own group members. If children find that how they talk and act is not understood or appreciated in school, they are apt to become disengaged and their rejection by the school forecasts their rejection of school. Since there is no evidence that any one way of talking is better than another, during the earliest years children should be expected to talk like their loved ones. If schools want children to use standard English, teachers will need to give and accept love because it is through relationships with meaningful others that young children learn language.

Third, teachers need to begin instruction with interactive styles and content that are familiar to the children. Whether this means speaking in the child's language, or using styles of address and patterns of management that are familiar and comfortable for children, the purpose is to establish a base line of shared knowledge. Teachers and children alike need to know that they have a basis for communication. While fluency in a child's primary language may not be an achievable goal for many teachers, they can become more adept at understanding, planning, and implementing a culturally sensitive curriculum. Such curricula must encompass more than "tasting" parties and dress up clothes; they must be more than stereotyped tours through the amusing and odd practices of people from different parts of the world or different racial groups. They require teachers who have come to grips with their own ethnocentricity and are able to deal with themselves and others fairly—teachers who know the difference between style and substance. Preservice and in-service programs for teachers will need to focus much more on helping teachers bridge cultural difference if language curricula are to be meaningful.

Where discrepancies exist between the cultural patterns of home or community and the school, teachers must plan to bridge these gaps. The essential task is to create new and shared meanings between teachers and children, new contexts that give meaning to the knowledge and skills being taught. Behaviors embedded in critical identity issues are more difficult to change than those that have more superficial meaning to the core of the individual. The challenge is to find personally interesting and culturally relevant ways of creating new contexts for children, contexts in which school skills are meaningful and rewarding. Learning mediated by teachers who are personally involved—affectionate, interested, responsive—in the lives of young children has greater "sticking power" than when the adult is perceived as impersonal and socially distant.

Fourth, school learning is most likely to occur when family values reinforce school expectations. This does not mean that parents must teach the same things at home that teachers do in school. It does mean that parents and community must project school achievement as a desirable and attainable ego ideal if the children are to build it into their own sense of self. This means that interpretation of the school's agenda to parents is as important—perhaps more important—than many of the other tasks at which teachers spend their time.

Fifth, the same "contexts" do not have the same meanings to children from different groups, and the assessment of learning outcomes therefore presents a formidable problem as children misunderstand the meaning of a teacher's requests for information, knowledge, and skills. The meanings of words, gestures, and actions may be quite different without either the adult or the child recognizing the discrepancy. The same curriculum materials and methods may take on meanings different from what the teacher intended and they may be interpreted differently by the various children in the class depending upon their background. Evaluation of children's knowledge and understanding is difficult, and until teachers have built a common culture and a common language with the children, they will be unable to assess accurately what children know or can do. Formal assessment should be delayed until teachers and children have built a set of new meanings together so that the children understand the language and behavior called for in school.

A developmentally appropriate curriculum can not be standardized in a multicultural community. Thoughtful teachers can use developmental principles to create meaning for the new context of school, to attach new learning to that already achieved, and to safeguard children's self-image and self-confidence while they expand their knowledge and skills. It is not easy, but it is the only workable system.

FOOTNOTES

1. Edward E. Evans-Pritchard, *Social Anthropology and Other Essays* (Glencoe, IL: Free Press, 1962).

2. John H. Chilcott, "Where Are You Coming From and Where Are You Going? The Reporting of Ethnographic Research," *American Educational Research Journal* 24, no. 2 (1987): 206.

3. William Labov, "The Logic of Non-Standard English," in *Language and Cultural Diversity in American Education*, ed. Roger D. Abrahams and Rudolph C. Troike (Englewood Cliffs, NJ: Prentice-Hall, 1972).

4. Barbara Rogoff, Mary Gauvain, and Shari Ellis, "Development Viewed in Its Cultural Context," in *Developmental Psychology*, ed. M. H. Bornstein and M. E. Lamb (Hillsdale, NJ: Erlbaum, 1984), pp. 537-572.

5. Joan Lawson, "A Study of the Frequency of Analogical Responses to Questions in Black and White Preschool-age Children," *Early Childhood Research Quarterly* 1, no. 4 (1986): 379.

6. Erik Erikson, *Childhood and Society* (New York: W. W. Norton, 1950).

7. Monica McGoldrick, "Ethnicity and Family Therapy: An Overview," in *Ethnicity and Family Therapy*, ed. Monica McGoldrick, John Pearce, and Joseph Giordano (New York: Guilford Press, 1982), p. 4.

8. Barbara J. Shade, "Afro-American Cognitive Style: A Variable in School Success," *Review of Educational Research* 52, no. 2 (1982): 219.

9. Michael Cole and Jerome Bruner, "Cultural Differences and Inferences about Psychological Processes," *American Psychologist* 26, no. 10 (1972): 867-876.

10. Ellen Gray and John Cosgrove, "Ethnocentric Perception of Childrearing Practices in Protective Services," *Child Abuse and Neglect* 9 (1985): 389-396.

11. Barbara Bowman, "Culturally Sensitive Inquiry," in *What Children Can Tell Us: Eliciting, Interpreting, and Evaluating Information Received from Children*, ed. James Garbarino, Frances Stott, et al. (San Francisco: Jossey-Bass, 1989), pp. 92-107.

12. McGoldrick, "Ethnicity and Family Therapy."

13. Hinda Winawer-Steiner and Norbert Wetzel, "German Families," in *Ethnicity and Family Therapy*, ed. McGoldrick et al.; Behnaz Jalali, "Iranian Families," in *Ethnicity and Family Therapy*, ed. McGoldrick et al.

14. Fred Wise and Nancy Miller, "The Mental Health of the American Indian Child," in *Psychosocial Development of Minority Group Children*, ed. Gloria J. Powell (New York: Brunner/Mazel Press, 1983).

15. Ibid., p. 350.

16. Cole and Bruner, "Cultural Differences and Inferences about Psychological Processes"; Asa Hilliard and Mona Vaughn-Scott, "The Quest for the Minority Child," in *The Young Child: Reviews of Research*, vol. 3, ed. Shirley Moore and C. Cooper (Washington, DC: National Association for the Education of Young Children, 1982).

17. Shade, "Afro-American Cognitive Style," p. 227.

18. Phyllis Katz, "Development of Children's Racial Awareness and Intergroup Attitudes," in *Current Topics in Early Childhood Education*, 4, ed. Lilian Katz (Norwood, NJ: Ablex, 1982).

19. John H. Ogbu, *Minority Education and Caste* (New York: Academic Press, 1973).

20. Courtney Cazden, *Classroom Discourse: The Language of Teaching and Learning* (Portsmouth, NH: Heinemann, 1988).

21. Sue Bredekamp, *Developmentally Appropriate Practice in Early Childhood Programs Serving Children from Birth through Age 8* (Washington, DC: National Association for the Education of Young Children, 1987).

22. Hilliard and Vaughn-Scott, "The Quest for the Minority Child," p. 176.

CHAPTER III

Language and Cultural Issues
in the
Early Education of Language Minority Children

LILY WONG FILLMORE

The Problem

"Papa, I can't say it in Chinese. Can I say it in English? English is easier." English was not always easier for five-year-old Mei-Mei. Just two years ago, when Mei-Mei and her mother came to the United States from Beijing, she knew only Chinese. They had come to join Mei-Mei's father, a doctoral student at an American university. He had arrived a year earlier, and it had taken a year to arrange for his family to join him in what, at that time, promised to be a stay of at least four more years in the United States.

As soon as Mei-Mei and her mother were acclimated to their new social surroundings, the family decided that the two of them should go to school to learn English. Mei-Mei entered the preschool program in the married student housing complex where the family lives. Her mother enrolled in an adult education class to learn English and she attends class each day while Mei-Mei is at school.

Learning English has proven to be much easier for Mei-Mei than for her mother. While her mother practiced hour after hour, trying to coordinate tongue and throat in forming the quite impossible sound combinations of English, Mei-Mei, after a week or two of weeping, was playing happily with her classmates at school. Her inability to communicate with them slowed her down initially, but she soon discovered, as children do, that they could play together despite the language barrier. And while playing with her new friends, she soon found that she could figure out what they were saying if she listened

Some of the issues discussed in this chapter were discussed in earlier papers prepared for the Council of Chief State School Officers (1988), and for the National Association of State School Boards.[1] The latter paper was co-authored by Susan Britsch. I gratefully acknowledge the research assistance she provided me in the preparation of this chapter.

30

and observed them closely enough. By the end of the first year, Mei-Mei was chattering comfortably, if imperfectly, in English. By the end of the second year, she had achieved a native-like level of competence and fluency in the new language. Now in kindergarten, she expresses herself as easily and well in English as any of her five-year-old classmates. English has become, in the process, her preferred language. And therein lies the problem that is the focus of this paper.

Mei-Mei's parents encouraged her to use English with them at first. Her father was delighted by his daughter's alacrity in achieving what he knew to be a remarkable cognitive feat. He knew that many immigrant children have difficulty making progress in American schools because they do not speak English. His daughter would not have such problems when it was time for her to enter kindergarten because she was learning English in nursery school. He therefore welcomed Mei-Mei's use of English at home. Mother was especially pleased with Mei-Mei's use of English because she herself needed practice hearing and speaking English. The mother, unlike the child, was not finding English easy to learn. She was embarrassed about her lack of progress, and did not like to use it with her friends. Despite her near perfect attendance at her adult school class in English as a second language, despite endless hours of practice, she had mastered neither the tongue-twisting sounds of the language nor the intricacies of its inscrutable grammar. She was reluctant to practice speaking English with her husband because it did not feel right to do so. With Mei-Mei, it was different. Using English with the child meant that both were practicing what they were learning, and Mei-Mei did not seem to mind that her mother's efforts sounded more like Chinese than English.

Neither Mei-Mei's father nor her mother can say for certain when the child stopped speaking Chinese. Over the past year or so, she simply switched to English. The language of the home is still Chinese since Mother remains, despite her best efforts, a Chinese monolingual. Although she tries to speak English with Mei-Mei when she can, her command of the new language is so limited that she invariably switches back to Chinese to express herself. Father speaks English, but since Mother does not, he uses Chinese when he is at home. Because of Mei-Mei, however, the communicative environment in the home has changed. The parents speak to Mei-Mei in Chinese mostly, but she always responds in English. When Mother does not understand her, Mei-Mei patiently rephrases or repeats her response, or Father interprets for her. It is clear to the parents that Mei-Mei is losing her ability to speak and understand Chinese. The loss has been gradual. She gave up speaking the language, although she continued to understand her parents when they spoke it at first. Recently, however, the child has shown signs of not understanding all that her parents say to her. Her father is alarmed because Mei-Mei seems to be "forgetting" Chinese. He has begun to insist that she use Chinese when she is at home, and especially when she talks with Mother. But Mei-Mei can not. She has lost her facility in Chinese: "Please, Papa. Say it in English. I don't know what you are saying. It's too hard. English is better."

How typical is Mei-Mei's case? Did her parents, by encouraging her to speak her new language at home, cause the loss of the native language? Can children really lose their native languages? What are the mechanisms and consequences of this kind of loss, and what relevance does this problem have in a discussion of early education for language minority children in the United States? What policy or pedagogical issues should the potential loss of language raise for us? These issues are examined in the present chapter in relation to current discussions on early education policy toward America's language minority children.

Language Minority Children in American Schools

Each year many hundreds of thousands of children enter American schools knowing little or no English at all. Estimates on the number of such children vary and they are not especially reliable given rather great disparities in the criteria used by different agencies for identifying language minority children, and in their reporting practices. Over the past nine years, there have been no reliable statistics on the present size or characteristics of this population.[2] The last time figures were available (estimates based on 1980 Census data), there were 5.5 million school-aged children (between ages five and eighteen) who were said to be limited in their English proficiency (LEP). That figure was disputed, however, and was eventually adjusted to 2.4 million.[3] Whichever one of these figures is realistic, it is clear that the number has increased greatly over the past decade and it continues to grow. A 35 percent increase in their numbers was projected by the year 2000,[4] but one can only guess how many there are presently, and what proportion of the total falls into the age range (between 0 and 5 years of age) that is relevant to this chapter. The only firm statistics currently available are for Spanish speakers who constitute the largest group of LEP children in the country. The Census Bureau reports that there are presently some 239,000 three- to five-year-old Spanish-speaking children in the country.[5] There are many other language minority groups besides Hispanics, however, and all together they comprise a population of considerable size and diversity. A visit to elementary schools in most urban areas as well as in many rural ones gives the observer a glimpse of the future population of the society. In cities all along the east and west coasts and throughout the Southwest, one finds the schools filled to capacity with children from diverse language, ethnic, and cultural backgrounds. In cities like Los Angeles and San Francisco, the overwhelming majority of the children in the early grades are language minorities: they come from homes in which languages other than English are spoken.

In this discussion, language minorities (LM) will refer to children from homes in which English is not the predominant language of communication between parents and children. Many of these children do not speak English well enough to function in an all-English environment. Some of them are bilingual; they speak a language other than English with their parents in the home, but the children also know and can use English when it is needed. They comprise a linguistically and ethnically heterogeneous population. Many of these children are from recent immigrant or refugee families, but some of their families are natives or long-time members of the society.

These children present a problem to the schools because many of them cannot speak or understand English well enough to participate in instructional activities that are conducted exclusively in that language. And in most cases, English has been the exclusive language of instruction in American classrooms. Without assistance, many LM children fail to make the progress expected of them in school. Their achievement problems have been well documented both historically and currently.[6] It is clear that the schools have not provided these children with the help they need. The tendency, however, has been to blame the children and their parents for having problems rather than the school and the society for failing to address them.[7] This is not to say that the schools have not tried to help.

Over the past twenty-five years, American educators have tried to provide special help to LM children who are educationally at-risk in several ways. They have administered large doses of compensatory education on the assumption that the academic problems of LM students stem from shortcomings in basic skills, background, and in experiences. There has been a persistent belief that children who do not speak the variety of English used in school are linguistically deficient, and this deficiency, if not remedied, can seriously impede intellectual development. The remedy has been compensatory language instruction whereby children are drilled in the ways of thinking and talking that are valued in school.[8] The assumption supporting the instruction given to LM children in English as a second language (ESL) is that their inability to speak English is what ails them, and the cure is to teach them English. But none of these compensatory efforts has proven to be especially effective. They have not changed the educational odds for LM children.

The goal of bilingual education, one of the ways educators have tried to even the odds, has been to educate LM children not only in English, but in their home language as well. Since the mismatch between home and school language puts LM children at a disadvantage in the school, they will be helped by being taught partly in the language of the home, and partly in the language of school. The use of the school language enables the children to learn it as a second language. The use of the home language allows them to learn the content of the curriculum in language they understand. Supporters of the bilingual approach argue that use of the home language for instructional purposes can mitigate the linguistic impediment to academic progress for LM children.

This approach, however, has proven to be a controversial one, and has been the focus of a continuing debate over language choice in the society. The arguments are social and political at bottom, but they invariably center on the psychological and pedagogical soundness of bilingual education. Opponents of bilingual education have argued that it is wrong-headed and ineffective. Since LM children must learn English to survive in school and in the society, educating them in their home language is counterproductive, they argue. Bilingual education, we are told, does not provide enough exposure to English to enable children to learn it as a second language. Further, if LM children have as much difficulty managing instruction in one language, it simply complicates matters to teach them in two. Bilingualism, in this view, constitutes a handicapping condition, and is not in the children's best interest. They charge that the research on bilingual programs has shown them to be neither effective in promoting English development nor in improving the academic performance of LM students.[9]

This interpretation of the evidence on bilingual education has been disputed by other researchers.[10] In a recent review of research documents by the U.S. General Accounting Office,[11] it was found that the evidence weighed heavily in favor of bilingual education. In an even more recent examination of bilingual research, Cummins argues:

The research on most of these issues is sufficiently clear to show that the major psychoeducational arguments against bilingual education are spurious. In fact, massive amounts of research evidence refute the argument that insufficient exposure to English is a major cause of minority students' academic failure.[12]

The arguments against bilingual education are sociopolitical rather than educational, Cummins points out, and are without research or rational support. Their aim is to legitimize a return to past practices: insuring the rapid linguistic assimilation of LM children by schooling them in sink-or-swim English classes.

The debate continues, but unfortunately for LM children, educators are already backing away from bilingual instruction. Many current programs are bilingual in name only. The children in such programs are taught exclusively in English. The children's home languages, if they are used at all in school, serve only to keep these programs from being seen as sink-or-swim operations. The direct and indirect consequences of returning to such practices are predictable. The indirect consequences historically have been the systematic eradication of LM children's native languages and the undermining of cultural identities. The most direct consequence has been the high rates of school failure for LM students that led educators to consider bilingual instruction as an alternative to English-only instruction in the first place.

Beliefs about LM Children, Language Learning, and School Readiness

The controversy over bilingual education has led policymakers to consider alternative solutions to the "linguistic problem" LM children present to the society's schools. One alternative that seems to appeal to many educators is early English immersion. The idea is to provide three- to five-year-old LM children with preschool programs that are conducted entirely in English, thereby giving them an opportunity to learn English before they begin school and to acquire some of the skills and experiences that are prerequisites for later learning. The rationale for doing so is deceptively reasonable. The younger children are, the easier it is for them to learn a new language. As we saw in Mei-Mei's case, children can achieve a near-native level of proficiency in a second language in a year or two simply by interacting and playing with others who speak the language. If LM children could learn English before they enter elementary school, the reasoning goes, they would not require further language instruction or support in the form of bilingual education later on. Further, the benefits of early educational interventions for at-risk children are well established, and LM children would obviously profit from the experience of such a program. In one easy "two-fer" stroke, both the bilingual education issue and the compensatory education question are resolved.

This proposal is seldom mentioned in discussions of early education legislation throughout the country but it is nevertheless implicit in the thinking of educational policymakers. It raises a number of critical issues for advocates of language minority children and their families. First, are the underlying assumptions valid? That is, will LM children acquire a second language as easily as Mei-Mei did? Will the learning of English during the preschool years and an early education intervention experience reduce the need for special assistance in school later on? Secondly, will the plan have any negative consequences on the children who are targeted for this kind of educational intervention? Will the learning of English in the preschool years affect communication patterns in the homes of LM families as they appear to have in Mei-Mei's? Do the benefits of such programs outweigh their drawbacks? In other words, what are the arguments for and against this approach?

Can other LM children learn English as rapidly and easily as Mei-Mei? They can, provided the conditions for language learning are as optimal as they were for Mei-Mei. She was in a preschool program in which most of her classmates were native speakers of English—they were mostly the children of graduate students. Mei-Mei was therefore surrounded by classmates who could provide both incentive and assistance for learning English. Mei-Mei's classmates talked as they played with her, and the language they produced in the course of play gave her a linguistic model and served as input for her acquisitional effort. When she attempted to talk with them by adopting utterances she heard them using, they let her know, by their responses, whether or not she was on target. When she appeared not to be, they demanded clarification of her intended meaning, or provided corrective feedback on misusages, thereby revealing to her what native speakers of English regarded as appropriate or grammatically acceptable ways of saying things, given her communicative intentions. Her friends gave Mei-Mei the exposure she needed to English, and supported her efforts to use the language herself. At age three and four, children are in their most active period for language learning. This is the time when children enjoy a natural advantage for learning language. Whether the processes involved are biologically or socially triggered, children during the preschool years are able to manage almost effortlessly the learning of whatever language or languages happen to be spoken in their surroundings, provided they have adequate support for learning them, and provided nothing interferes with the process.

What might interfere with the process? The conditions under which children come into contact with a new language can be far less optimal for learning than the ones Mei-Mei found in her preschool. One important source of interference is the social setting itself in which the child comes into contact with speakers of the target language. For Mei-Mei, the setting was a nursery school classroom in which there were many native speakers of English with whom she could interact. The linguistic input they provided her was representative of English as it is spoken by little children from mainstream families. The form of the language she learned was that of native speakers of her own age and circumstances. But consider what she would have learned had she been in a preschool program designed just for LM children. All or nearly all of the children in such a program would have been non-English speakers.

If they had the same primary language, they would no doubt have communicated by means of that language and no harm would have come of the experience. But if the children had come from different language backgrounds, and especially if the teacher had emphasized the use of English at school, the children would have been forced to learn enough of the new language to communicate in it eventually. In such situations, the input on which the children base their learning of the language is largely the speech of classmates. Because nearly everyone is a learner of English, the speech they hear most of the time consists of approximations of the target language rather than standard forms. What the learners hear and practice is not the English of native speakers, but learner varieties that may deviate considerably from the standard. The children can not judge what is grammatical and what is not, so they can not offer one another the corrective feedback or support needed to insure mastery of the language. The variety of English learned under such conditions is likely to fall short of what the school expects. Teachers presumably can compensate for the shortcomings in the peer input by limiting the extent to which the children are able to interact with one another, and by providing the input and support needed by everyone. However, in order to do that, they would have to adopt a highly structured, and teacher-centered instructional approach, which is quite inappropriate for early education.

The most serious problem that can arise from the proposal we are considering, however, is not with the learning of English. Children can and do learn a second language easily. If the conditions are right, they learn a standard age-appropriate variety of the language. If the conditions are not right, they learn an imperfect variety, but they learn it nevertheless. An even greater concern is what happens to the native languages of LM children as they learn English. We saw how, in Mei-Mei's case, one apparent consequence of learning English has been the gradual erosion and loss of her native language. How common is this?

While there has been little systematic study of the effects of early immersion in English on the maintenance of mother tongues, there is enough evidence to suggest that they are considerable. An examination of data collected on patterns of language use and preference in the late 1970s revealed that after just one year in a Project Head Start program, children who entered as Spanish speakers had shifted substantially to English. The program was experimenting with a bilingual curriculum, but as often happens, the use of English in the classroom outweighed the use of Spanish. Sandoval-Martinez reports that when the children began the program, 78 percent of their total language output was in Spanish.[13] After one year, the percentage had gone down to 58 percent. Should this be a cause for alarm? One of the objectives of programs like Head Start is to give the LM children in them an opportunity to learn English, and such a finding can be taken as evidence that the program was meeting that objective. But were the children adding English to their linguistic repertoire, or were they in fact replacing their native languages with a school language as Mei-Mei has done? What was happening in their homes? These are questions that have not been raised in studies of LM children in early education programs.

This is not to say that there is no evidence at all on this matter. The linguistic history of immigrant groups in this society has been subtractive rather than additive bilingualism. The group may enjoy a brief period of bilingualism, but before long English takes the place of the ethnic language, and it becomes an English monolingual group.[14]

The process of shift seen in Mei-Mei's case is similar to that found in many LM families. Over the past decade and a half or so, I have studied the learning of English by over 200 Latino and Chinese children. Most of them were the children of immigrant and refugee families, and their progress in English was followed longitudinally. In one study, the course of English development was tracked over a three-year period. The effects of English on language use in the homes of those children were considerable. After just one year in the study, 65 percent of the Chinese and 41 percent of the Latino subjects were using English at home with their non-English-speaking parents. The Latino subjects were more inclined to use English with their siblings and playmates: 53.8 percent of them showed a preference for English over Spanish when talking with their siblings, and 74 percent preferred using it in their interactions with friends outside of school. What we see in these figures is evidence of the beginnings of language shift. The children in these studies were five and older when they first came into contact with English. They had had two years more of uninterrupted native language development than Mei-Mei had when she first came into contact with English. Are children at a greater risk of losing their native language at a younger age? There is evidence to suggest that this is indeed the case.

In a study of her child's language learning experience, linguist Ruth Berman documented the process by which three-year-old Shelli lost her primary language soon after coming to the United States with her parents.[15] The Berman family was spending a sabbatical year at the Berkeley campus of the University of California, so Shelli, who spoke only Hebrew at the time she came to America, was placed in an all-day nursery school to learn English. Shelli learned English very quickly—within six weeks of entering school, she had switched to speaking English only. Her mother observed that after another four months, all traces of Hebrew had disappeared from her speech. At seven months, her productive competence in English was reported to be equivalent to that of her three-and-a-half-year-old American classmates. By then, Shelli had given up entirely the productive use of Hebrew. She would not tolerate being addressed in Hebrew, and she appeared genuinely unable to understand anything said to her in Hebrew. Since both Shelli's mother and father spoke English, they were able to accommodate to the change by shifting the language of the home to English. Israeli visitors who came to stay with the family during its year-long stay in Berkeley could not communicate with Shelli, however. Shelli returned to Israel at the end of her parents' sabbatical year and eventually recovered her Hebrew, but it took time to do so. The loss of her native language, it appeared, was real and quite complete.

Over the years, I have informally documented the language learning experiences of twelve preschool age children of visiting scholars. These children have been quite different from the immigrant and refugee children whose language learning I have studied formally. They were the children of educated and privileged families who, like the Bermans, were in the United States for a one-year stay. The families of these children came from Germany, Switzerland, Finland, the Netherlands, Japan, and Brazil. Each family agreed to keep records of their children's language and social adjustment for me during their year in Berkeley. Since all of the visiting scholars were linguists working on language acquisition, they were inclined to do so anyway. All of the children attended English-only nursery schools during their stay in Berkeley, and to one extent or another, they all learned English.

Two-thirds of the families (eight of twelve) reported a switch to English over the course of their year in Berkeley. One child, four-year-old Linus from Finland, asked his mother not to speak to him in Finnish when he was with his American playmates. This child had had a difficult time adjusting to nursery school because he could not communicate with his English-speaking classmates. Once he had picked up enough English to get by, he appeared not to want them to know he spoke anything else. Linus did not master English as quickly or completely as Shelli, but by the end of his stay in Berkeley, English was his preferred language. Another child, four-year-old Hans from Switzerland, was puzzled and out of sorts initially at his nursery school. He had attended school before coming to Berkeley with his parents, but like Linus, he was initially stymied by his inability to communicate with his classmates. He spent the first several months sulking and misbehaving at school. I observed Hans on a field trip with his classmates one day in downtown Berkeley. He was lagging behind his teachers and classmates, walking backwards in a way that seemed to reveal how alienated he was from his classmates. Soon after that incident, his parents reported that he had begun to pick up some English phrases. He had made a friend at school and was more willing to go to school each day. Before long, Hans was suggesting to his parents that they should speak to him in English. It was permissible for them to speak to one another in German, but they should talk to him in English. Like Linus, Hans in no way mastered English over the course of the year, but by the time he returned to Switzerland, he was showing a definite preference for English and an erosion in his primary language proficiency and use. His parents reported that it took him several years after returning home to relearn German, and to reach a level of proficiency that was equivalent to that of his age-peers. Hans, now an adolescent, studies English in school, and he is said to be good at it. Linus lost the English he learned as soon as he returned to Finland. Like Hans, he studies English in school now and is relearning it.

Not all of the children in this small sample lost their native language over the course of the year but, as noted earlier, all of them were affected in one way or another by the experience of being in an all-English nursery school environment. It seems that at this age, children have simply not reached a stable enough command of their native language for it not to be affected by contact with a language that they perceive to be more socially desirable. In the cases I have described, each child was aware of the language barrier that prevented him from interacting with classmates initially. The home language comes to represent the social and cultural barriers that stand in the way of easy participation with the social world outside the home. Once the children learned a little English, they demonstrated that the barriers had been removed in the most definitive way they could. They were eager to show, by their use of English, that they were full participants in their new social world.

In the cases just discussed, the children were in the United States for a short time only, and thus, the loss of their primary languages was temporary. They were able to relearn them after returning to their places of origin. The children's language switch did not seriously disrupt the communicative patterns in the family because the parents were able to speak English. This is not the case in the immigrant and refugee families I have studied, nor will it be the case in Mei-Mei's family. There a switch to English can mean the eventual breakdown of communication between parents and children.

In families where the parents speak no English, or where they do not speak it well enough to communicate easily, the loss of the native language is tragic. It is not immediately apparent, of course. Language loss is rarely as dramatic as in the case of Shelli. For a year or two, the children may comprehend the parental language (as Mei-Mei still does), even if they do not use it productively. The parents speak to the children; the children respond in English. Gradually, however, the language is affected because when children and parents do not use the same language, communication begins to break down. The parent says what must be said, but does not go beyond that level of basic necessity. When that happens, the language input the child receives from the parents is no longer supporting the development that should be taking place in the primary language. Gradually, the child's command of the home language erodes to the point where the child no longer understands what the parents say. Communication between them becomes strained and limited—too limited to convey the lessons that parents should be teaching their children at that stage in their development.

How big a loss is this to the child? Should educators and policy-makers be concerned about the loss of minority languages and the breakdown of communication in the home? One might argue that the society is not responsible for what happens in the home. It does have a responsibility to facilitate the learning of English, and to help LM children make the transition from the home to school. Is it even desirable for children to maintain the primary language? A preschool teacher's comment seems to summarize the way many people in the society feel about these issues: "Look, these kids need English before they go to school. So what if they lose their first language? In this world, you have to give something to get something! They lose their mother tongue, but they gain English, and with it, access to what they can learn in school. That's not such a big price."

And what about the lessons to be learned in the home? What about the cost to the family and children? When what is lost is the means of communication in a family, the children lose access to all the things that parents can teach them. Where the parents are able to speak English, the loss is not complete. If the parents are willing to switch to English too, they can go on socializing their children in the values, beliefs, and practices that are important to the family and community. When the parents are not able to do so, what is lost is closeness and family unity. That may be too big a price for the children to pay for an easier transition from home to school.

Language, Culture, and Early Educational Policy

Is this loss an inevitable part of the assimilation process? It is not, but it happens, unless steps are taken to prevent it from happening. We need to consider the assumptions underlying our educational policies toward LM children, and the long-term consequences these policies will have, not only in terms of what happens to the children in school but what happens to the family in the home as well. The society should not adopt educational policies that diminish the role families must play in the socialization and education of their children, nor should it contribute to the breakdown of family unity. Not everything that children need to learn can or should be learned in school. Families are responsible for preparing their children for the learning they must do outside the home, and with the exception of dysfunctional families they generally do. The problem is that this preparation is not recognized or valued by many of the people who are responsible for educating LM children.

We have seen how educators tend to assume that LM children do not do well in school because they lack the linguistic and experiential backgrounds that are prerequisites for school. This assumption allows them to justify the practice of putting them into intervention programs that are designed to teach them English before they reach school age, and which provide them with the skills and experiences they putatively lack. The preparation that parents give children for school is seldom recognized as such or appreciated. Although educators are generally aware that cultural differences exist, few in fact recognize or accept the validity of such differences as reflected in the early experiences of LM children. When they show up in school, they are seen, not as children who speak different languages or who have different styles of learning and behaving, but as children who do not speak English, and who are therefore unprepared for school. The preparation that is deemed as standard and necessary for school participation is based on the mainstream model: children are expected to talk, behave, and learn as children do when they have been socialized in mainstream English-speaking families. In the eyes of many educators, the real test for school readiness is English. A better understanding of how different groups socialize children for learning is a prerequisite, both for the design of early educational programs for LM children, and for the preparation of professionals to work in those programs. But what do we know of such matters?

Ethnographic research in child language socialization has revealed the many ways in which different cultural groups can prepare children for learning, and has pointed out the need to recognize the different patterns of learning behaviors and abilities that result from the socializing experiences that children have undergone.

Groups differ in the extent to which they rely on speech as the primary means by which they teach children what they need to know about the world. Heath's ethnographic research on the socialization practices of working-class blacks and whites and of mainstream families in a rural Appalachian community has shown how greatly groups can differ in their beliefs about how children learn, the roles parents play in their education, and how they prepare children for literacy.[16] The practices of teaching children about shared experiences by talking about them and of inviting children to respond to questions about the world as it is presented in books (which educators take to be the standard or normal way for parents to socialize children) are characteristic only of mainstream families, Heath found. Both the black and white working-class families she studied followed quite different practices in interacting with their children, and in offering them opportunities to learn about ways of talking and relating with their social environment. In neither of these groups was there as strong an emphasis on learning through discourse, nor was teaching as proactive as in the mainstream families she described.

According to researchers who have studied the socialization of American Indian children in various communities,[17] the modes of learning which are most highly valued are the visual and experiential rather than the verbal. Children are encouraged to learn through observation and practice. Adults tend not to push or to exhort children to try doing things, nor do they provide verbal instructions or explanations while the children are engaged in figuring things out. The child decides when he or she is ready to demonstrate comprehension and mastery of a new skill, and at that time the family takes note of the accomplishment.

In her study of child socialization in Mexican families, Valdés found that parents also emphasize observation and independence in learning.[18] Children are encouraged to observe and to participate in the performance of household tasks when they feel ready to do so. It is assumed that the child is able to judge when he or she is ready, and when he undertakes a task, the performance is the best that he is able to manage at the time. Adults provide guidance if it is needed or requested, but they rarely offer much in the way of unsolicited verbal instructions.

Cheung found that Chinese parents follow child socialization practices that differ sharply from the ones just mentioned for Mexican and American Indian parents.[19] The Chinese parent believes that children learn nothing unless they are properly taught. The parents' role is to see that their children learn all the values, skills, attitudes, and beliefs that characterize the well-prepared and civilized individual. They judge themselves and are judged by others on how well they instruct their children. Nothing is left to chance. Parents decide when children are ready to acquire particular skills, and they train them in the performance of the instructional task. The instruction given to the child consists more of exhortations and criticism than explanation or direction. There is an emphasis on training children to do things well. They are given only those tasks that the parents regard as appropriate to the child's age and level of development, and then the children are guided and "jaw-boned" into a level of performance acceptable to the adult.

Such different patterns of socialization can result in quite different approaches to learning on the part of different groups of LM children. By the time these children arrive at school at age five or six, they are all well prepared to learn, but their preparedness may or may not be recognized by their teachers at school. The expectation at school is that children have had the kinds of socialization experiences provided by mainstream parents. If children have not undergone the kind of verbal socialization that mainstream children have had, their teachers may regard them as being deficient in their preparation for school.

It is important to recognize the consequences that early education programs for LM children can have on the family's ability to perform its socializing role. As noted earlier, one of the assumptions underlying the compensatory approach to educating LM children is that their parents are doing an inadequate job preparing them for school. The belief is that these children cannot succeed in school or later in life unless they become more like mainstream children. They are therefore given early education programs that provide them with the mainstream language and cultural experiences they lack. More harm than good can come of programs founded on these beliefs. The problem, we have seen, is that these very experiences can cause children to turn away from the influence of their parents in some very fundamental ways. Admittedly, there are positive benefits to be had from an early immersion in the ways of speaking and learning that are the most highly valued by the school. The children will find it easier to make the transition to school eventually. But what of the negative consequences on the family and children? Such programs achieve little if they contribute to a breakdown in parent and child relations. What is at stake is nothing less than the family's continued role in the socialization of its children.

Societal Responsibility to Families and Children

This chapter began with a story of a child, a story that is still being worked out. Mei-Mei is just now entering kindergarten, and in time, we will learn whether or not she has abandoned her mother tongue entirely, and therefore lost her only means of communication with her mother. The chapter ends with the story of another child, Ong. Ong is now fifteen years old. He is a student in a San Francisco high school where he attends special education classes. His command of English is, at best, shaky. He did well in the primary grades, but he has had problems handling the demands of school since junior high. Ong came to the United States from Vietnam with his father and brother when he was just two years old. His mother was killed shortly after Ong was born, and his father is badly crippled from injuries suffered while escaping from Vietnam. On the day I met Ong, he was visibly upset. He had attended a musical performance the night before with his ESL class. The performance was of Vietnamese folk music put on by a troupe of visiting musicians from Hanoi. He told me that his father had scolded him for going and was very angry with him. Why?

"Because those people are communist. Because they are bad. They kill my mother, he say."

How does Ong feel about that?

"I don't know. I don't know what happen. I was just a kid when I leave Vietnam. I know they kill my mother, but I don't know why."

We talked about the war briefly. It was a war in which there was a lot of harm done to people on both sides, but it was a war between brothers. It is hard to say who is right or wrong in such a war. It is important now that it is over to try to understand, and to work out the differences. Ong knew all that, but his father is mad at him.

"Talk to him," I said. "Let your father know how you feel about this. Find out how he feels about it. It is really important for you to discuss these things with your dad."

Ong looked at me, puzzled. "I can't," he responded.

"Of course you can," I said. "He's angry with you, but he needs to talk about it as much as you do."

"I can't talk with him. I don't know how."

"What do you mean, you don't know how?"

"I don't know how to say it in Vietnamese, and he don't understand English," Ong replied.

Ong's dilemma sums up the tragedy of language loss. What is lost is the ability for parents and children to communicate about the deep and critical experiences of growing up. What the parent has to teach the child and what the child is able to share with the parent are irretrievably lost when their means of communication are lost to them.

Ong has been instructed exclusively in English since he first entered school. He learned English, but not well. He expresses himself adequately in his second language, but not richly or fully. At the same time, he has effectively given up the use of his primary language, so in a sense he does not have a full command of either language.

What then is the conclusion to be drawn from this discussion? Am I suggesting that LM children should not be given preschool experiences? Quite the contrary. It is necessary, however, to consider the kind of early education programs that LM children need. Can we provide opportunities for them to learn English and to acquire some of the experiences and skills that their teachers will expect them to have without the negative consequences that I have described here? There is clearly a need to study this and the other questions I have raised concerning the preschool population that is the focus of this chapter. Given the diversity of that population, the research would clearly have to examine broadly the issues that have been raised here. The design, implementation, and evaluation of appropriate program models call for early education professionals who have a clear understanding of these cultural and linguistic issues. That calls for special funds for program development and for staff development.

One obvious solution is to provide early education programs for children that emphasize the development of native language skills and culture before introducing English and elements of the common culture of the society to them. Another is to invite parents to participate in helping their children to make the transition to school by letting them know what teachers regard as necessary preparation and experiences for school. This would allow them to figure out how best to provide those experiences for their children. Parents should also be warned about the potential loss of the family language as their children learn English in school. They should be encouraged to insist on their children's continued use of the primary language at home as they learn English. Anything less than that would be a disservice to families and children.

Footnotes

1. Lily Wong Fillmore and Susan Britsch, "Early Education for Children from Linguistic and Cultural Minority Families" (Paper prepared for the Early Education Task Force of the National Association of State Boards of Education, 1988).

2. Ibid.

48 LANGUAGE AND CULTURAL ISSUES

3. J. Michael O'Malley, *Children's English and Services Study: Language Minority Children with Limited English Proficiency in the United States* (Rosslyn, VA: InterAmerica Research Associates, 1982).

4. Rebecca Oxford, Louis Pol, D. Lopez, P. Stupp, S. Peng, and Murray Gendell, *Projections of Non-English Language Background and Limited-English Proficient Persons in the United States to the Year 2000* (Rosslyn, VA: InterAmerica Research Associates, 1980).

5. Bureau of the Census, U. S. Department of Commerce, *Statistical Abstract of the United States* (Washington, DC: U. S. Department of Commerce, 1987).

6. See, for example, George L. Sánchez, "Group Differences and Spanish-Speaking Children: A Critical Review," *Journal of Applied Psychology* 61, no. 5 (1932): 549-558; David K. Cohen, "Immigrants and the Schools," *Review of Educational Research* 40, no. 1 (1970): 13-27; Thomas P. Carter and Roberto D. Segura, *Mexican-Americans in School: A History of Educational Neglect* (New York: College Entrance Examination Board, 1979); National Center for Education Statistics, *The Education of Minority Persons in the United States*, Spring, 1976, NCES Bulletin 78-B-4 (Washington, DC: U. S. Department of Education, 1978); Laurence Steinberg, Patricia Lin Blinde, and Kenyon S. Chan, "Dropping-Out among Language Minority Youth: A Review of the Literature," NCER Working Paper no. 81-3W (Los Alamitos, CA, National Center for Bilingual Research, 1982).

7. Jim Cummins, *Empowering Minority Students* (Sacramento, CA: California Association for Bilingual Education, 1989).

8. Carl Bereiter, Siegfried Engelmann, Jean Osborn, and Phillip A. Reidford, "An Academically Oriented Preschool for Culturally Deprived Children," in *Preschool Education Today*, ed. Fred M. Hechinger (New York: Doubleday, 1966); Russell Gersten and John Woodward, "A Case for Structured Immersion," *Educational Leadership* 43 (September 1985): 75-79.

9. See, for example, Keith A. Baker and Adriana A. de Kanter, *Effectiveness of Bilingual Education: A Review of the Literature* (Washington, DC: Office of Planning and Budget, U. S. Department of Education, 1981). It should be noted that much of this research has been done on programs for school-aged children. The conclusions that critics of bilingual education have drawn from their interpretation of this research have unduly influenced educational policymakers who are concerned with preschool children.

10. See, for example, Ann C. Willig, "A Meta-Analysis of Selected Studies on the Effectiveness of Bilingual Education," *Review of Educational Research* 55 (1985): 269-317.

11. U. S. General Accounting Office, *Bilingual Education: A New Look at the Research Evidence*, Briefing Report to the Chairman, Committee on Education and Labor, House of Representatives (Washington, DC: General Accounting Office, 1987).

12. Cummins, *Empowering Minority Students*, p. 20.

13. Steven Sandoval-Martinez, "Findings from the Head Start Bilingual Curriculum Development Effort," *NABE: Journal of the National Association for Bilingual Education* 7, no. 1 (1982): 1-12.

14. The reasons for language shift are sociolinguistic, and are related to status differences between the minority language and English, and to the pressures operating in the society against linguistic and cultural diversity. These issues, however, are beyond the scope of this chapter, and are mentioned only as they figure in the discussion of the children and educational policies that are the foci of attention here.

15. Ruth A. Berman, "The Re-emergence of a Hebrew-English-Speaking Child," *Working Papers on Bilingualism* 19 (1979): 157-159.

16. Shirley Brice Heath, *Ways with Words: Language, Life, and Work in Communities and Classrooms* (New York: Cambridge University Press, 1983).

17. Susan U. Phillips, *The Invisible Culture: Communication in Classroom and Community on the Warm Springs Indian Reservation* (New York: Longman, 1983); Susan Britsch, "Child Language Socialization in a Tachi-Yokuts Home: A Pilot Study" (Unpublished manuscript, University of California, Berkeley, 1987).

18. Guadalupe Valdés, "Brothers and Sisters: A Closer Look at the Development of 'Cooperative' Social Orientations in Mexican-American Children" (Paper presented at the Annual Convention of the California Association of School Psychologists, Oakland, CA, 1986).

19. Christinia Cheung, "The Socialization of Chinese-American Children" (Paper presented at the AERA Mini-Conference, Berkeley, CA, 1988).

CHAPTER IV

Pedagogical Issues in Early Childhood Education

LILIAN G. KATZ

To confront a child with tasks for which he is not ready, with the implication that he should succeed, gives him a feeling of failure, undermines his security. Instead, we must guide him into those learning situations that he can attack effectively and with sufficient success to yield satisfaction, encouragement, and growth.

Carleton Washburne

Washburne's admonition, directed primarily at elementary education, is more than fifty years old! For more than twice that long the field of early childhood education has been marked by unrelenting dissension concerning appropriate pedagogical practices. Lazerson points out that early in this century controversy in the field raged over such issues as the relative emphasis on symbolism versus realism, the extent of free play versus teacher direction, and the nature and importance of creativity.[1] In the 1930s, Gardner attempted to put the continuing controversies to rest once and for all with a comparative study of two schools: School A characterized by practices known in the United States as "open" or "informal" methods, and School B, using formal didactic methods of educating young children.[2] In spite of findings in favor of School A, the debate resumed barely a generation later.

During the expansion of early childhood programs in the 1960s, Winsor noted that it was ironic to find the "very nursery movement which had its beginnings in progressive education described as 'traditional' " in contrast with the new academic curricula advocated for compensatory early childhood education.[3] The advocates of formal didactic pedagogical practices in this period frequently implied that "traditional" nursery and kindergarten pedagogy was merely laissez faire, offering little more than free play and some socialization experiences.[4]

Since the 1960s, the issues in early childhood practices have been cast in terms of polar dimensions such as child-centered versus adult-centered, structured versus unstructured, didactic versus nondidactic, child-initiated versus teacher-initiated, play versus instruction, socialization versus academics, and several variations of each. In actual implementation these dimensions are most likely confounded and overlap considerably.[5]

A number of factors may account for the length and persistence of the debates over pedagogical practices in the field. It has often been noted that educational ideologies swing back and forth in pendulum fashion; a particular approach to early childhood education is enthusiastically embraced at a given time, followed within a few years by a countermovement, which in turn is followed by overcorrections for the preceding swing, and then another zealous movement to correct previous overcorrections, ad infinitum. The curriculum developed by Bereiter and Engelmann in the 1960s[6] (now known as DISTAR) can be seen as an overcorrection of their perception of the traditional preschool and kindergarten curriculum and its apparent ineffectiveness. However, a clear pattern of overcorrections of DISTAR is not apparent.

Ideally this dissension could be settled by referring to pertinent empirical data. Although many studies bearing on the comparative effects of alternative practices have been reported in the last twenty years, their findings and conclusions are interpreted in many different ways.[7] Numerous measurement, methodological, and logistical problems are inherent in conducting longitudinal studies of alternative approaches to early childhood pedagogy. Furthermore, a robust design for such comparative studies would almost certainly pose daunting ethical problems as well.

As we enter the last decade of the century, the controversy centers primarily on the accelerating "downward shift of what were next-grade expectations into lower grades."[8] Since next-grade expectations are typically academic and narrow rather than intellectual and open, their appropriateness for younger children has become a major issue for all who have a stake in the healthy development of young children. Indeed, the controversy over the "push-down" of the primary curriculum became sufficiently acute in the 1980s to prompt the largest membership association of early childhood practitioners, the National Association for the Education of Young Children (NAEYC), to issue a substantial position statement against it in 1986, and to recommend a set of appropriate practices covering children from birth up through the age of eight years.[9]

The NAEYC Position Statement on appropriate practices for young children argues that practices are acceptable to the extent that they take into account what is known about children's development; the position assumes that such knowledge can provide a basis upon which curriculum and pedagogy appropriate to the age and maturity of both the group and of individual learners can be generated. However, the relationship between the body of knowledge called child development and pedagogical practices is not a simple or direct one.[10] Indeed, it is difficult to determine just where knowledge and principles of child development fit into the processes of determining appropriate practices. The matter is further complicated by the fact that there are criteria other than development by which the appropriateness of pedagogical practices might be judged, viz. cultural, social, ethical, health, logistical, or even financial criteria.

The number of factors that account for the actual nature of early childhood educational practices is potentially very large. It seems reasonable to hypothesize that major ones among them fall roughly into three large categories. One is the body of knowledge and principles of child development. Another includes characteristics of the parents served, such as their goals, expectations, aspirations, and their understandings and preferences with respect to appropriate experiences for their children. A third category of factors includes what teachers are willing and able to do; teachers may be willing to implement some practices, but for a variety of reasons may be unable to do so, and vice versa.

The Venn diagram in figure 1 is a schematic representation of how these three factors might intersect. It may be that in some situations not any of the three factors intersect, or only two of them (child development knowledge and the teacher variables) do. Furthermore, the extent to which they intersect may vary greatly. Nevertheless, the goal of specialists in the field is to enlarge the area of overlap of all three of the circles as much as possible.

In the meantime, those in decision-making roles must proceed to plan and implement programs for young children in the absence of clear empirically derived conclusions and guidelines. The aim of this chapter is to discuss the main issues that have to be addressed in determining the appropriateness of pedagogical practices, and to suggest some principles applicable to the processes involved.

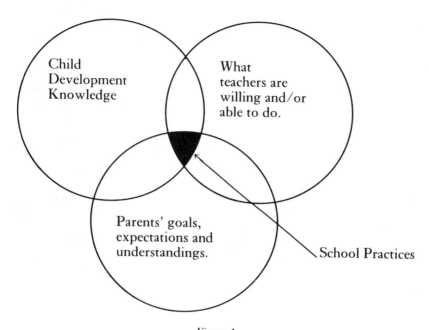

Figure 1
Schematic representation of major factors that account for school practices.

Identifying Appropriate Pedagogical Practices

In view of the long-standing tradition of diverse approaches to pedagogy in the field, how can those responsible for planning and implementing pedagogical approaches for young children select the best approach for their own communities? Are decision makers faced with either/or choices between opposing camps? Is a compromise or eclectic position feasible so that a community can have the best of all pedagogical worlds? Is there an optimum mix of several approaches? Responses to these questions are proposed by beginning with three interrelated a priori questions: (1) What should be learned? (2) When should it be learned? (3) How is it best learned?

Responses to the first question provide the *goals* of the program for which pedagogical practices are to be adopted. The second question is the *developmental* one in that it draws upon what is known about the development of the learner. In other words, child development helps to address the *when* questions of program design. The third question turns specifically to matters of appropriate pedagogy itself; it includes consideration of all aspects of implementing a program by which the program's goals can be achieved.

It is apparent, however, that responses to one of the three questions are inextricably linked to responses to the other two. Thus *what* should be learned and *how* it is best learned depends on *when* the learning is to occur. Similarly, *how* something is learned depends upon what it is, as well as upon the developmental characteristics of the learner. For example, virtually all stakeholders in early childhood education would place literacy high on the list of answers to the question about what should be learned. However, they are likely to diverge considerably upon the question of *when* as well as *how* it should be learned, the latter considerations being related to each other. Terms like "emergent literacy" and "preliteracy" have recently appeared in the early childhood literature partly in order to address the confounding of the "when" and "how" questions. The confounding of the three questions is acknowledged; however, for the sake of discussion, they are taken up separately in this chapter.

What Should Be Learned?

The values and preferences of the parents served by the program would seem to have first claim among criteria for determining what should be learned. However, parents are rarely a homogeneous or monolithic group with clear consensus upon the goals of their children's education. Divergent answers to the question of what should be learned are as likely to be offered within school boards, parent groups, and school faculties, as between them. Furthermore, since the answers are based on values, ideals, and assumptions about the future needs of the learners, they cannot be determined empirically; they thus inevitably become the subject of dispute.[11] While the community and clients' preferences determine the goals, the special expertise of professional educators should be brought to bear on addressing the questions of when and how the goals can best be implemented.

FOUR TYPES OF LEARNING GOALS

Whatever specific learning objectives are identified by clients and educators, they are all likely to fit into each of four types of learning goals: knowledge, skills, dispositions, and feelings, defined as follows:

1. *Knowledge* during the preschool period can be broadly defined

as ideas, concepts, schemas, facts, information, stories, myths, songs, and other such contents of mind that come under the heading of what is to be learned. Three Piagetian categories of knowledge social, physical, and logico-mathematical are often used in discussions of the knowledge goals in early childhood education.[12]

2. *Skills* are defined as small, discrete, and relatively brief units of behavior that are easily observed or inferred from behavior (e.g., skills of cutting, drawing, counting a group of objects, making friends, and solving problems).

3. *Dispositions* are broadly defined as relatively enduring "habits of mind," or characteristic ways of responding to experience across types of situations (e.g., persistence at a task, curiosity, generosity, meanness, the disposition to read, to solve problems). Unlike an item of knowledge, or a skill, a disposition is not an end state to be mastered once and for all. It is a trend or consistent pattern of behavior and its possession is established only if its manifestation is observed repeatedly.

4. *Feelings* are subjective emotional or affective states (e.g., feelings of belonging, of self-esteem, confidence, adequacy and inadequacy, competence and incompetence). Feelings about or toward significant phenomena may vary from being transitory to enduring, intense or weak, or perhaps ambivalent. In early childhood education attitudes and values can also be included in this category; in education for older children they merit separate categories.[13]

In principle, pedagogical practices are appropriate if they address all four categories of learning goals equally and simultaneously. Pedagogical practices that emphasize the acquisition of knowledge and the mastery of skills without ensuring that the dispositions to use the knowledge and skills so learned are also strengthened are not appropriate. Similarly, if the desired knowledge and skills are mastered in such a way that feelings of distaste for their use or for the school environment accumulate throughout the learning process, then the pedagogy may be judged inappropriate. Similarly, if a pedagogical approach succeeds in generating feelings of joy, pleasure, amusement, or excitement, but fails to bring about the acquisition of desirable knowledge and skills, it cannot be judged appropriate.

Most stakeholders in early childhood education are likely to agree on broad goals in all four categories of learning. For example, most state and school district curriculum guides for kindergarten list such goals as knowledge and skills related to literacy and numeracy, various items of cultural knowledge, plus dispositions like the "desire to learn," creativity, cooperativeness, and so forth. The list of goals related to feelings usually includes "positive feelings about themselves," or "self-confidence."[14] Once the knowledge, skills, dispositions, and feelings to be learned have been agreed upon, the next question is *when* they should be learned.

When Is It Best Learned?

In the introductory chapter of *Child Development and the Curriculum*, published more than fifty years ago as the Thirty-eighth Yearbook of the National Society for the Study of Education, Carleton Washburne stated that

> . . . before education can be really effective we must understand child nature. We must know better than we now do what the developing organism is reaching out for at each successive stage. We must know much more than we now do about the experiences, knowledge, and concepts of the child at each level of development. We must learn how to measure at successive levels the child's capacity for adding to his experiences and interpreting them. We must measure the assimilability of new experiences to which the developing organism is to be exposed. At present we are in the first crude beginnings of this stage of scientific approach to our problem.[15]

In the fifty years since Washburne's observation, much has been learned about children's development that can help to address the issues in early childhood pedagogy. Indeed, early childhood education has traditionally drawn heavily on studies of children's development. The study of development is typically a major component of early childhood teacher preparation. It is widely assumed that mastery of the knowledge and principles of child development can form a basis for pedagogical decisions most likely to enhance growth and learning and to minimize potential harm to young children.

Typically discussions of curriculum and pedagogical practices use the concept of development to refer to what is known about the typical characteristics of children at each age. Many curriculum guides, for instance, include sections describing typical characteristics of four-year-olds, five-year-olds, etc. However, characteristics of children at particular ages are only one aspect of their development— the *normative* one. The concept of development can be seen as having two distinctive but related dimensions, the *normative* and the *dynamic*, each of which should be taken into account when deciding what and how children should learn.[16] Each dimension is defined briefly below.

NORMATIVE DIMENSION OF DEVELOPMENT

Common use of the concept of development draws on the *normative* dimension. This dimension addresses matters such as what most children can and cannot do at a given age or stage. For example, what is typical and what is most frequently observed in children at two, three, five, and nine years of age? We apply the normative dimension when we discuss how many words most children know at a particular age, and the average age at which they can be expected to take their first step, to understand time, to conserve volume, and so forth. When we say that an activity is developmentally appropriate, cite grade level achievement, or apply Gesell-type measures to children's behavior, we employ the normative dimension of the concept of development.

DYNAMIC DIMENSION OF DEVELOPMENT

The other major dimension is the *dynamic one*. Rather than compare behaviors across a group of children of the same age, the dynamic dimension addresses within-individual growth through time. While the normative dimension deals with aspects of development that are thought to be universal, the dynamic dimension focuses on the unique or idiosyncratic patterns of development of the individual.

The dynamic dimension can be further analyzed into three interrelated subcategories. One deals with the ways that individual human beings *change* over time and with experience. This subcategory addresses the sequence of learning, the transformations that occur in capabilities from one age or time period to another, and the order in which the stages of development and learning occur. Thus some specialists study the progressive, sequential changes, stages, or transitions involved in going from babbling babyhood to becoming a competent speaker of a language by age four or five.

Another subcategory of the dynamic dimension of development is *delayed impact*. This concerns the way early experience may affect later functioning, particularly with respect to affective and personality development. It attends to determinants of behavior that may be unconscious but caused by early experiences no longer easily accessible to conscious attention. It is this aspect of development, for example, that leads to widespread concern among early childhood specialists about whether early separation of an infant from its mother may have a delayed impact on later mental health. Delayed impacts may be both positive and negative. For example, either the loving or abusive behavior of a new parent toward his or her infant may be the result of delayed impacts of their own very early experiences that are no longer recalled.

A third subcategory of the dynamic dimension is the long-term *cumulative effect* of repeated or frequent experiences. An experience might have no effect or a benign effect on a child's development if it occurs only once in a while, but might be harmful if experienced repeatedly or frequently over a long period of time. A teacher might not become concerned if the directions for completing school tasks confuse a child once in a while; but repeated or frequent experience of being confused may have strong cumulative effects on the child's self-confidence and self-perceptions as a learner, and thus become a source of concern to the teacher. Similarly, occasional exposure to horror movies might not affect a child; but the cumulative effects of frequent exposure to them might cause long-term deleterious effects.

In a similar way, an activity might seem to have little positive effect on a child's development if it occurs only occasionally but may yield substantial benefits cumulatively. For example, some parents and educators might question the value of block play or dramatic play to a child's development. If this kind of play is available only occasionally, it may produce few if any positive effects; however, the cumulative effects of repeated opportunities to engage in such peer-interactive, open-ended, expressive, creative, child-governed activities may be both positive and substantial.

Taking into account both the normative and dynamic dimensions of development suggests that, in principle, just because children *can* do something does not mean that they *should*. The determination of what most children of a given age can do is a normative assessment; the determination of what the same group should do depends upon anticipated dynamic long-term consequences of an undertaking for each individual. For example, though it is likely that most young children can learn phonics at age four—a normative assessment—it does not follow that they should do so. Judgment concerning whether instruction in phonics (or any other skill, for that matter) must be based on at least two considerations: the dynamic developmental trajectory of each individual in a group, and the potential long-term consequences of such a practice in terms of its possible cumulative effects. Individuals may vary with respect to their vulnerability to negative cumulative effects of a pedagogical practice that may be benign if experienced infrequently.

The distinction between what children can do and what they should do is especially serious in early childhood education because most young children are eager to please their teachers and appear willing to do almost anything asked of them. Most even enjoy the activities offered, at least until their novelty wears off. However, children's willingness and enjoyment are potentially misleading criteria for judging the appropriateness of pedagogical practices. Instead, estimates of the possible delayed impacts and cumulative effects of practices must be considered.

The two dimensions of development, and especially the sub-categories of the dynamic dimension—*change, delayed impact, cumulative effects*—provide a framework for considering the appropriateness of the learning goals derived from answering the question, What should be learned? For example, from a normative perspective, extensive studies of young children suggest that, in principle, pedagogical practices should address helping them make better, deeper, and more accurate sense of their own environments and experiences. As children increase in age and experience, it is the responsibility of educators to help them make better, deeper, and more accurate sense of the environments and experiences of others who are distant in time and place. Similarly, the view of children's intellectual development currently held by contemporary developmentalists suggests that, in principle, the younger the children, the more likely knowledge can be acquired if it is context- or situation-bound.[17] Furthermore, Piagetians have made the case that children's intellectual development progresses in fairly predictable and invariant sequences or stages. Thus both the normative and stage/sequence aspects of development deserve consideration in selecting what knowledge is to be acquired in an early childhood program. Similarly, normative and stage/sequence considerations are appropriate in identifying the skills to be included among the goals of a curriculum or program.

When it comes to identifying the dispositions and feelings to be fostered or weakened by a pedagogical approach, the other two subcategories of the dynamic dimension—delayed impacts and cumulative effects—merit consideration. For example, the introduction of formal instruction in phonics at age four or five may be acceptable on normative grounds; but in view of its timing and the amount of instruction likely to be required when starting that early, the potential delayed or cumulative effects—positive or negative—of adopting this practice must be considered. Opponents of the practice argue that, even if the knowledge and skill involved in reading is acquired, the cumulative effects of an early start may be to damage the disposition to read, and that it may engender negative feelings

surrounding literacy and literature that are undesirable (e.g., boredom
or dislike). Advocates of early reading instruction, on the other hand,
assert that postponing its introduction unnecessarily deprives the
learner of whatever knowledge and experiences can be acquired
through reading.[18]

In principle, then, an appropriate pedagogy or curriculum is one
that takes into account the acquisition of knowledge and skills in such
a way that the disposition to use them and positive feelings toward
them are also strengthened. Some might argue that, given the
vulnerability of children, it may be that the younger the child the
more consideration should be given to goals in the disposition and
feeling categories of learning. However, because neither of these two
types of learning can be addressed directly, but are by-products of
interactions involving the other two categories, they cannot easily be
given priority in curriculum planning. It is reasonable to assume that
dispositions and feelings are always being strengthened or weakened,
either intentionally or by default; they do not wait upon particular
lessons or instructions.

How Is It Best Learned?

This question takes us directly to matters of pedagogy, including
teaching methods, activities, materials, and all other practical matters
designed to achieve the learning goals and to take into account what is
known about learners' development. Thus answers to the *what* and
when questions are blended to yield principles of practice that constitute
a general pedagogical approach to early childhood education.

Learning in the four categories of goals is facilitated in different
ways. In the case of both knowledge and skills, learning can be aided
by instruction as well as by other processes; but dispositions and
feelings cannot be learned from direct instruction. Dispositions appear
to be acquired from models, to be strengthened by being manifested
and appreciated, or weakened when not sufficiently manifested,
acknowledged, or effective.

Feelings related to learning experiences are likely to be learned as
a by-product of experiences rather than from instruction. Both
dispositions and feelings can be thought of somewhat like incidental
learnings in that they are incidental to the processes by which
knowledge and skills are acquired. To label feelings as incidental is not
to belittle them, or to devalue the role of the pedagogue in their
development; rather, it is to emphasize that they cannot be taught

didactically. Children cannot be instructed in what feelings to have.

We consider first the principles of pedagogical practice applicable to each of the four categories of learning goals and follow with a discussion of pedagogical principles generally applicable to most of the goals of an early childhood program.

PRINCIPLES RELATED TO THE ACQUISITION OF KNOWLEDGE

Recent insights into children's development suggest that, in principle, the younger the child, the more readily knowledge is acquired through active and interactive processes; conversely, with increasing age children become more able to profit from reactive, passive-receptive pedagogical approaches or instructional processes. This developmental principle suggests that pedagogical practices are appropriate when the knowledge to be learned is relatively easily accessible through the child's own firsthand, direct experiences and when it is accessible from primary versus secondary sources.[19] This is not to say that children do not acquire knowledge and information from secondary sources like stories, books, and film. The extent to which they do so is related to whether young children can connect the material within the secondary sources to the images and knowledge they already possess.[20] With increasing age and experience children become more able to profit from secondhand, indirect experiences and secondary sources (e.g., textbooks). This principle is consistent with the concept of "situated cognition" that has recently been proposed to account for the nature of learning at all ages. As Brown, Collins, and Duguid explain:

To explore the idea that concepts are both situated and progressively developed through activity, we should abandon any notion that they are abstract, self-contained entities. Instead, it may be more useful to consider conceptual knowledge as, in some ways, similar to a set of tools. Tools . . . can only be interpreted in the context of their use.[21]

Thus, pedagogical practices are appropriate if they provide young children with ample opportunity to interact with adults and with children who are like and unlike themselves, with materials, and directly with real objects and real environments. However, interactions cannot occur in a vacuum; they have to have content. Individuals cannot interact in a vacuum. They must interact *about* something.

What criteria can be used to determine what knowledge or content is appropriate for young children? For example, should young children spend up to ten minutes per day in a calendar exercise? Should young children in southern Florida be making styrofoam snowflake crystals in January? Should substantial proportions of time be allocated to observance of public holidays and festivals? Why? And why not? What factors, data, or other matters should be taken into account in answering these questions? One way to approach these questions is to derive principles of practice from what is known about the nature of children's intellectual development.

In principle, a substantial proportion of the content of interaction in early childhood education settings should be related to matters of actual or potential interest to the children. Since not all of children's interests are equally deserving of attention, some selection of which interests are the most worthy of promotion is required. Current views of children's learning and their active construction of knowledge suggest that those interests most likely to extend, deepen, and improve their understandings of their own environments and experiences are most worth strengthening.

Child development data suggest furthermore that, in principle, the younger the learner, the more integrated the curriculum should be; conversely, as children increase in age and experience, their capacities to profit from subject- or discipline-based study increases. Young children do not differentiate their ideas, thoughts, and interests into categories like science, language, and mathematics. They are more likely to gain knowledge and understanding by pursuing a topic to which scientific, linguistic, mathematical, and other discipline-related concepts can be applied.

PRINCIPLES RELATED TO THE ACQUISITION OF SKILLS

Skills can be acquired and strengthened through a variety of processes, viz., observation, imitation, trial and error, coaching, and instruction. They can be improved with optimum drill and practice. Contemporary views of the nature of learning also suggest that, like physical and social skills, intellectual skills are best learned when they occur in a meaningful situation.[22] In principle, the younger the child, the more likely it is that skillfulness is strengthened by *application* in meaningful contexts.[23] As children increase in age and experience, and are more able to grasp the relationship between skillfulness and drill, they can more easily understand and accept the need for practice and exercise of disembedded or decontextualized skills, even if they do so reluctantly.

PRINCIPLES RELATED TO BOTH KNOWLEDGE AND SKILLS

Consideration of both the knowledge and skills to be learned in the light of what is known about children's development suggests that in principle, the younger the children, the more important it is that what they are to learn about (knowledge) and learn to do (skills) should have more *horizontal* than *vertical* relevance. Vertical relevance is that which prepares the pupils for the next school experience rather than for the one in which it is occurring; it is a type of "education for the next life." Horizontal relevance means that what the children are learning about and learning to do is applicable and meaningful to them on the same day, on the way home, and in their contemporary lives outside the educational setting. As children increase in age and experience they become more able to acquire knowledge and skills that have no immediate application or meaning for them.

Social competence. Contemporary research suggests that the first six or seven years of development are a critical period in the development of social competence, and that failure to achieve at least a minimum level of peer interactive competence can have long-term negative consequences.[24] Social competence requires such social knowledge as understanding others' points of view and feelings, and such skills as turn-taking, negotiating, approach strategies, and many others. Data from child development research suggests that, in principle, an appropriate pedagogy for young children is one that provides ample opportunity for them to be engaged in activities in which cooperation and coordination of effort are functional and consequential.

STRENGTHENING DESIRABLE DISPOSITIONS

The goals listed among the objectives of most early childhood programs invariably include dispositional outcomes. Among them are: having the desire to learn, being cooperative, being creative, being eager to approach and solve problems, and other such desirable dispositions. The assumption underlying these goals is that mastery of knowledge and skills must be accompanied by robust dispositions to employ them.

As suggested earlier, dispositions cannot be taught directly. Dispositions appear to be learned or strengthened to the extent that they are observed by children in significant models, that they are manifested, and that their manifestations are appreciated rather than rewarded. This suggests that desirable dispositions must be observable by the learners in the adults around them. It also implies that, in principle, if dispositions are to be strengthened, ample opportunity for their exercise must be available. For example, if children's dispositions to be problem solvers are to be strengthened, they must have real and meaningful problems to solve in the course of their daily activities.

A distinction is drawn here between rewarding and appreciating dispositional behavior. Although these two types of response to children's behavior probably overlap, they differ more in manner and in what they communicate to the children than in actual form or content. Let us take the example of a teacher who follows up a question raised by a child a day or two earlier by saying something like "Remember when you asked about X? I found out that it is such-and-such and found a book about it too," etc. In this example, the teacher's comment is positive and appreciative without distracting the child from his original interest. By contrast, research in child development indicates that rewards tend to distract children from the content of the problem at hand. After all, rewards can only work if children are aware of them.[25] This kind of teacher response also provides children with a model of the disposition to look things up, and to pursue a topic. Given the cumulative negative effects of rewards on children's dispositions related to learning, a pedagogy is appropriate if it strengthens intrinsic motivation by appreciating children's efforts and by encouraging them to evaluate their own work.

Contemporary research on children's dispositions to learn indicates that excessive emphasis on skilled performance on academic tasks has cumulative negative effects on their mastery, effort, and challenge-seeking dispositions.[26] The findings of the research in this area suggest that, in principle, pedagogical practices that emphasize child-initiated learning tasks are more likely to strengthen dispositions toward mastery, effort, and challenge-seeking.

FEELINGS RELATED TO SCHOOL EXPERIENCES

One of the most typical learning goals found in curriculum guides is that children should learn to "feel good about themselves." Most curriculum guides include feelings of confidence, competence, and acceptance by others.

Like dispositions, feelings cannot be taught directly; they are experienced and strengthened in the context of the ongoing relationships and activities that give rise to them. One of the issues in the dispute over developmentally appropriate practices is that when they focus on a narrow range of academic tasks (e.g., workbooks, lessons in phonics), a substantial proportion of the learners will likely be unable to respond to the work effectively. Indeed, there is some evidence to suggest that when a single instructional approach is employed with any group of children that is diverse in background, ability, and development, about one third will likely feel left out and develop feelings of incompetence or inadequacy.[27] Thus, in principle, a pedagogical approach is appropriate if it adopts a variety of methods of teaching and makes a wide variety and range of activities available to the children.[28]

GENERAL DEVELOPMENT AND APPROPRIATE PEDAGOGY

Current understandings of development suggest that, in principle, the younger the learner, the larger proportion of time should be allocated to informal activities. However, there are at least three kinds of informal activities: (1) spontaneous dramatic play, (2) arts and craft activities, and (3) cooperative work on extended group investigations or similar exploratory and constructive projects in which the teacher role is consultative rather than didactic. Some time can also be allocated to varieties of music and literature-related activities, which may occur in small- or whole-group teacher guided activities.

Based on current research on children's learning, it is reasonable to assume that between 20 and 30 percent of all children will need some systematic help from an adult in learning some of the skills included among the goals in early childhood education. However, there is a distinction between systematic instruction and common use of the term direct instruction.[29] Systematic instruction is typically given to an individual and sometimes a pair or trio, and is planned by a teacher for the individuals based on extensive observation and analysis of their particular needs.[30] It can be provided within the classroom and minimize both the stigma and logistical problems associated with "pull-out" programs. The individual instruction that almost all children require from time to time can be offered while others are engaged in spontaneous play or engaged in cooperative and individual work on worthwhile topics.

Summary

The main argument in this chapter is that considerations of *what* young children should learn, and *when* and *how* they should do so, have to be addressed jointly in order to formulate an appropriate pedagogical approach for them. In the light of current research related to these questions it is suggested that such a pedagogy for young children should be largely informal in structure, should attend to the children's dispositional and emotional development as well as to the acquisition of appropriate knowledge and skills. Such a pedagogy is appropriate also if it is primarily *intellectual* rather than *academic* in focus, if it provides a balance of opportunities for both individual and cooperative group work on intellectually engaging tasks, and if systematic instruction is available to individual children as needed periodically.

The pedagogical approach proposed here would bring pedagogical practices into line with what is known about young children's development and learning. A remaining challenge to early childhood educators is to bring parents' understandings, expectations, and preferences into closer agreement with these recommended practices.

FOOTNOTES

1. Marvin Lazerson, "The Historical Antecedents of Early Childhood Education," in *Early Childhood Education*, ed. Ira J. Gordon, Seventy-first Yearbook of the National Society for the Study of Education, Part 2 (Chicago: University of Chicago Press, 1972), p. 41.

2. Dorothy G. M. Gardner, *Testing Results in the Infant Schools*, 2d ed. (London: Methuen & Co., 1948).

3. Charlotte B. Winsor, "The Progessive Movement," in *Education Before Five*, ed. Betty D. Boegehold, Harriet K. Cuffaro, William H. Hooks, and J. Klopf Gordon (New York: Bank Street College of Education, 1989), p. 34.

4. Alfred E. Baldwin, "A Is Happy B is Not," *Child Development* 36 (1965): 583-601. See also, Lilian G. Katz, "Perspectives on Early Childhood Education," *Educational Forum* 36 (1973): 393-398.

5. Douglas R. Powell, "Comparing Preschool Curricula," in *Early Schooling: The National Debate*, ed. Sharon L. Kagan and Edward F. Zigler (New Haven, CT: Yale University Press, 1987), p. 195.

6. Carl Bereiter and Siegfried Engelmann, *Teaching Disadvantaged Children in the Preschool* (New York: Prentice-Hall, 1966).

7. Powell, "Comparing Preschool Curricula." See also, David Elkind, "The Resistance to Developmentally Appropriate Educational Practice with Young Children: The Real Issue," in *Resource Guide to Public School Early Childhood Programs*, ed. Cynthia Warger (Alexandria, VA: Association for Supervision and Curriculum Development, 1988), pp. 53-62.

8. Lorrie A. Shepard and Mary L. Smith, "Escalating Academic Demand in Kindergarten: Counterproductive Policies," *Elementary School Journal* 89 (1988): 136. See also, Doris Pronin Fromberg, "Kindergarten: Current Circumstances Affecting Curriculum," *Teachers College Record* 90 (Spring 1989): 392-403.

9. Sue Bredekamp, *Developmentally Appropriate Practice in Early Childhood Programs Serving Children from Birth through Age 8* (Washington, DC: National Association for the Education of Young Children, 1987). See also, Nebraska Council of School Administrators, *Developing Minds through Active Learning: A Position Statement on Early Childhood Education,* n.d., n.p. A similar position statement on appropriate practices for early childhood education is in preparation by the Association for Supervision and Curriculum Development.

10. Bernard Spodek, "Development, Values, and Knowledge in the Kindergarten Curriculum," in *Today's Kindergarten: Exploring the Knowledge Base, Expanding the Curriculum,* ed. Bernard Spodek (New York: Teachers College Press, 1986), pp. 32-47. See also, Nancy Karweit, "Quality and Quantity of Learning Time in Preprimary Programs," *Elementary School Journal* 89 (1988): 119-134, and Lilian G. Katz and Sylvia C. Chard, *Engaging Children's Minds: The Project Approach* (Norwood, NJ: Ablex, 1989), especially chapter 2.

11. Richard W. Clark, "Who Decides?" in *Critical Issues in Curriculum,* ed. Laurel N. Tanner, Eighty-seventh Yearbook of the National Society for the Study of Education, Part 1 (Chicago, IL: University of Chicago Press, 1988), pp. 175-204.

12. Connie K. Williams and Constance Kamii, "How Do Children Learn by Handling Objects?" *Young Children* 42 (1986): 23-26.

13. In the case of young children, undesirable and inappropriate attitudes and values are assumed to be a function of faulty developmental progress rather than of general institutional socialization. For example, dishonesty or greed in a five-year-old are more likely to be interpreted as symptoms of idiosyncratic developmental patterns than as problems of attitudes and values.

14. See, for example, State of Iowa, *Kindergarten: A Year of Beginnings* (Des Moines, IA: State of Iowa, 1983); State of Connecticut, *A Guide to Program Development for Kindergarten,* Part 1 (Hartford, CT: State Board of Education, 1988); Oklahoma State Department of Education, *Beginnings: Early Childhood Education in Oklahoma,* 3d ed. (Oklahoma City, OK: State Department of Education, 1986); Patricia Morgan Roberts, ed., *Growing Together: Early Childhood Education in Pennsylvania* (Harrisburg, PA: Pennsylvania Department of Education, 1989).

15. Carleton Washburne, "Introduction," in *Child Development and the Curriculum,* ed. Guy M. Whipple, Thirty-eighth Yearbook of the National Society for the Study of Education, Part 1 (Bloomington, IL: Public School Publishing Co., 1939), p. 3.

16. Eleanor E. Maccoby, "Socialization and Developmental Change," *Child Development* 55, no. 2 (1984): 317-328.

17. John S. Brown, Allan Collins, and Paul Duguid, "Situated Cognition and the Culture of Learning," *Educational Researcher* 18, no. 1 (1989): 32-42.

18. Douglas Carnine, Linda Carnine, Joan Karp, and Paul Weisberg, "Kindergarten for Economically Disadvantaged Children: The Direct Instruction Component," in *Resource Guide to Public School Early Childhood Programs,* ed. Warger, pp. 73-98.

19. Shirley Brice Heath, "Redefining Culture: Society, Anthropology, and Education" (Paper presented at the Annual Meeting of the American Educational Research Association, Washington, DC, 1987).

20. Kieran Egan, *Teaching as Story Telling: An Alternative Approach to Teaching and Curriculum in the Elementary School* (Chicago: University of Chicago Press, 1986).

21. Brown, Collins, and Duguid, "Situated Cognition and the Culture of Learning," p. 33.

22. Ibid.

23. Lauren Resnick, *Education and Learning to Think* (Washington, DC: National Research Council, 1987), especially p. 42. See also, Annemarie Sullivan Palincsar, "Less Charted Waters," *Educational Researcher* 18 (May 1989): 5-7.

24. Jeffrey Parker and Steven Asher, "Peer Relations and Later Personal Adjustment: Are Low-Accepted Children at Risk?" *Psychological Bulletin* 102 (1987): 358-389.

25. For a review of the literature related to the negative effects of rewards, see Katz and Chard, *Engaging Children's Minds*, chapter 2.

26. Ibid.

27. Ibid.

28. Lilian G. Katz, James D. Raths, and Rosalle Torres, *A Place Called Kindergarten* (Urbana, IL: ERIC Clearinghouse on Elementary and Early Childhood Education, University of Illinois, 1987).

29. For a review of the pertinent research, see Katz and Chard, *Engaging Children's Minds*, chapter 2.

30. This approach to systematic instruction is very similar to the approach known as Reading Recovery. See, for example, Gay S. Pinnell, Diane E. DeFord, and Carol A. Lyons, *Reading Recovery: Early Intervention for At-Risk First Graders* (Arlington, VA: Educational Research Service. 1988).

Section Two
ISSUES OF PARTNERSHIPS
AND LINKAGES

CHAPTER V

Continuity in the Early Years:
Transitions between Grades and Systems

BETTYE M. CALDWELL

That development is continuous, albeit marked by apparent spurts
and plateaus, is a truism. The education which should parallel and help
to shape that development is, on the other hand, characterized by
sharp discontinuities. Moving from one branch to another—e.g.,
elementary school to secondary school—is more than simply climbing
up one rung on the educational ladder. It involves a move into a new
culture, a new ecology with a different set of procedures and
requirements. Adaptation to the new setting requires more than
merely learning where the lockers are and how to use them.

Nowhere is this discontinuity more striking than in the
educational settings available during the early years of life. With the
most appropriate labels for this period (viz., primary, elementary)
long since preempted for programs designed for older children,
educational programs for the early years have had to accept an
assortment of semantic compromises typically compounded out of the
syllable "pre" and some other term with a reasonably clear
connotative meaning—preschool, prekindergarten, preprimary, etc.
Yet these compromises produce discomfort on both sides of the time
line, causing representatives of those already claiming the position of
primacy to highlight differences in their approach in order to validate
their claim to the label and forcing those who must accept the "pre"

status into a defensive posture to prove their legitimacy. It is perhaps difficult for practitioners to feel proud of what they do if it is seemingly not viewed by society as valuable in itself but only as preparatory for what follows. And that which follows is considered valuable enough that it is regarded as a birthright of all citizens, is made universally available, and is supported by public funds.

Such evidence of status and public trust have not, until very recently, been accorded the field of early childhood. As a consequence it has grown somewhat haphazardly into a nonsystem of programs with different goals and objectives, different constituencies, and different criteria of quality. And, whereas the semantic confusion *between* early childhood and subsequent programs is subtle, revealing only subconscious attitudes about the value of the different segments of the educational progression, such confusion is rampant *within* the early childhood years. What do we really call these programs? Are they preschools, nursery schools, kindergartens, prekindergartens, early childhood education, play schools, or Head Start centers? Or are they day care centers, child care centers, day nurseries, family day care? Or are they, heaven forbid, "baby sitting"? Continuity between and among different segments of the early childhood endeavor is weak or nonexistent. Whoever heard, for example, of a director of a child care center who sent a report of accomplishments to a child's kindergarten or first-grade teacher? Or a kindergarten teacher who valued the opinion of a child care worker enough to ask for one? Until very recently, such a simple act of support for continuity would not have been possible because few, if any, programs kept records of achievement (or lack of same) worth sending along to professionals at the next level. In general, early childhood programs operated under different auspices (education, social service, religious groups, etc.) and were as isolated from one another as from the educational mainstream into which the participating children were promoted.

The Climb toward Legitimacy

Early childhood programs have always had their devotees and their advocates, and even their intellectual and scientific heroes and heroines. In today's world, the name "Montessori" undoubtedly has higher recognition value than "Thorndike"—perhaps even more than sacred names like "Mann" and "Dewey." Furthermore, every important child development theory of the twentieth century[1] has paid attention to and placed stress on the early years as being critical for subsequent development. However, something in the customary descriptors of program goals (mainly social and emotional development), operational procedures (half-day programs, much time spent in routines, long naps if all-day attendance), and apparently passive pedagogy (much free play, teacher mainly a responder rather than an initiator) tended to deny the field the aura of respectability claimed for the remainder of the education domain. And, as child care was presumed to be only for "care and protection" and referred to as "custodial" or "institutional," certainly it did nothing to improve the status of the early years as a legitimate field of intellectual endeavor.

The field got its big boost toward legitimacy in the first half of the 1960s with the publication of three seminal books: Bruner's *The Process of Education* (1960), Hunt's *Intelligence and Experience* (1961), and Bloom's *Stability and Change in Human Characteristics* (1964).[2] At the risk of oversimplifying, these books, based on and supported by research from such diverse fields as animal ethological studies, clinical deficit or deprivation studies, and attempts to accelerate developmental progress,[3] generated three principles which in time gained the status of aphorisms:

1. Young children can learn a great deal more than we have given them credit for, provided we teach them properly.

2. As encounters between a young child and the environment are critical for development, the nature of these encounters should not be left to chance.

3. More intellectual development takes place from conception to age four years than during any comparable period in the remaining years of life.

The research on which these summaries were based had already begun to spawn a few innovative early childhood programs, perhaps most notably those of Deutsch and Deutsch, Gray and Klaus, Bereiter and Engelmann, and Weikart.[4] Gordon, Caldwell and Richmond, and Levenstein responded more literally to the age implications of the data and began early intervention programs for infants and toddlers.[5] But by far the biggest impact was the launching of Project Head Start in 1965.[6] With the birth of Head Start, serving roughly a half million children a year, early childhood (here defined according to typical administrative divisions as dealing with children younger than six) joined the big numbers game in the field of education and became, perhaps for the first time, a continuing part of public policy for children and families.[7]

Since the early 1960s, with the launching of Head Start and the ever-increasing visibility of the small but innovative experimental enrichment programs, the field of early childhood has steadily gained status. Endorsements of its merits seem to increase daily, with the corporate world and economic forecasters among the most recent converts and publicists.[8] However, its new status as an important service has not earned it the right to be considered the first rung on the educational ladder. As indicated earlier, all too often it is still considered *pre*educational. Ask most people when children start school and they will answer, "When they go to first grade."

Perhaps one reason for this lack of public conviction that educational settings attended by young children are *real* schools is the diversity of settings in which early childhood programs operate and the cacophony of labels applied to them. If you wanted to find an educational program for young children, you probably would not go to an elementary school campus. Rather you might drive by the nearest church, or note a fenced yard with more than the usual amount of play equipment, or turn in the driveway where you see a sign reading "Fair Park Day Care" (which, on the other side for traffic going the opposite way, reads "Fair Park Child Care"). Or you might be attracted by a plywood facade shaped and painted like the administration building of a university campus and given some "cute" label like "Kiddie's Kollege" or "Li'l Darlins" or you might spot a small house lovingly decorated with nursery rhyme decals and a sign by the front gate reading "Miss Velma's Babies" (with a second line in small print reading, "I Took Care of Your Mother, Honey"). If you were reasonably knowledgeable about who funds most corporate child care you might look in a hospital. Of course, if you were really wise about young children, you would simply drive with your window down and listen for the noise of happy children playing!

This tongue-in-cheek description—unfortunately all too accurate—highlights the generalization that educational programs for children younger than six years in this country are a hodgepodge in terms of type, quality, and auspice. This heterogeneity is poignantly reflected in Table 1, which presents a summary of the enrollment patterns of

TABLE 1

EARLY CHILDHOOD ALTERNATE CARE ARRANGEMENTS, 1987

POPULATION CATEGORY	GROUP SIZE (THOUSANDS)		
	AGES 0-2	AGES 3-4	BIRTH TO 5
All Children	9,629	6,454	16,083
With Working Mothers	4,921	3,497	8,418
	(51%)	(54%)	(52%)
Child Care Arrangements			
With parent(s) at work	1,226	783	2,009
	(13%)	(12%)	(12%)
In-home or relative	1,628	908	2,536
	(17%)	(14%)	(16%)
Other home	1,265	621	1,886
	(13%)	(10%)	(12%)
Centers or schools	802	1,186	1,988
	(8%)	(18%)	(12%)

Source: Patricia P. Olmsted and David P. Weikart, *How Nations Serve Young Children.* Ypsilanti, MI: High/Scope Educational Research Foundation, 1989, p. 381. Reproduced with permission.

young children in some type of alternate care in America. In spite of the sincerity of commitment to children reflected by the decision to provide a service in this field, representatives of the different types of programs really do not trust one another, much less the educational system which follows. Furthermore, in programs for young children, there appears to be a built-in bias against specifying goals and objectives and against compiling information about children's progress that will be sent forward to personnel at the next level in hopes of thereby facilitating the child's functioning at that level—or even to personnel in a different contemporary program (e.g., one child care center to another). Furthermore, at the next level, one can often detect a touch of arrogance about the value of information provided by those who worked with the child previously. After all, if they are not "real" educators and the child was not in a "real" school (just day care, or, horror of horrors, baby-sitting) of what value would such information be anyway?

This extreme heterogeneity and absence of sincere networking among staff in different types of early childhood programs, plus the fact that whatever system exists is in actuality a nonsystem, militate significantly against continuity from early childhood to elementary education. Under such conditions, the transition is bound to be difficult for the children and minimally efficient for those who will be their mentors at the next level.

Lasting Effects: Evidence of Effective Transitions

How does one determine whether a transition has been effective? In this context, we seem to judge early childhood programs according to a set of standards different from those implicitly used at subsequent stages. For example, if a child reaches junior high school *at a level* specified as being appropriate according to state or national norms, we are satisfied. If not, we are probably more prone to look for explanations in the child than in the quality of the elementary education she or he received.

Not so with regard to early childhood. Here, we expect children who have participated in such programs to be *ahead*—and to stay ahead. Some of this may be the legacy of adoption of such terms as "Head Start," which imply that participating children will function better than their age mates, not merely better than they would have functioned without the experience. Also it is a legacy of impressive evidence that an immediate benefit can be created and can be demonstrated. The professional literature is now rife with studies showing immediate positive cognitive and academic gains associated with participation in a quality early childhood program[9] and equally impressive evidence of reasonably durable effects,[10] although there appears to be a fade-out of measurable cognitive and academic benefits by age eight or nine.[11] However, research that has followed the subjects into young adulthood[12] appears to support either latent or re-emerging psychological benefits, such as reduced likelihood of delinquency, and economic benefits, such as fewer placements in special education and grade repetitions. So impressive and so timely have been these economic benefits that they are often cited as the primary reason for establishing early childhood programs. A formula often given is that every dollar invested in a quality early childhood education program will save close to five dollars in remedial societal activities (special education, welfare, prison, etc.) in the future.[13]

It should be noted that, without exception, these data pertain only to the effects of early childhood education and care on poor, disadvantaged, at-risk children. At this juncture, some twenty-five years after the renaissance of early childhood in America, we still have virtually no research on the effects of such programs on cognitive, academic, and social behavior of children from middle-class families. An exception is an important study done over twenty years ago at the University of North Carolina,[14] which showed that at-risk children did indeed gain in IQ at the end of approximately a year in a highly creative infant day care program but that children of educated parents tended to gain even more. These results, obtained in a study with a very small sample of children younger than three years of age, have not been replicated to the best of my knowledge. In fact, in another North Carolina study done at the same time and using only middle-class children,[15] no differences in intellectual functioning were detected between children who had participated in the infant day care program and controls who had not. The generalization most typically offered to describe the impact of early education and care programs on middle-class children is that there are no cognitive advantages or disadvantages associated with participation in them.[16] Suffice it to say, our modern failure to research the effects of such early educational experiences on middle-class children is the equivalent of a metaphorical black hole in our cosmos of data on the effects of early experience. It is almost as though there is a conspiracy of fear about what we might find.[17]

One major study that included middle-class children in its sample was the Brookline Early Education Project.[18] This project, which served children from infancy to age five, conceptualized early childhood programs as preventing school-related difficulties (rather than as accelerating children ahead of their peers). Major components of the project included a variety of educational and support services to parents, half-day educational programs when the children reached age two, and diagnostic and referral services for any developmental problems observed in the enrolled children. The project was an official part of a public school district. The services were available to all parents residing in the district who wished to participate. Although inclusion of a total community should provide a fairly wide social class spread, residential patterns of Brookline predetermined a predominantly middle-class sample. When the project children were in second grade, they were found to have significantly fewer classroom behavior problems and less difficulty in reading. These findings were true for children from all social classes, but more intensive outreach by project staff was necessary to produce effects in children of less educated parents. Nonetheless, it was clear that the array of parent and child programs available to the families did indeed facilitate the transition into public school.

Models Serving Disadvantaged Children that
Stress Continuity

Shortly after early results from Head Start evaluations with their quick-spurt-fast-plateau pattern began to circulate,[19] educational theorists and policymakers began to search for ways to sustain whatever gains might have appeared during the early education programs. Bronfenbrenner analyzed the available early enrichment literature and concluded that only those programs with a heavy parent component were associated with lasting effects.[20] Others reshuffled objectives and formulated new explanations, and in the process a number of models for improving developmental continuity were born. The reconceptualization involved in such efforts also led to the formulation of a fourth principle relevant to early intervention. This was:

4. *Appropriate environmental encounters during the early years are necessary to achieve, but not sufficient to sustain, developmental advances.*

In this section a few of the models specifically designed to improve developmental continuity will be described. By far the most notable and important of these was Project Follow Through. Also of merit are several models such as the Abecedarian Project of Ramey and others,[21] the author's Kramer Model,[22] and the new and exciting Zigler Model for the "School of the 21st Century."[23]

FOLLOW THROUGH

While everyone in America (and many other parts of the world) has heard about Head Start, its related program, Follow Through, is much less well-known. Early childhood people should love Follow Through, regardless of what it might have accomplished, as it is the only educational program that bases its legitimacy upon our efforts and existence. Instead of forcing us to be known disparagingly as *pre*-something-else, the label chosen for this model identifies it as unequivocally *post*-early-childhood. Not bad!

Whether by design or accident, Follow Through attempted to rectify some of the mistakes made in the design and establishment of Head Start. Whereas Head Start was created in the heat of enthusiasm and optimism, Follow Through was born when optimism had been somewhat dimmed by a deluge of disappointing data. Head Start could promise; Follow Through had to explain. The entire start-up time for Head Start was from February to June of 1965; Follow

Through was carefully planned for more than a year. Whereas the implementation of Head Start (not the conceptual underpinning) represented bootstrapping and rampant empiricism, Follow Through had the benefit of the thinking of the best social scientists of the period. During the early years parents had no influence on the type of early childhood curriculum that would be available in their children's Head Start; parents in Follow Through from the outset selected from a curriculum smorgasbord the specific educational menu they wanted for their children. Whereas a major evaluation of Head Start came only four years after the launching of the program and was then planned retroactively, a national evaluation of Follow Through based on the thinking of the country's best social scientists was planned on a rational basis at the outset.

This is not the place to offer a comprehensive review of the voluminous literature on the effects of Follow Through. Several important reviews and critiques have appeared, most of which have been summarized by Rhine.[24] The Rhine volume also includes a report on the evaluations conducted by the designers of each of the Planned Variations (as the curriculum offerings were called). Here our concern is primarily with the feasibility of the concept of implementing a program that accepts the legitimacy of our fourth principle—the necessity to create an educational environment which can sustain any gains previously made in an early childhood program.

Although planned specifically to build upon and help sustain the benefits achieved in Head Start, Follow Through had to be implemented on its own. Curricular enhancement in elementary school cannot realistically deal with a unit smaller than a single classroom. Yet, as not all children enrolled in a given Head Start program would move ahead to the same elementary school, some of the children in a Follow Through classroom would have attended a Head Start center and some would not—while still others might have participated in one of the other diverse early childhood programs available in a community. Thus evaluations of Follow Through are literally not evidence of benefits of continuity and sustained support; for some of the children, the data merely show what can be accomplished when compensatory efforts begin at either kindergarten or first grade rather than at age four or younger.

For the purpose of determining whether Follow Through facilitated a smooth transition from early childhood into elementary programs, most of the evaluation studies are not too useful. Some of the evaluations[25] have focused on whether classroom events were actually different in schools that had chosen different program sponsors (i.e., whether the curricula as implemented were faithful to the models they were supposed to represent) and, in general, differences could indeed be detected. Others merely compared children who attended Follow Through classrooms with comparable children who had attended "regular" classrooms in the same school.[26] When it has been possible to identify in the records those Follow Through children who also attended Head Start or a comparable early childhood program, effect sizes for positive benefits are generally greater for the Head Start children. The best example of this is a long-term follow-up of children in Follow Through classrooms in Philadelphia.[27] The children who had also attended Head Start (or a comparable early childhood program called Get Set) tended to be below the median of the Follow Through children in absences, in missing school when achievement tests were given, in grade retention, and above the median on achievement test scores up to the third grade.

Such data, encouraging as they are, still do not tell us whether the children who performed at better levels in Follow Through were the same children who had gained significantly in Head Start—a test of our fourth principle. The results could just as well reflect a spurt shown by a different Head Start subgroup at a later age. With no information available about how the children were functioning at the end of their Head Start experience, we cannot know whether the Follow Through program helped to sustain gains made during the earlier period or whether Head Start prepared the children better for what would be offered in Follow Through. Although it would be interesting to know this, it is not essential in order to appreciate the improvement associated with a smooth transition from early childhood into elementary school.

THE ABECEDARIAN PROJECT

This project, carried out in Chapel Hill, North Carolina, under the general direction of Craig Ramey for over a decade, is methodologically quite different from Follow Through.[28] That is, it has been a tightly controlled, carefully supervised early intervention project serving only a small number of subjects in several cohorts, rather than a national program serving thousands of children with obviously much less control over program quality and program fidelity. It is one of the few infant intervention programs in which subjects have been randomly assigned to the different groups. In the project, children were enrolled from approximately six weeks of age until they entered kindergarten in high-quality day care that offered a carefully targeted curriculum and comprehensive health maintenance. Parents have been involved in as many ways as possible. In addition to stimulation for cognitive growth, the program has featured units designed to foster the acquisition of prosocial skills.

This program is modern enough to have had the advantage of findings from other studies which showed a plateauing of effects in early elementary school, along with a catch-up phenomenon for controls once they entered school. Accordingly, when their subjects reached first grade level, the North Carolina group again randomly divided both enriched and control children into two subgroups. Half of the children in each group were assigned a Home/School Resource Teacher who provided liaison between the school and the home, made frequent home visits, prepared homework assignments that built upon what the children were doing in school, worked with the mothers, etc. Thus there were then four evaluation groups instead of two: Early Enrichment/Elementary Support, Early Enrichment/Elementary Control, Early Control/Elementary Support, Early Control/Elementary Control. It is fascinating to note that, in terms of both IQ scores and achievement test data,[29] the groups ranked in exactly the order described at the third-grade level. That is, those who had early enrichment with transitional support functioned best, and those who had neither functioned least well. The other two groups occupied a middle ground. These findings are fascinating and point impressively to the value of providing some assistance to children at the time of transition to more formal education.

THE KRAMER MODEL

A few special facilities have been developed at various times since the launching of Head Start which had developmental continuity as a major objective. One of these was the Kramer Project in Little Rock, Arkansas, established in 1969.[30] Having been convinced early in my career of the validity of the first three principles cited above, I had previously operated an early intervention program for infants and toddlers in upstate New York. As the children in that project reached school age, I became acutely aware of the disjunction that existed between anything educational that occurred prior to kindergarten or first grade and events thereafter. I became convinced that early education would never have much impact in this country until it became an integral part of public education. At that point in history, evaluations of various early intervention projects were beginning to produce the quick spurt/early fade-out pattern, and the fourth principle began to dominate my thinking. It seemed at least one thing was essential in order to avoid that phenomenon, namely, to design a setting in which sensitive support could be offered during the early primary years that would help to sustain whatever gains had occurred during earlier years.

An equally basic objective of the Kramer Project was minimally concerned with vertical developmental continuity but might be described as a concern for horizontal continuity. At that time, the precipitous rise in the percentage of working mothers with children under six had begun, and the necessity for educational programs that served children under ten years of age to provide extended care appeared a social imperative. Thus the concern with developmental continuity was fused with a desire to determine whether an existing public elementary school could be converted to an extended day and extended year child care program. Today I refer to this restructured education-care complex as "educare." Funding for the project was obtained from the Children's Bureau to cover the cost of the early childhood program and the extended care for the older children, and the Little Rock School District turned over one of its regular elementary schools, Kramer School, as a site for the project. Unique then and now among public schools, Kramer was open year-round from 6:45 a.m. to 6:15 p.m.

At that time Arkansas schools did not even offer kindergarten, so an elementary school that enrolled children from six months to twelve years of age was a novelty, and the idea that "Babies Go to School" was more likely to make headlines than anything else about the project during its early years. Although the mechanics of converting a regular public elementary school into a day care facility is perhaps of greatest interest in today's world, the extent to which we facilitated transition from the early childhood component of the project into the primary school is of most relevance for this chapter. And, in brief, even when both components existed within the same building and were under the same administrator, an adaptive transition was difficult.

The main reason for the difficulty was the simple one of subject attrition. Like the Philadelphia Follow Through study cited earlier,[31] attrition rates up to 70 percent were not uncommon for a particular class in a given year. When you are dealing with an entire school district, such attrition does not defeat your efforts to have enough children to measure some attribute or function. However, when you are one small elementary school with only one class per grade level, attrition defeats your best efforts at measurement. Actually, in our program attrition was greater at the junction of the two divisions of the program, i.e., precisely at the point where we had wanted to keep the children. As has been frequently documented, mobility is high among low-income families. But, because of the free child care that we offered, our families seemed to make extra efforts to remain in the same neighborhood until their children reached first grade. Once that milestone had been reached, however, remaining at Kramer meant less to the families. It is interesting today to note that when people refer to Kramer (to what a landmark school it was, etc.) they rarely mention anything innovative we did at the elementary level but refer instead to its "creative early childhood program." And the way these people remember the program is not too far off from what it really was—an early childhood program *tacked onto* but not truly *integrated into* an elementary school.[32]

But, in spite of measurement difficulties, transition activities abounded and were natural in the setting. Instead of having to take a field trip to see what kindergarten was like, Kramer children walked across the hall. Kindergarten children who showed early precocity in reading spent some time each day in the first grade classroom. Likewise, we had one kindergarten-first grade transition room which was exquisitely "developmentally appropriate" some two decades before the phrase was coined. We were as concerned about the sudden withdrawal of hands-on learning opportunities for first graders as people are today about the downward extension to kindergarten of more abstract learning requirements. And a second grader who showed reading progress might be given a reward of reading a simple story to the four-year-olds.

In terms of social behavior, the school provided many opportunities in which this developmental orientation found expression. For example, one of the most effective reinforcers for some of the older children with behavior problems was the privilege of "working" in the baby house or toddler room for an hour—something that could be allowed only when they were in control of themselves. For fire and tornado drills, the older children had specific assignments to carry out one of the very young children, thus helping them develop a sense of responsibility. Whenever the older children put on a play, the small ones got to sing a little song or participate in some way. (There was never an empty seat in the auditorium; it was the one sure way to get parents to the school.) When there were assemblies, all children, including the youngest babies, attended—with older children who had earned the privilege holding them on their laps. Perhaps one of the most innovative and useful activities was the design and installation of a child development unit for children in grades four through six which used the very young children as "laboratory students."

These activities have been described in some detail as they are the very essence of developmental continuity and of effective transitions from early childhood into the elementary years. The old Kramer model (still in existence in Little Rock in Winthrop Rockefeller School) bears many similarities to the exciting model proposed by Zigler and referred to as the "School of the 21st Century."[33] There are some important differences between the two models, however. In his model, Zigler will extend the school downward only to three-year-olds rather than infants, and the official educational program for the children will be limited to half a day. At that time, certified teachers will work with another group, and the child care hours will be under the supervision of Child Development Associates. At Kramer, children as young as six months were enrolled, and the same teachers remained with their groups for a full school day (though not for the late afternoon hours). These structural differences between the models will probably result in minimally observable programmatic differences. What is important at this point in history is that educational planners take cognizance of the need for schools of the twenty-first century to enroll children at a younger age, to provide comprehensive educare services rather than a segmented version of either education or care, and to facilitate smooth transitions from one level to all others.

Smoother Transitions for All Children

Thus far everything that has been included in this chapter has pertained to disadvantaged children, to children at risk for academic failure and future economic dependency. The early childhood research of the last twenty years has by and large neglected all other children, a fact that many researchers have lamented.[34] Even so, considerable work has been taking place in regard to ways of achieving developmental continuity for children who can generally be expected to make it no matter what the schools offer.

It is of interest that historically people have worried more about the transition from kindergarten to first grade. Now, according to many professionals and parents, an even more critical transition is from child care or an early education program into kindergarten.[35] Nationally there is considerable anxiety that too much formal instruction is being pushed down from first grade into the kindergarten, and many states (e.g., New Jersey, South Carolina) are developing guidelines to help prevent this.[36] In this context it is relevant to mention that much of the apparent push is coming from parents,[37] many of whom are convinced that their children have "already learned in their day care what kids used to learn in kindergarten" and are demanding that the kindergarten curriculum be adapted so as to take advantage of this prior learning.

In their national survey of early childhood programs in the public schools, Mitchell, Seligson, and Marx offer the caution that continuity alone is not necessarily a good thing.[38] That is, in the schools they visited they often found the most continuity in the most developmentally inappropriate programs. Administrators and teachers had ostensibly improved continuity by making the curriculum for four-year-olds more like that in the kindergarten—likewise kindergarten more like first grade. Continuity tended to be poor when the four-year program was developmentally appropriate and the kindergarten a first grade facsimile. Mitchell, Seligson, and Marx comment on this with some concern: "This pattern should be viewed with alarm. Both prekindergarten and kindergarten should focus on an upward extension of earlier development rather than a downward extension of schooling."[39]

Many concrete efforts are being made to improve the transition from early childhood into elementary programs, whether kindergarten or first grade. The U.S. Department of Health and Human Services issued a helpful pamphlet intended as a guide for parents and for teachers on both sides of the barrier.[40] Head Start has stepped up efforts to improve transition[41] and has made special awards to a number of centers that are making special efforts along these lines. Also encouraging is the launching of a National Transition Study in the fall of 1989 by the U. S. Department of Education.[42] In this study, case studies will be conducted in a number of elementary schools that are attempting to find ways to smooth the transition from either home or some other early childhood program into kindergarten. Results of this study should offer promising leads for all types of schools attempting to facilitate the passage.

Barriers to Continuity

But barriers are there. In this last section, I will briefly cite five deterrents to smooth passage (most of which have at least been hinted at in earlier sections of the chapter).

1. *Curriculum and pedagogy.* No matter how much we might want to envision a smooth curve from infancy to adulthood in learning tasks and achievements, the progression is saltatory. Regardless of whether this mirrors or distorts intrinsic developmental patterns, it is the way things are. And no matter how much we might want to define early childhood as birth to age eight (as does the National Association for the Education of Young Children), most people envision a fairly sharp segmentation at or around six years. Walsh suggests that the kindergarten has now been fully absorbed into the elementary school and that the changes early childhood professionals deplore are not so much first grade practices as elementary school practices.[43] He further analyzes the conflict as raging between the "school effectiveness" position and the "developmentalist" position, implying that currently proponents of the former are winning.[44]

There can be little question that parents expect educational programs to reflect their perceptions of their children's developmental advances and to be disturbed if, at any given transition point (e.g., three to four), they do not detect pedagogical differences. Even young children themselves tend to expect a significant change at entry to first grade. As one five-year-old friend of mine recently put it, when I asked him the difference between kindergarten and first grade, "You play in kindergarten and you work in first grade." Obviously my little friend was reflecting what others had said to him—parents, friends, older siblings perhaps. But regardless of the source, the expectation is there.

In early childhood programs, *children* are taught; in elementary school, *subjects* (reading, arithmetic, social studies) are taught. Furthermore, styles of teaching will—or should—be different. In first grade and beyond, the teacher talks more, and children are expected to talk less (but learn more language). Rates of reinforcement are likely to go down. What is to be learned is more determined by city and state requirements than by a given child's own interests. There is significantly less hands-on and more abstract learning.

All these curricular and pedagogical differences can be handled—and are, indeed, expected—by most children. But, should a given child not be precisely ready to conform to what is expected with this new format, there is sure to be transition difficulty. And, whatever else we might not know about a group of new first graders, we do know that there will be individual differences among them. The acceptability and authenticity of this curricular and pedagogical hiatus, however, is deeply ingrained in our culture and is an indisputable deterrent to smooth transition for many children.

2. *Auspices.* Whenever we move from one type of program sponsorship to another, there is sure to be some degree of disjunction. Early childhood programs in America have no consistent auspice or operational format—private nonprofit, private for profit, church sponsored, publicly operated as part of antipoverty action or welfare reform, public school based, etc. In general, no one wants to give up sponsorship, and many of these groups are suspicious of the quality in any program other than their own. Records containing information that could help a child function in the next setting might be withheld "because they might misuse the information or hold it against the child." Unfortunately, such suspicions might be entirely accurate.

Although I am willing to forecast an increasingly important role for the public schools in early childhood program sponsorship over the next decade, I certainly do not see—or wish to see—a move toward a monopolistic system. Private child care and private schools fit very comfortably into the American private enterprise ethic, just as does the necessity for having a strong and effective public school system. At this point in history, schools have not earned the trust of parents and professionals to the extent that there is any sort of ground-swell toward consolidating the auspices under which early childhood programs are offered into a comprehensive educare system.

3. *Peer turnover.* Much has been written about the negative effects on children of turnover among staff who work with them. Little attention has been paid, however, to the importance of peer constancy as a support for transition and its absence as a barrier. And peer constancy is frequently missing. A group of children may remain together for three or four years in child care or Head Start, only to be sent to elementary schools in different parts of the city where new friendship patterns and new turf rules have to be established all over again. A study done some years ago by Schwartz, Strickland, and Krolick provided some data on this issue.[45] A group of children who had been previously enrolled in a high quality infant day care center with an age ceiling of three years were transferred to an ongoing early childhood program for three- to five-year-olds. Following the transfer, the children who had been together in the infant center played with one another more than with the other children and were somewhat slow to develop new social attachments. But, of course, they were already attached to their peers from the other center. The

value of this sort of support during transitions has probably been underestimated and needs to be understood more completely.

4. *Mixed signals to parents.* It is my conviction that one reason we are having such ferment about the proper curriculum for early childhood programs is that parents, just as much as professionals, are aware of the three catalytic principles that have revitalized early childhood in America. Some of them might even be able to articulate the fourth. As a consequence, they are demanding that we live up to our promise to help their children develop optimally by providing educational experiences appropriately matched to their children's level of development. Something exists in all parents that makes them want to see their children progress rapidly; it is, for good or ill, the American way. After assuring them that it can be done—and can't be done without our help—we then pull back and implicitly say, "Well, we never said it *should* be done." Many parents then seem to lose confidence in our judgment and take it on themselves to assure their children's principal that their child already knows how to read, can do simple sums, and is not going to enjoy "just playing" in kindergarten for a whole year.

The implications of this sort of impasse between parents and professional early childhood personnel are clear. We now have to do as good a job of convincing parents that we know as much about *how* to teach young children as we did about the importance of teaching them in the first place. After a generation of hearing from us that they know more about their children than we do, they are not going to believe us without evidence. Right now, we are offering more polemic than persuasion.

5. *Public policy.* Many chapters in this volume relate to our need to have a consistent public policy pertaining to young children and families in this country. Without such a policy, transition from one educational level to another will never be smooth. We have at present a nonsystem, with funding coming from a variety of sources and targeted to children representing different categories—the poor, the handicapped, etc. We are basking in the sunshine of public acceptance as never before, with general recognition that our nation will not be able to keep pace with other industrial nations in the years ahead unless our young children acquire a strong and secure foundation for development during their early years. Hopefully, public policy itself is at a transition in the history of this country and early childhood professionals and advocates can help it achieve a smooth passage into coherency and effectiveness for young children.

FOOTNOTES

1. Bettye M. Caldwell and Julius B. Richmond, "The Impact of Theories of Child Development," *Children* 9 (1962): 73-78.

2. Jerome S. Bruner, *The Process of Education* (Cambridge, MA: Harvard University Press, 1960; J. McV. Hunt, *Intelligence and Experience* (New York: Ronald Press, 1961); Benjamin S. Bloom, *Stability and Change in Human Characteristics* (New York: John Wiley & Sons, 1964).

3. Bettye M. Caldwell, "The Rationale for Early Intervention," *Exceptional Children* 36 (1970): 717-726.

4. Cynthia P. Deutsch and Martin Deutsch, "Brief Reflections on the Theory of Early Childhood Enrichment Programs," in *Early Education: Current Theory, Research, and Action*, ed. R. D. Hess and R. M. Bear (Chicago: Aldine, 1968), pp. 83-90; Susan W. Gray and Rupert A. Klaus, "An Experimental Preschool Program for Culturally Deprived Children," *Child Development* 36 (1965): 887-898; Carl Bereiter and Siegfried Engelmann, *Teaching Disadvantaged Children in the Preschool* (Englewood Cliffs, NJ: Prentice-Hall, 1966); David P. Weikart, "A Comparative Study of Three Preschool Curricula" (Paper presented at the Biennial Meeting of the Society for Research on Child Development, Santa Monica, CA, March 1969).

5. Ira J. Gordon, *Early Child Stimulation through Parent Education*, Final report to the Children's Bureau, U.S. Department of Health, Education, and Welfare (Gainesville, FL: Institute for Development of Human Resources, University of Florida, 1969); Bettye M. Caldwell and Julius B. Richmond, "The Children's Center in Syracuse, New York," in *Early Child Care: The New Perspectives*, ed. Laura L. Dittman (New York: Atherton Press, 1968), pp. 326-358; Phyllis Levenstein, "The Mother-Child Home Program," in *The Preschool in Action: Exploring Early Childhood Programs*, ed. Mary Carol Day and Ronald K. Parker (Boston: Allyn & Bacon, 1977), pp. 27-49.

6. Stone Canyon Press, *America Invests in the Future: Project Head Start A Briefing* (Dallas, TX: Stone Canyon Press, 1989).

7. This assertion might be challenged on the grounds that the WPA nurseries during the 1930s and day care centers established during World War II under the Lanham Act also represented the establishment of early childhood programs as a public policy. However, in both of these instances the early childhood programs were created out of necessity as a part of adult-oriented policies finding work for unemployed teachers in the first instance and freeing mothers to work in war industries in the second. The earlier day nursery movement, which actually impacted very few children, was also conceptualized as a service for adults and was supported largely by philanthropic organizations rather than by public monies.

8. Committee for Economic Development, *Investment Strategies for the Educationally Disadvantaged* (New York: Committee for Economic Development, September 1987).

9. See, for example, Caldwell and Richmond, "The Children's Center in Syracuse"; V. G. Cicirelli, *The Impact of Head Start: An Evaluation of the Effects of Head Start on Children's Cognitive and Affective Development* (Washington, DC: National Bureau of Standards, Institute for Applied Technology, 1969); Howard L. Garber, "Preventing Mental Retardation through Family Rehabilitation," in *Infant Education: A Guide for Helping Handicapped Children in the First Three Years*, ed. Bettye M. Caldwell and Donald J. Stedman (New York: Walker and Co., 1977), pp. 63-79; Susan W. Gray, Barbara K. Ramsey, and Rupert A. Klaus, *From 3 to 20: The Early Training Project* (Baltimore: University Park Press, 1982); Levenstein, "The Mother-Child Home Program"; Craig T. Ramey, "Preventing Mental Retardation That Is Socially Caused," in *Prevention of Developmental Disabilities*, ed. M. DiBenedetto (Columbus:

Ohio State University, 1979), pp. 17-25; Weikart, "A Comparative Study of Three Preschool Programs"; Ruth Hubbell McKey, Larry Condelli, Harriet Ganson, Barbara J. Barrett, Catherine McConkey, Margaret C. Plantz, *The Impact of Head Start on Children, Families and Communities*, Department of Health and Human Services Publication No. 85-31193 (Washington, DC: CSR, Inc., 1985).

10. Irving Lazar, Richard B. Darlington, Harry Murray, Jacqueline Royce, and Ann Snipper, "Lasting Effects of Early Intervention," *Monographs of the Society for Research in Child Development* 47, nos. 2-3 (1982): 1-151; John R. Berrueta-Clement, Lawrence J. Schweinhart, W. Steven Barnett, Ann S. Epstein, and David P. Weikart, "Changed Lives: The Effects of the Perry Preschool Program on Youths through Age Nineteen," *Monographs of the High/Scope Educational Research Foundation*, No. 8 (Ypsilanti, MI: High/Scope Educational Research Foundation, 1984); Gray, Ramsey, and Klaus, *From 3 to 20*.

11. Bettye M. Caldwell, "Staying Ahead: The Challenge of the Third Grade Slump," *Principal* 66, no. 5 (1987): 10-14.

12. Berrueta-Clement et al., "Changed Lives"; Louise B. Miller and Rondeall P. Bizzell, "Long-Term Effects of Four Preschool Programs: Sixth, Seventh, and Eighth Grades," *Child Development* 54, no. 3 (June 1983): 727-741.

13. Committee for Economic Development, *Investment Strategies for the Educationally Disadvantaged*.

14. Halbert B. Robinson and Nancy M. Robinson, "Longitudinal Development of Very Young Children in a Comprehensive Daycare Center: The First Two Years," *Child Development* 42, no. 6 (1971): 1673-1683.

15. Mary Elizabeth Keister, *A Demonstration Project: Group Care of Infants and Toddlers*, Final report submitted to the Children's Bureau, Office of Child Development, U. S. Department of Health, Education, and Welfare (Washington, DC: U. S. Department of Health, Education, and Welfare, 1970).

16. Edward F. Zigler, "Addressing the Nation's Child Care Crisis: The School of the Twenty-first Century," *American Journal of Orthopsychiatry* 59, no. 4 (1989): 484-491.

17. This question had plenty of attention in the late 1930s and early 1940s a fact which is now often forgotten. Perhaps the best summary can be found in George D. Stoddard and Beth L. Wellman, "Environment and the IQ," in *Intelligence: Its Nature and Nurture*, Part 1, *Comparative and Critical Exposition*, ed. Guy M. Whipple, Thirty-ninth Yearbook of the National Society for the Study of Education (Bloomington, IL: Public School Publishing Co., 1940), pp. 405-442.

18. Donald E. Pierson, Deborah K. Walker, and Terrence Tivnan, "A School-based Program from Infancy to Kindergarten for Children and Their Parents." *Personnel and Guidance Journal* 62, no. 8 (1984): 448-455.

19. Max Wolff and Annie Stein, *Study I: Six Months Later: A Comparison of Children Who Had Head Start, Summer 1965, with Their Classmates in Kindergarten* (Washington, DC: Research and Evaluation Office, Project Head Start, Office of Educational Opportunity, 1966).

20. Urie Bronfenbrenner, *A Report on Longitudinal Evaluations of Preschool Programs*, Vol. 2: *Is Early Intervention Effective?*, DHEW Publication No. OHD 74-25 (Washington, DC: U. S. Department of Health, Education, and Welfare, 1974).

21. Craig T. Ramey et al., "An Introduction to the Carolina Abecedarian Project, in *Infant Education for Handicapped Children*, ed. Bettye M. Caldwell and Donald J. Stedman (New York: Walker and Co., 1977), pp. 101-121.

22. Phyllis T. Elardo and Bettye M. Caldwell, "The Kramer Adventure: A School for the Future," *Childhood Education* 50 (January 1974): 143-152.

23. Zigler, "Addressing the Nation's Child Care Crisis."

24. W. Ray Rhine, *Making Schools More Effective* (New York: Academic Press, 1981).

25. Jane Stallings, "Implementation and Child Effects of Teaching Practices in Follow Through Classrooms," *Monographs of the Society for Research in Child Development* 40, nos. 7-8 (1975): 1-133.

26. A complication in much of this research and much of all early intervention evaluation is the kindergarten year. Some Follow Through programs began during the kindergarten year; others during first grade. The evaluations were made typically following some specified duration of participation in Follow Through, viz., three years. If the Follow Through program began during the kindergarten year, then the results would pertain to early childhood-elementary transition. If it did not begin until first grade, then technically it did not include an evaluation of an early childhood program followed by sustained elementary support, merely an evaluation of a special curriculum at the early elementary level. Unfortunately, the children who came into Follow Through might or might not have been enrolled in Head Start or some other early childhood program. The inability to sort out these differences in much Follow Through research makes it very difficult to evaluate the program's effectiveness as a type of sustained support for early intervention.

27. Carol E. Copple, Marvin G. Cline, and Allen N. Smith, *Path to the Future: Long-term Effects of Head Start in the Philadelphia School District* (Washington, DC: Head Start Bureau, U. S. Department of Health and Human Services, September 1987).

28. Ramey, "An Introduction to the Carolina Abecedarian Project."

29. Craig T. Ramey and F. A. Campbell, "The Carolina Abecedarian Project: An Educational Experiment Concerning Human Malleability," in *The Malleability of Children*, ed. J. J. Gallagher and Craig T. Ramey (Baltimore: Paul H. Brookes, 1987).

30. Elardo and Caldwell, "The Kramer Adventure"; Bettye M. Caldwell, "A Comprehensive Model for Integrating Child Care and Early Childhood Education," *Teachers College Record* 90 (Spring, 1989): 404-414.

31. Copple, Cline, and Smith, *Path to the Future*.

32. It may well have been that the children were the only ones who truly understood what the school was all about. The big ones understood why the little ones were there, even though their presence curtailed the amount of playground space available to the older ones or might mean that they had to delay their lunch for fifteen minutes until the slower moving toddlers got out of the cafeteria. A few of the elementary teachers never grasped the full significance of the project and either directly or deviously tried to sabotage some of the activities, but, by and large, they moved on to other schools on their own initiative.

33. Zigler, "Addressing the Nation's Child Care Crisis."

34. Julia D. Harris and Jean M. Larsen, "Parent Education as a Mandatory Component of Preschool: Effects on Middle-class, Educationally Advantaged Parents and Children," *Early Childhood Research Quarterly* 4, no. 3 (1989): 275-288.

35. John M. Love and Bruce Yelton, "Smoothing the Road from Preschool to Kindergarten," *Principal* 68, no. 5 (1989): 26-27.

36. K. Glicksman and T. Hill, *Easing the Child's Transition between Home, Child Care Center, and School: A Guide for Early Childhood Educators* (Trenton, NJ: New Jersey Department of Education, 1981); Dorothy Ham and Janet Perry, *Continuity of Learning for Children Ages 4, 5, and 6 in South Carolina Public Schools* (Columbia, SC: South Carolina Department of Education, 1988).

37. L. Lynn Harris and Bettye M. Caldwell, "Parental Preferences for Kindergarten Curriculum" (Unpublished paper, University of Arkansas at Little Rock, 1989).

38. Anne Mitchell, Michelle Seligson, and Fern Marx, *Early Childhood Programs and the Public Schools: Between Promise and Practice* (Dover, MA: Auburn House Publishing Co., 1989).

39. Ibid., p. 227.

40. Sue Bredekamp et al., *Easing the Transition from Preschool to Kindergarten* (Washington, DC: U. S. Department of Health and Human Services, 1987).

41. Ruth Hubbell et al., *Final Report: The Transition of Head Start Children into Public School*, Vol. 1 (Washington, DC: Department of Health and Human Services, CSR, Inc., 1987).

42. Love and Yelton, "Smoothing the Road from Preschool to Kindergarten."

43. Daniel J. Walsh, "Changes in Kindergarten: Why Here? Why Now?" *Early Childhood Research Quarterly* 4, no. 3 (1989): 377-391.

44. I was very impressed by the Walsh article, in that I had so strongly insisted at Kramer that general educational practices be no different for the early childhood teachers and the elementary teachers, i.e., salary schedule, committee service, break times, etc. According to his interpretation, I may unwittingly have been contributing to the elementary school's victory over the kindergarten rather than the reverse, as I had intended.

45. J. Conrad Schwartz, George Krolick, and Robert G. Strickland, "Effects of Early Day Care Experience on Adjustment to a New Environment," *American Journal of Orthopsychiatry* 43, no. 3 (1973): 340-346.

CHAPTER VI

Parents and Programs: Early Childhood as a Pioneer in Parent Involvement and Support

DOUGLAS R. POWELL

The image of parents and teachers functioning as partners in a young child's education has commanded a highly respected position in the ethos of early childhood education since the field's inception. In the early days, the early childhood educator's work with both children and parents was clearly defined and closely intertwined, as suggested in the title of the 1929 yearbook of the National Society for the Study of Education: *Preschool and Parental Education.* In more recent times, the imagery has become kaleidoscopic in nature, manifest in disparate approaches to the partnership concept and diverse assumptions about the appropriate relationship between families and early childhood programs.

The revered status of the home-school partnership image in the early childhood field stems from basic premises about families and societies, and the anticipated effects of close working relationships between parents and program staff.[1] The premises include: (a) the doctrine of parental rights, a core American value which places responsibility for determining the child's best interest first and foremost with parents; (b) the assumption that families exert a significant influence on a child's development, with the corollary assumption that preschool experiences must be extended and reinforced in the home if the preschool is to have long-term effects on the child; and (c) the principle of citizen participation in democratic institutions.

Rationales for close program-family ties generally point to anticipated outcomes in three areas. It is assumed that *child competence* will be enhanced if important adults in the child's life agree on and are consistent about the way they deal with the child. *Parents' self-development* also is to be affected through parental participation in programs. Having control over one's destiny in a program is seen as a way to help parents improve their feelings of competence and self-worth. Parent involvement rationales pertaining to this anticipated outcome generally reflect Smith's argument that individual competence is developed through the provision of opportunity, respect, and power; opportunities that do not carry a sharing of power result in paternalism and a corresponding decrease in self-respect and increase in dependency.[2]

A third anticipated outcome is increased *responsiveness and resourcefulness of programs serving children and families,* including early childhood programs and other institutions such as public schools. Participation in early childhood programs typically is viewed as training in how to relate to and enhance institutions that serve children and families. Anecdotal reports indicate that the parent cooperative preschool movement in this country produced "mother graduates" who readily assumed positions of responsibility as parent-teacher association officers and volunteers in public schools.[3] Some initiatives have viewed parent involvement as a way to strengthen parents' skills in facilitating institutional change. One of the early rationales for parent participation in Head Start, for example, was that involvement in program decision making would be a beginning step toward changing human service institutions that may be insensitive to parental needs and interests.[4] It also is assumed that parent involvement will increase program resources through parents' contributions to service delivery (e.g., classroom workers), and as fund raisers and advocates for societal support of children's programs.

Parent involvement was defined primarily as parent education for approximately the first fifty years of the nursery school movement. Programs sought to inform parents about child development and appropriate child-rearing practices through lecture, discussion, and experiential methods. While the parent education tradition continues to play an important role in early childhood programs, it is undergoing a paradigm shift in ideological framework, content, and methods that emphasizes the provision of social support as well as information regarding the family's child-rearing role. Since the mid-1960s, parent involvement also has been conceptualized as a mechanism for enhancing the resourcefulness and responsiveness of early childhood programs and other community institutions. Within this framework, the parent-teacher partnership has been defined as a shared decision-making relationship involving open two-way communication and, in some programs, structural mechanisms for ensuring parental influence on program operations.

Thus, two paradigms of parent involvement—parents as learners, and parents as program decision makers and resources—provide contrasting frameworks for the early childhood field's policies and practices surrounding relations between programs and families.[5] This chapter reviews major practices within these two paradigms of parent involvement: program efforts to support parents' child-rearing roles, and strategies for facilitating program responsiveness and resourcefulness through parent involvement. It concludes with an identification of critical challenges for the 1990s in view of the lessons learned from existing and previous practices.

Supporting Parents' Child-Rearing Roles

The dissemination of scientific knowledge about child development to parents has been a persistent effort in the early childhood field's attempts to support parental child rearing. One of the original purposes of the nursery school was to serve as a forum for educating parents about the nature and nurture of young children. As noted in the 1929 NSSE yearbook, the assumption was that learning to become a parent through "imitation and the trial-and-error method" was "glaringly" inadequate but was the only resource available to the average parent.[6] The yearbook included chapters on the use of the nursery school as a laboratory to train parents in child development and appropriate child-rearing practices.

The child study movement shifted the content of "expert" guidance in child rearing from religious, folklore, and intuitive sources to science. In a 1931 essay entitled "Mother's Heart Plus Mother's Head," William John Cooper, then U.S. Commissioner of Education, argued that child rearing in an industrial society requires careful preparation. "No longer may we assume that it is an inborn capacity," he wrote. "So to mother's heart must now be added mother's head."[7] Nearly fifty years later, U.S. Commissioner of Education Terrel Bell echoed Cooper's sentiments in suggesting that every child deserves a trained parent.[8]

Nursery schools established in the 1920s typically provided an array of parent education activities, including conferences with teachers, home visits, parent group meetings focused on child-rearing topics, and a consultation service for parents to explore child-rearing problems and concerns on an individualized basis with a professional. Parents also were encouraged to observe children in the nursery school setting.[9] The Works Progress Administration (WPA) nursery schools continued this parent education tradition during the Depression years. WPA funds supported teachers and other experts to facilitate parent discussion groups in nursery schools and other settings.[10] It was common in WPA nursery schools for parents to meet on a weekly basis with a parent educator who led them in discussions on family problems; helped them to identify and use community resources; and provided support for their self-development and learning. Parents appeared to be "very interested in and responsive to information from the science of child development."[11]

The parent cooperative movement, which dates to 1916, also has served as a major vehicle through which parents could learn about child development by assuming responsibility for and participating in a preschool classroom. Co-op preschool programs enabled parents to engage in "practice teaching for parenthood"[12] by working alongside an experienced early childhood educator. Programs also provided frequent lecture and discussion sessions on child development topics, guided observation and study of children's behavior, and experience in planning program activities for young children.[13]

The parent education tradition was well represented in the early intervention programs of the 1960s and 1970s. Nearly all of the major program models contained a parent education component. The Perry Preschool program, for example, supplemented the preschool classroom with a weekly home visit in which teachers worked with child and parent for one and a half hours.[14] Some model programs targeted the parent as the primary recipient of early intervention services. Gordon's Parent Education Infant and Toddler Program, and Levenstein's Mother-Child Home Program are illustrative of parent-as-teacher approaches developed in the 1960s. The purpose of the Gordon program was to enhance the development of infants through weekly visits to their homes by parent educators who taught mothers activities to carry out during the week with their infants. Gordon assumed that by helping a mother learn how to provide an educationally stimulating environment, her child might have a supportive environment all the time and not just during the weekly visits.[15] In the Mother-Child Home Program, "toy demonstrators" conducted weekly or semiweekly home play sessions with mother and toddler together around toys and books provided by the program. The intent was to prevent school failure by tapping "the rich educational potential of the mother-toddler relationship."[16]

Since its creation in 1965, Head Start has afforded the early childhood field a major opportunity to experiment with different approaches to working with parents.[17] Head Start performance standards call for parents to be involved in (a) the classroom as paid employees, volunteers, or observers; (b) activities for parents that they have helped to develop (e.g., parent education meetings); and (c) working with their children in cooperation with the staff of the center. Parent participation in program policy decisions also is mandated (see a subsequent section in this chapter). Examples of structured approaches to parent education in Head Start include the "Exploring Parenting" and "Getting Involved" series. Head Start also has generated ambitious, experimental program models aimed at supporting the family's child-rearing function. These initiatives have included Home Start, a home-based early education program; the Parent Child Centers; and the Child and Family Resource Program (discussed below).

The social and political currents of the 1960s, and the dramatic changes in family structure, function, and life-styles in the 1970s set the stage for profound shifts in parent education as practiced in early childhood settings. During this turbulent era, early intervention programs were criticized for assuming that participating families provided deficient child-rearing environments. For example, Baratz and Baratz argued that interventions aimed at low-income African-American children were based on an "inadequate mother hypothesis" that assumed the ghetto mother did not provide adequate social and sensory stimulation and failed to emphasize the importance of school achievement.[18] Criticisms also were made of an exclusive or primary intervention focus on the child or the mother-child dyad at the expense of attending to other elements of the family system, including a family's relations with the environment. Especially influential was Bronfenbrenner's report on the effects of early intervention, which argued that parents need *ecological* intervention in the form of family support systems.[19]

In response to these developments in the 1960s and 1970s, the parent education tradition in the early childhood field is undergoing major changes in ideological framework, content, and methods.[20] One emerging direction entails a realignment of relations between program and participants. The 1960s set in motion an alteration of the traditional balance of power between program staff and parents that emphasizes program staff serving as facilitators and collaborators vis-a-vis parents, and not as experts who engage in diagnosis and prescription regarding parents' child-rearing needs. The term *empowerment* typically is used in the field to describe this change.

Another emerging direction is increased programmatic attention to the social context of parenting. Early childhood programs are experimenting with ways to strengthen parents' sources of social support as a buffer against stressful situations and transitions. In some programs, the provision of supportive ties for parents is viewed as an equal or greater influence on parent functioning than the provision of child development information. Hence, the term *parent support* often is used in lieu of or in addition to the conventional *parent education* label. The name change reflects a substantive shift in the assumptions about influences on parent behavior and beliefs.

Representative of these emerging directions in the field are the Family Matters program,[21] the Family, Infant, and Preschool Program of the Western Carolina Center,[22] and the Child and Family Resource Program.[23] The Family Matters program experimented with a parental empowerment process that placed parents, not program experts, in the role of determining goals and activities to be pursued within the program. The program adhered to an ecological perspective that emphasized parents' personal social networks, and parents' roles in mediating the influences of larger systems (e.g., neighborhood, school, workplace) on their children's development. The Family, Infant, and Preschool Program exemplifies a movement toward increased interest in the social context of parenthood. The program, which serves handicapped and developmentally at-risk children, has evolved from a child-focused early intervention program to a family-systems-oriented program. In this Western Carolina Center program, all intervention efforts revolve around an identification of family members' needs from the family's (not the program's) perspective. The Child and Family Resource Program was an experimental Head Start initiative of the 1970s that viewed the family as the focus of program services. Working with family members, program home visitors conducted comprehensive assessments of the strengths and needs of participating low-income families, and generated an action plan that would help move the family toward its desired goals.

Programmatic attention to parents' needs regarding child-rearing information and support continues to be an active domain in the early childhood field. For instance, Minnesota's Early Childhood and Family Education program, founded in 1975, expands on a yearly basis in local communities. This program provides parent group discussions, home visits, child development classes, and other approaches to enhancing and supporting the competence of parents in providing optimal child-rearing environments. The state of Missouri has launched an ambitious New Parents as Teachers initiative which involves home visits and group meetings for new parents. Other states, including Illinois, Maryland, Connecticut, and Kentucky, also are investing in programs aimed at parents of children under five years of age.

Many full-day child care centers provide supportive services to families. Information on the range of services offered is dated (1976-1977) but extensive (national probability sample of 3,167 centers). The supply study component of the National Day Care Study surveyed approximately one out of six child care centers in each of the fifty states plus the District of Columbia.[24] The study found that counseling on child development was provided by 86 percent of the centers. Sizable percentages of centers also provided family counseling (55 percent), assistance in obtaining food stamps or financial aid (45 percent), and assistance in obtaining community services (52 percent). Only 10 percent of the centers provided none of these services.

There is evidence that early childhood programs support parents in their child-rearing roles through informal helping relationships among parents and between parents and staff. Both center-based and family day care providers have been found to assume an active helping role in responding to parents' questions and concerns regarding a range of child-related topics. Staff responses include asking questions, offering sympathy, presenting alternatives, and just listening.[25] An ethnographic study of preschool programs found a viable program "underlife" where staff informally provided such help as after-school chauffeuring, legal and medical advice, and career counseling.[26] About one-fourth of the child care center personnel involved in another study indicated that they considered some of their parents to be friends, and interacted frequently with these persons in settings (e.g., church) outside the child care center.[27]

In spite of the long and rich history of diverse efforts in the early childhood field to enhance parents' child-rearing roles, there is a limited amount of research evidence on the effectiveness of early childhood initiatives that provide services aimed at enhancing parents' child-rearing functions. Most of the existing investigations have focused on intensive parent- or family-oriented early childhood programs aimed at low-income populations. Evaluations of these types of initiatives have found positive short-term effects on child competence (i.e., IQ) and maternal behaviors.[28] A ten-year follow-up study of a long-term and comprehensive program for impoverished mothers uncovered long-term effects on such family characteristics as level of education, family size, and financial self-support.[29] Analyses suggest that the number of service-oriented contacts (e.g., home visit) with a family (i.e., eleven or more)[30] and the range of services offered to the family[31] may be associated with the magnitude of program effects.

Little is known about the effects of early childhood programs that employ modest approaches to parent education and support such as periodic lectures and/or discussions on child- or parent-related topics for parents of children enrolled in a preschool program. Research on middle-class populations is especially sparse.

Enhancing Program Responsiveness and Resourcefulness

As noted earlier, parent involvement has been employed as a strategy for enhancing the responsiveness and resourcefulness of early childhood programs to child and family needs. Most interest in program responsiveness stems from concern about the child's experiences with continuity between family and program. It is assumed that close coordination and communication between families and early childhood programs will lead to reduced levels of home-school discontinuity and concomitant improvements in the quality of the child's socialization experiences. This rationale has been used to recommend or justify the practice of frequent sharing of home and school information between parents and staff, and the practice of parental involvement in program decisions that contribute to program sensitivity to family values and circumstances.

COMMUNICATION TOWARD SUPPORTIVE LINKAGES

There is strong theoretical support for parent-staff communication aimed at fostering supportive linkages between program and family. Among theoretical treatments of relations between parents and nonfamilial child-rearing settings, Bronfenbrenner has offered the most elaborate set of propositions about the conditions that enhance the development of children (as well as adults) who function in multiple settings.[32] He suggests that a setting's developmental potential is improved when there are supportive linkages between settings; when a child's entry into a new setting is made in the company of one or more persons with whom the child has participated in other settings (e.g., parent accompanies child to preschool); when there is open two-way communication between settings that includes the family in the communications network; and when the mode of between-setting communication is personal (i.e., face-to-face versus printed announcement).

The National Association for the Education of Young Children has issued standards of professional practice in early childhood programs which call for parents to be well informed about and welcome as observers and contributors to the program. The standards are used by the National Academy of Early Childhood Programs (NAECP) to accredit programs for young children. The guidelines indicate that in high-quality programs (a) information about program philosophy and operating procedures should be given to new and prospective families; (b) children and parents should be oriented to the center through pre-enrollment visits, parent meetings, or similar means; (c) staff and parents should communicate regarding home and center child-rearing practices; (d) parents should be welcome as visitors in the center at all times; and (e) a communication system should be established to share day-to-day exchanges between parents and staff.[33]

There is scattered and dated research information on the actual frequency and content of communication between parents and personnel in early childhood programs. In one study of a university-based child care center committed to the concept of parent involvement, parents were found to spend an average of 7.4 minutes a day in the center, including time spent dropping off and picking up their child, conferences with center staff, observation of children, and participation in group meetings. During the seventy consecutive days observed for this study, there were three parent-teacher conferences lasting no more than 10 minutes each.[34] Another study of twelve urban child care centers found that a majority of parents and early childhood personnel communicated in person weekly or more frequently, typically during the child drop-off and pick-up times. The most frequently discussed topic was what the child's day is like at the center. Parent- and family-related topics were discussed infrequently. Parent-teacher conferences and staff visits to the child's home were infrequent or nonexistent. A majority of parents and staff believed that the center should not be kept informed of family activities on a routine basis.[35] A potential problem of communication during the drop-off and pick-up transition times is that individuals may be preoccupied with other matters. Also, at many child care programs the personnel on duty during late afternoon pick-up time typically have not been with the child all day and therefore may have limited information to share on the child's day. Thus, perhaps it is not surprising that the study uncovered a high level of parent and caregiver dissatisfaction with parent-staff discussion of activities at the center.

Overall, relations between parents and early childhood providers may be stronger in family day care than in center-based arrangements. Parents using family day care have reported closer personal relationships with caregivers than parents using child care centers.[36] One study found that center providers spent 13.7 minutes per week with each parent while family day care providers spent 54.7 minutes per week with each parent.[37] The higher ratio of providers to children in centers may translate into less available time for interaction with parents.

Research data on the effects of interaction between parents and early childhood personnel on children are virtually nonexistent. There has been no empirical examination of the assumption that parent-staff collaboration leads to improved home-school continuity, which in turn leads to improved child competence. Hence, the aforementioned theoretical grounds are significantly stronger than the research foundation of rationales for establishing and maintaining cooperative relations between families and early childhood programs.[38] There also is limited research understanding of what parents and early childhood personnel do with the information they receive from one another. How parents and staff process and act on the messages they transmit to each other is a fertile area awaiting systematic research attention.

PARENTS AS PARTICIPANTS IN PROGRAMS

The placement of parents in volunteer or paid program staff positions, and in decision-making roles regarding program services are strategies the early childhood field has utilized to ensure program responsiveness. These practices characterize preschool programs in the parent cooperative movement, which traditionally has served a middle-class population. They also are found in Head Start and some other government-sponsored early intervention initiatives, which often are targeted at low-income populations.

Mechanisms for enabling parental influence on the responsiveness of educational services for children with special needs were established in 1975 through federal legislation mandating educational services for all handicapped children. The Education of All Handicapped Children Act of 1975 (Public Law 94-142) specified a role for parents in decisions about child testing and placement in special education programs, and the right to initiate due process hearings. These provisions were maintained in the recent Education of the Handicapped Act Amendments (Public Law 99-457), which provide assistance to states in offering early intervention services to infants and toddlers.

The responsiveness of early childhood programs to child and family characteristics is a particularly critical issue for programs serving low-income and ethnic minority populations who frequently are targeted for receiving early childhood intervention programs and traditionally have been disenfranchised from mainstream political power structures. It has been proposed that discontinuity between home and school is a major cause of the high rate of low academic achievement among low-income and some ethnic minority populations.[39] In anticipation of the growth of public school programs for four-year-olds, the National Black Child Development Institute issued a set of ten "safeguards" for programs for four-year-olds in the public schools that call for parental involvement in program decisions about curriculum and program policy.[40] The guidelines suggest parents should assume active roles in evaluating program operations, and that a standing parent committee should work with teachers surrounding curriculum issues.

Head Start has served as a national field-based laboratory for experimenting with the placement of parents in preschool classrooms and program decision-making roles. Head Start was founded in 1965 during an era of political and social unrest and War on Poverty initiatives. The Economic Opportunity Act of 1964 called for the "maximum feasible participation" of citizens in community action programs. In its early years, Head Start actively pursued bold and often controversial methods toward implementing the maximum feasible participation concept. One of the more innovative responses was offered by the Child Development Group of Mississippi where the Head Start program for a poor African-American community was run totally by the people themselves.[41] Since 1970, the national Head Start office has adhered to performance standards that require parental involvement in decisions about program operations (in addition to other forms of parent involvement discussed previously in this chapter). Specifically, each local program is to establish and maintain a Head Start Policy Council comprised of at least 50 percent parents of Head Start children presently enrolled in that delegate agency program plus representatives of the community. Head Start staff members cannot serve on the council in a voting capacity. Parent members of the policy council must be elected by parents of Head Start children currently enrolled in the program. By federal policy mandate, one of the many charges to the local council is the hiring and firing of the Head Start director and staff.

Even though Head Start parents continue to represent a majority of local Head Start policy councils, a historical assessment of Head Start parent involvement practices suggests that the political organizing role envisioned for Head Start parents has diminished over the years, and an emphasis on parent education currently dominates the Head Start parent involvement component.[42] Existing data indicate that sizable proportions of parents participate in various paid and volunteer capacities in Head Start. However, the extent of involvement reportedly is uneven, with a "core of parents contributing a disproportionate share of time."[43] For example, one study found that on the average, parents volunteered thirty-two hours a year, but 35 percent of the parents accounted for 71 percent of the total time volunteered.[44]

Information on the level of parent involvement in full-day child care centers in this country is dated. It comes primarily from the supply study component of the National Day Care Study discussed earlier.[45] In this national probability sample, 35 percent of the centers indicated that parents were involved in reviewing center budgets and programs. Parent participation in staff selection occurred at 22 percent of the centers, and parents served as volunteers at 28 percent of the centers. At 35 percent of the centers, parents reportedly used the center for social activities, and at 33 percent of the centers parents were involved in raising funds for program operations. At 41 percent of the centers, parents were not involved in any of these five ways. Parent involvement was considerably higher in nonprofit centers than in proprietary centers. Sixty-seven percent of the centers not receiving any government funds for any child reported that parents were not involved in any of the participation modes noted above; this was the case for 36 percent of nonprofit centers. Also, lower percentages of proprietary centers than nonprofit centers indicated no parent participation in staff selection and in reviews of budgets and programs.

Studies involving low-income populations suggest that higher levels of parent involvement in early childhood programs (i.e., as classroom workers) are related to positive aspects of parental functioning. Active parent involvement in Head Start has been found to be positively associated with parents' psychological well-being, including greater feelings of mastery and life satisfaction[46] and reduced levels of anxiety and depression.[47] Research design limitations, however, make it difficult to determine whether the program is the causal factor in these relationships between participation and individual functioning. Anecdotal data offer rich accounts of the direct impact of program participation on parental self-esteem.[48]

As noted earlier, one of the visions of advocates of parent participation in early childhood programs is that parents would strengthen their skills in dealing with community agencies and therefore be able to encourage other institutions (e.g., public schools) to be more responsive to the needs of children and their families. While it is methodologically difficult to carry out research on whether this expectation has been realized, an early Head Start study found that in centers with high parent participation the parents were more active in affecting institutional change in the community than in Head Start centers where parent participation was low. The study also discovered that in centers with lower levels of parent participation the parents expressed less confidence in their ability to influence their local school system.[49]

There are abundant anecdotal reports in the literature that parent participation in early childhood initiatives has led to increases in program resources through parents' advocacy work. The reports represent publicly funded early childhood centers in California,[50] the National Head Start Association,[51] and the federal Follow Through program.[52]

Challenges of the Future

As demonstrated in this chapter, policies and practices regarding relations between parents and early childhood programs historically have been predicated on two different assumptions about the usefulness of resources that parents bring to an early childhood program. In one view, it is assumed that parents need expert guidance and information about child development and appropriate child-rearing involvement, while a second view assumes that parents possess resources that can be marshalled and nurtured toward the end of strengthening program resources and responsiveness. The boundaries and inherent conflicts between the parent-as-learner and parent-as-program-resource paradigms have subsided a good deal in the past decade largely due to the aforementioned shifts in the field's approach to parent education and support. Emerging ideologies and methods of supporting parents emphasize family strengths and a proactive parental role in determining the ways in which programs support parents. The growing interest in program responsiveness to and respect for parental interests regarding the family's child-rearing function is in sharp contrast to earlier views of parents as uninformed and perhaps misguided rearers of young children.

A superordinate challenge is for the field to develop a workable image of parent-program relations that incorporates elements of the conventional paradigms. Of necessity, a vision of parent involvement must address the persistent conflict between this country's deeply held doctrine of parental rights and the growing professionalization and institutionalization of early education and care. Most serious discussions of relations between parents and early childhood program personnel ultimately reduce to fundamental questions about the status of parental prerogatives and the autonomy of early childhood personnel. Freedom from lay control of the content and method of services is a tenet of professionalism and a characteristic of most human service institutions. Yet in America, the private matter of early child rearing is not a task that is easily relinquished to nonfamilial institutions and professionals. The challenge is to generate policies and practices that permit a two-way flow of influence between parents and programs that is respectful of the expertise and perspectives of all parties involved. In practical terms, for example, the field needs easily replicated mechanisms of ensuring that needs assessments conducted in family-oriented early intervention programs actively incorporate parents' world views and perceptions of their children, and do not simply impose professional judgments of needed changes within a family system. As another example, the field needs parent-program relationship strategies that permit a respectful accommodation of parental desires for structured academic curriculum and professional judgments about developmentally appropriate practices with young children. These are not new issues, but their importance is elevated by the expansion of institutional structures for the delivery of early education and care, and by efforts of professional groups (notably NAEYC) to encourage widespread adoption of standards and practices in early childhood education and care.

Workable schemes of parent-program relations also must take careful account of the rapid and profound changes in family structure and life-style. The challenge is to develop strategies for working with families that accommodate the limited availability of growing numbers of parents to support program activities through traditional avenues. Many existing practices of working with parents are based on outdated images of the nuclear family in America, yet many of today's parents have limited time or energy to pursue the typical models of parent involvement in early childhood programs. The parent-staff partnership concept seems to be particularly vulnerable in full-day child care where, as noted earlier, research data suggest there are generally low levels of parental involvement. This finding is not surprising in view of the staffing patterns at most child care centers and in view of the dramatic changes in American families, including high numbers of single-parent households and dual-worker life-styles represented among users of full-day child care. Studies reviewed earlier in this chapter point to the rich possibilities of targeting informal exchanges between parents and staff as an important avenue for initiating and sustaining collaborative relations.

Unfortunately, there is limited research information to guide the development of new policy and program initiatives regarding parent involvement. A troubling paradox is that the field of early childhood education and care has sustained a long-standing commitment to parent involvement in the face of a severely limited research base. There are thin empirical grounds for many of the parent-staff relationship practices recommended by professional groups and leaders.[53] It appears that the field's historical commitment to working with parents has been fueled by the philosophical premises noted at the outset of this chapter, and by knowledge from practice informally garnered by generations of early childhood educators. There is a crucial need for research on the nature and effects of different patterns of program-family interaction in diverse program settings. Collectively, the existing research is limited in quantity as well as in the populations studied, measures employed, and conceptualizations of the program-family interface. Needed research directions include the consideration of working- and middle-class populations, inclusion of measures of child functioning that transcend cognitive outcomes, and differentiated views of the program-parent relationship that capture in precise terms the variegated transactions between parents and personnel in early childhood programs.

Also needed is thoughtful analysis of early childhood programs as case studies of program-parent relations. Programs operating under the aegis of Head Start and the parent cooperative movement are good candidates for identifying the conditions under which different forms of parent involvement are likely to flourish. Particular attention needs to be given to *structural provisions* for parent involvement. As discussed earlier, in Head Start there are specific federal mandates for parental roles in program operations, and the design of programs operating within the parent cooperative movement call for parents to assume key organizational roles. More information is needed about the relation of parent involvement mandates and organizational decision-making roles for parents to the facilitation of program responsiveness to families. Also in need of attention is the role of *staff competence* in working with parents. Most professional education programs emphasize work with young children and require little or no academic course work or supervised experiences in working with parents. The skills required for effective work with young children do not transfer to working with adults, and hence there appears to be a need for preservice and in-service education pertaining to parent development and strategies for involving parents in program operations. Head Start would be a useful case study in this regard in that thousands of staff members have received training in working with parents through the Child Development Associate credential program. Assessment of *staff resources* for facilitating parent involvement also requires the field's consideration. The experience of Head Start suggests that ambitious parent involvement plans necessitate staff time that is not divided among competing interests. In Head Start, at least one staff member (the family services coordinator) has the responsibility to work with parents in each local delegate program.

A tangible way for the early childhood field to address these challenges is to generate and promote guidelines on appropriate professional practices with parents in early childhood settings. The aforementioned NAECP guidelines are a useful beginning point but do not offer the scope and specificity necessary for defining the elements of parent support and involvement in early childhood programs. Advances in the relationship between families and early childhood programs require a thoughtful delineation of the components of developmentally appropriate practices with parents akin to the landmark report on developmentally appropriate practices with young children issued by NAEYC in 1987.[54] This challenge requires serious consideration of the ways in which early childhood programs can address the needs of parenthood as a stage of adult development and as an increasingly difficult task in a rapidly changing social context. Fortunately, the field has a long and diverse history of pioneering program experiences to draw upon as it anticipates and guides the nature of program partnerships with families of the 21st century.

FOOTNOTES

1. Douglas R. Powell, *Families and Early Childhood Programs* (Washington, DC: National Association for the Education of Young Children, 1989).

2. M. Brewster Smith, "Competence and Socialization," in *Socialization and Society*, ed. Joan A. Clausen (Boston: Little, Brown, 1968).

3. Katharine Whiteside-Taylor, "Cooperative Nursery Schools Educate Families," *Teachers College Record* 4 (1953): 332-339.

4. Jeanette Valentine and Evan Stark, "The Social Context of Parent Involvement in Head Start," in *Project Head Start: A Legacy of the War on Poverty*, ed. Edward Zigler and Jeanette Valentine (New York: Free Press, 1979).

5. Greta G. Fein, "The Informed Parent," in *Advances in Early Education and Day Care*, ed. Sally Kilmer (Greenwich, CT: JAI Press, 1980), pp. 155-185.

6. Committee on Preschool and Parental Education, "Training for the Field of Parental Education," in *Preschool and Parental Education*, ed. Guy M. Whipple, Twenty-eighth Yearbook of the National Society for the Study of Education, Part 1 (Bloomington, IL: Public School Publishing Co., 1929), p. 435.

7. William J. Cooper, "Mother's Heart Plus Mother's Head," in *Education for Home and Family* (Washington, DC: National Congress of Parents and Teachers, 1931), p. 32.

8. Terrel Bell, "The Child's Right to Have a Trained Parent," *Elementary School Guidance and Counseling* 9 (1975): 271.

9. Committee on Preschool and Parental Education, *Preschool and Parental Education*.

10. Orville G. Brim, *Education for Child Rearing* (New York: Russell Sage, 1959).

11. Millie Almy, "Foreword," in Powell, *Families and Early Childhood Programs*, p. vi.

12. Katharine Whiteside-Taylor, *Parents and Children Learn Together* (New York: Teachers College Press, 1968), p. 144.

· 13. Whiteside-Taylor, "Cooperative Nursery Schools Educate Families."

14. Lawrence J. Schweinhart and David P. Weikart, "Effects of the Perry Preschool Program on Youths through Age 15 A Summary," in Consortium for Longitudinal Studies, *As the Twig Is Bent: Lasting Effects of Preschool Programs* (Hillsdale, NJ: Erlbaum, 1983), pp. 71-101.

15. R. Emile Jester and Barry J. Guinagh, "The Gordon Parent Education Infant and Toddler Program," in Consortium for Longitudinal Studies, *As the Twig Is Bent*, pp. 103-132.

16. Phyllis Levenstein, John O'Hara, and John Madden, "The Mother-Child Home Program of the Verbal Interaction Project," in Consortium for Longitudinal Studies, *As the Twig Is Bent*, p. 237.

17. Edward F. Zigler and Johanna Freedman, "Head Start: A Pioneer of Family Support," in *America's Family Support Programs: Perspectives and Prospects*, ed. Sharon L. Kagan, Douglas R. Powell, Bernice Weissbourd, and Edward F. Zigler (New Haven, CT: Yale University Press, 1987), pp. 57-76.

18. Stephen S. Baratz and Joan C. Baratz, "Early Childhood Intervention: The Social Science Base of Institutional Racism," *Harvard Educational Review* 40 (1970): 29-50.

19. Urie Bronfenbrenner, *Is Early Intervention Effective? A Report on Longitudinal Evaluations of Preschool Programs*, Vol. 2 (Washington, DC: Office of Child Development, U.S. Department of Health, Education, and Welfare, 1974).

20. Douglas R. Powell, "Emerging Directions in Parent-Child Intervention," in *Parent Education as Early Childhood Intervention*, ed. Douglas R. Powell (Norwood, NJ: Ablex, 1988), pp. 1-22.

21. Moncreiff Cochran, "Parental Empowerment in Family Matters: Lessons Learned from a Research Program," in *Parent Education as Early Childhood Intervention*, ed. Powell, pp. 23-50.

22. Carl J. Dunst and Carol M. Trivette, "A Family Systems Model of Early Intervention with Handicapped and Developmentally At-Risk Children," in *Parent Education as Early Childhood Intervention*, ed. Powell, pp. 131-179.

23. Ruth Ann O'Keefe, "What Head Start Means to Families," in *Current Topics in Early Childhood Education*, Vol. 2, ed. Lilian G. Katz (Norwood, NJ: Ablex, 1979), pp. 43-67.

24. Craig Coelen, Fred Glantz, and Daniel Calore, *Day Care Centers in the U.S.* (Cambridge, MA: Abt Associates, 1979).

25. Robert Hughes, "The Informal Help-Giving of Home and Center Childcare Providers," *Family Relations* 34 (1985): 359-366.

26. Carole E. Joffe, *Friendly Intruders: Childcare Professionals and Family Life* (Berkeley, CA: University of California Press, 1977).

27. Douglas R. Powell, "The Interpersonal Relationship between Parents and Caregivers in Day Care Settings," *American Journal of Orthopsychiatry* 48 (1978): 680-689.

28. Susan R. Andrews, Janet B. Blumenthal, Dale L. Johnson, Alfred J. Kahn, Carol J. Ferguson, Thomas M. Lasater, Paul E. Malone, and Doris B. Wallace, "The Skills of Mothering: A Study of Parent Child Development Centers," *Monographs of the Society for Research in Child Development* 47, no. 6 (1982): 1-83, Serial No. 198; Diana T. Slaughter, "Early Intervention and Its Effects on Maternal and Child Development," *Monographs of the Society for Research in Child Development* 48, no. 4 (1983): 1-91, Serial No. 202; Jeffrey R. Travers, Marrit J. Nauta, Nancy Irwin, *The Effects of a Social Program: Final Report of the Child and Family Resource Program's Infant-Toddler Component* (HHS-105-79-1301) (Cambridge, MA: Abt Associates, 1982); Jester and Guinagh, "The Gordon Parent Education Infant Toddler Program."

29. Victoria Seitz, Laurie K. Rosenbaum, and Nancy N. Apfel, "Effects of Family Support Intervention: A Ten-Year Follow-up," *Child Development* 56 (1985): 376-391.

30. Christoph M. Heinicke, Leila Beckwith, and Anne Thompson, "Early Intervention in the Family System: A Framework and Review," *Infant Mental Health Journal* 9 (1988): 111-141.

31. Craig T. Ramey, D. M. Bryant, and T. M. Suarez, "Preschool Compensatory Education and the Modifiability of Intelligence: A Critical Review," in *Current Topics in Human Intelligence*, ed. Douglas Detterman (Norwood, NJ: Ablex, 1985), pp. 247-296.

32. Urie Bronfenbrenner, *The Ecology of Human Development: Experiments by Nature and Design* (Cambridge, MA: Harvard University Press, 1979).

33. National Academy of Early Childhood Programs, *Accreditation Criteria and Procedures of the National Academy of Early Childhood Programs* (Washington, DC: National Association for the Education of Young Children, 1984).

34. Edward F. Zigler and Pauline Turner, "Parents and Day Care Workers: A Failed Partnership?" in *Day Care: Scientific and Social Policy Issues*, ed. Edward F. Zigler and Edmund W. Gordon (New York: Free Press, 1982), pp. 174-182.

35. Powell, "The Interpersonal Relationship between Parents and Caregivers in Day Care Settings."

..

36. Alan R. Pence and Hillel Goelman, "Silent Partners: Parents of Children in Three Types of Day Care," *Early Childhood Research Quarterly* 2 (1987): 103-118.

37. Hughes, "The Informal Help-Giving of Home and Center Childcare Providers."

38. Powell, *Families and Early Childhood Programs.*

39. Roland G. Tharp, "Psychocultural Variables and Constants: Effects on Teaching and Learning in Schools," *American Psychologist* 44 (1989): 349-359.

40. National Black Child Development Institute, *Safeguards: Guidelines for Establishing Programs for Four-Year-Olds in the Public Schools* (Washington, DC: National Black Child Development Institute, 1987).

41. Polly Greenberg, *The Devil Has Slippery Shoes: A Biased Biography of the Child Development Group of Mississippi* (New York: Macmillan, 1969).

42. Valentine and Stark, "The Social Context of Parent Involvement in Head Start."

43. Ruth H. McKey, Larry Condelli, Harriet Ganson, Barbara J. Barrett, Catherine McConkey, and Margaret C. Plantz, *The Impact of Head Start on Children, Families, and Communities,* Department of Health and Human Services Publication No. 85-31193 (Washington, DC: CSR, Inc., 1985), p. 17.

44. U.S. Comptroller General's report to Congress, cited in McKey et al., *The Impact of Head Start on Children, Families, and Communities.*

45. Coelen, Glantz, and Calore, *Day Care Centers in the U.S.*

46. Faith L. Parker, Chaya S. Piotrkowski, and Lenore Peay, "Head Start as a Social Support for Mothers: The Psychological Benefits of Involvement," *American Journal of Orthopsychiatry* 57 (1987): 220-233.

47. For a review, see McKey et al., *The Impact of Head Start on Children, Families, and Communities.*

48. For example, see James L. Robinson and Willa B. Choper, "Another Perspective on Program Evaluation: The Parents Speak," in *Project Head Start,* ed. Zigler and Valentine.

49. Midco Educational Associates, *Investigation of the Effects of Parent Participation in Head Start, Final Technical Report* (Denver, CO: Midco Educational Associates, 1972).

50. Joffe, *Friendly Intruders.*

51. O'Keefe, "What Head Start Means to Families."

52. Patricia P. Olmsted and Roberta I. Rubin, "Parent Involvement: Perspectives from the Follow Through Experiment," in *Parent Education and Public Policy,* ed. Ron Haskins and Diane Adams (Norwood, NJ: Ablex, 1983).

53. See Powell, *Families and Early Childhood Programs.*

54. Sue Bredekamp, *Developmentally Appropriate Practice in Early Childhood Programs Serving Children from Birth through Age 8* (Washington, DC: National Association for the Education of Young Children, 1987).

CHAPTER VII

Early Childhood Teacher Training:
Linking Theory and Practice

BERNARD SPODEK

The field of early childhood education is populated with a wide range of practitioners. They vary in many ways—in the work they do, the fields from which they come, and the preparation they have. Some practitioners function in highly esoteric roles, conducting research, developing and testing theory, or writing scholarly tracts. Others engage in very down-to-earth activities, feeding children, cleaning and changing their clothes, wiping their noses, and helping them deal with the day-to-day problems that arise as part of growing up.

No one challenges the professionalism of the first group of practitioners. They generally have strong academic backgrounds and high levels of qualifications. However, questions have been seriously raised about the professionalism of the second group. In this chapter, I discuss the nature of professionalism and how it applies to early childhood practitioners, gatekeeping related to early childhood professionalism, the elements necessary for the preparation of early childhood professionals, and some of the dilemmas facing the field as it strives toward higher levels of professionalism.

Conception of an Early Childhood Professional

The word "professional" is used in many ways. In its everyday usage, we consider anyone a professional who follows an occupation as a means of earning a living. Thus, we talk about professional ballplayers, professional stockbrokers, professional carpenters, or professional dishwashers. The term "professional" is used here to separate those who do the work for a living from those who receive no pay for the same activity, in spite of the fact that the amateur might be as competent, or even more competent, than the professional. Given this use of the word, early childhood personnel would be considered professional if they received pay for their work.

110

The term "professional" is used in a more formal sense to recognize members of the learned professions. These originally included doctors, lawyers, and the clergy, but the list of the learned professions has been expanded beyond that small group. It is in this latter sense that the term professional is applied here. Professionalism reflects a level of practice in a field that requires a high degree of knowledge and skill developed over a lengthy period of preparation.

Professions are social institutions that are established to provide essential services. They are concerned with an area of social need. Professionals possess a specialized body of knowledge and skills based on an undergirding theory that is gained over a protracted period of preparation. Professionals are involved in basic decisions relating to their field and are typically organized into associations that support autonomous practice. They are relatively free of on-the-job supervision and enjoy a high level of public trust. The authority of professionals to practice derives from their clients. Standards of admission and continued practice, which are based upon long periods of preparation, are set by associations of professionals who also establish and enforce codes of ethics.[1]

Inquiring into the nature of the teaching profession, Howsam and his colleagues concluded that teaching could not be considered fully professional since practitioners did not meet all the criteria of professionals.[2] Instead, they considered teachers in general as semiprofessionals. Given the characteristics of early childhood practice, it is doubtful whether many early childhood teachers reflect even this level of semiprofessionalism.

Generally, when we inquire into teaching as a profession as Howsam and his colleagues have, we study teachers at the elementary or secondary school level. These teachers are graduates of college- or university-based teacher education programs lasting four or five years and leading to at least a bachelor's degree. The minimum level of their proficiency is attested to by a state teaching certificate. This certificate usually specifies the content area and/or the age level of the children the individual is considered competent to teach. It is issued by a state department of education to testify that the individual possesses at least a minimum level of teaching proficiency in a particular field.

Early childhood education is generally defined as the education of children from birth or three years of age through eight years of age. Early childhood teachers vary greatly in their preparation to practice and in their levels of skill and competency. Teachers of kindergarten and the early primary grades in public school programs generally have the same level of preparation and meet standards for certification that are similar to those for teachers of older children. Early childhood teachers in nonpublic schools, including those in child care centers, Head Start programs, and other preschools, often lack the teacher preparation and certification of their public school counterparts. They may be graduates of one- or two-year programs at community colleges, or they may have completed a preparation program at a vocational center. Some will have had their training in secondary school vocational training programs. Some will have had only informal training gained in in-service programs. Unfortunately, some practitioners have had no preparation at all.

While a few teachers in the private sector have teaching certificates, most only meet the minimum standards of state day care licensing agencies. Some years ago, the Child Development Associate credential was established as an alternative way of signifying competence among early childhood practitioners. However, this credential, which will be discussed more fully later, is held by only a small minority of child care practitioners. Thus, we have no single standard for entry into the early childhood profession, if we can characterize the field as a profession. We also have no standard requirement for preparation to practice in the field.

Professionalism in Early Childhood Education

One means that professions use to maintain their high degree of professionalism is to control entry into the field by requiring high levels of preparation as well as a demonstration, often by an examination, of a minimum required level of knowledge and competence. In some fields, a period of internship or guided practice is required as well. Completion of preparation and successfully passing the required examination leads to some form of license, given by the state or the professional association. Continued professional development and maintenance of professional behavior may be required for the license to remain in effect.

TEACHER CERTIFICATION

In the field of education, such a license takes the form of a state teaching certificate, as mentioned earlier. While many states offer such a teaching certificate in early childhood education, others provide some form of early childhood endorsement on an elementary teaching certificate. Not only can the type of teaching certificate vary; the age and/or grade range of the certificate or endorsement varies as well. Some early childhood certificates permit their holders to teach classes from kindergarten through grade three. Others permit the holder to teach children from preschool (children aged three and four) through grade three or even from birth through age eight. Sometimes only a kindergarten endorsement is available.

In order to receive an early childhood teaching certificate, individuals normally must have completed an approved program of early childhood teacher preparation. Most of these programs are at the bachelor's degree level, though some programs require a full five years of teacher preparation or are at the postbachelor's level. In most cases, state departments of education set standards for programs that lead to state teaching certificates. These standards generally include the amount and range of general education courses to be taken as well as the nature of the professional component of the program. Specific courses may be prescribed along with minimal hours for student teaching and other field experiences.

Most states evaluate the quality of the teacher training institution and its education faculty as well as the nature of the program leading to state teacher certification. Some of these institutions also have their programs accredited by the National Council for the Accreditation of Teacher Education (NCATE), which has adopted some of the guidelines for early childhood teacher education programs that were originally developed by the National Association for the Education of Young Children.[3]

In many states and in some large municipalities, successful completion of an examination is also required for certification or licensure. This examination may cover knowledge in the specific field of teaching, may be an examination of basic academic skills, or may be a more complex examination. In some places the National Teachers Examination is used while others have had examinations specifically designed for them.

Calls for reforms in teacher education have been heard in recent years. At the same time, requests for admission to teacher education programs have increased. Jointly, these two conditions have influenced teacher training programs to become increasingly selective. Few four- or five-year programs of teacher education are in institutions that practice open enrollment, admitting every candidate who applies. Generally, criteria for admission include high school grade point average or class standing, and college entrance examination scores, either the Scholastic Aptitude Test (SAT) or the

American College Test (ACT). Teacher education programs in these institutions may be further selective, adopting requirements beyond those for admission to the college or university. These added requirements might include minimum grade point averages in general education courses, as well as interviews, writing samples, or other indicators of academic competency or potential success as a teacher. While the same information might continue to be requested from all applicants, programs become more or less selective by modifying the criteria used for admission, for example, by requiring a higher or lower test score or grade point average so that the number of successful applicants for admission will closely match the number of spaces available in the program.

CREDENTIALS FOR PRESCHOOL TEACHERS

Entry into the nonpublic school sector of the field of early childhood education has been more accessible than has been public school teaching. Standards for admission and continued practice are significantly less stringent, especially for teachers in preschools and child care centers. In most states, the licensing and supervision of preschools is outside the domain of state departments of education and requirements for practice are not the same as for public school teachers. Teaching in these centers does not generally require a teaching certificate and a level of preparation lower than a bachelor degree teacher training program is usually accepted. Completion of a one- or two-year postsecondary program, or the accumulation of a minimum number of credits in child care courses may be expected. Sometimes requirements are even lower than that, with experience serving in lieu of preparation.

Because there has been no teaching certificate available for preschool or child care practitioners, the Child Development Associate (CDA) credential has been proposed as an alternative. This credential originated in 1971 to serve the needs of the Head Start program. By the end of 1989, over 30,000 CDA credentials had been awarded. While this number may seem large, it actually represents only a small proportion of those who practice in the field.

The CDA credential was rooted at its inception in the ideology of the competency-based teacher education movement. Assessment was originally to be based upon demonstration of competencies through meeting observable performance criteria. Presently, the assessment consists of the combined judgments of an evaluation team who view the candidate's portfolio, interview persons who have professional contact with the candidate, and observe the candidate in practice. A new assessment procedure is presently being designed.

The CDA credential is based upon an evaluation in thirteen functional areas to assess the candidate's ability (1) to establish and maintain a safe, healthy learning environment; (2) to advance physical and intellectual competence; (3) to support social and emotional development and provide positive guidance; (4) to establish positive and productive relationships with families; (5) to insure a well-run, purposeful program responsive to participant needs; and (6) to maintain a commitment to professionalism.[4]

The candidate is not required to complete an early childhood teacher education program in order to receive the CDA credential. However, a number of community colleges have based the content of their programs on the CDA competencies and use their program to prepare their students to be evaluated for the CDA credential.

The CDA credential is presently undergoing modification to become more available to practitioners at a national level and new requirements and forms of evaluation are being developed. Two routes are being considered at present. One would require completion of a training program including course work and field work, a self-study, completion of a written test, and an on-site evaluation. The second route would include only a written test and an on-site evaluation.[5]

LEVELS OF PROFESSIONALISM

Many practitioners in the field of early childhood education have neither a teaching certificate nor a CDA credential. It is also questionable whether all practitioners need the levels of preparation attested to by these credentials. The National Association for the Education of Young Children has suggested that there be four levels of professionalism for early childhood practitioners, each with its own requirements:

1. *Early Childhood Teacher Assistants*, level one, are entry level practitioners who work under the direct supervision of professionals. They are expected to have a high school diploma or its equivalent and to participate in professional development activities.

2. *Early Childhood Associate Teachers*, level two, would implement program activities and be responsible for a group of children. They are expected to have a CDA credential or its equivalent.

3. *Early Childhood Teachers*, level three, would provide care and education for groups of children. They would have a bachelors degree in early childhood education or child development.

4. *Early Childhood Specialists*, level four, would supervise and train staff, design curriculum, and possibly administer programs. They are expected to have at least a bachelors degree in early childhood education or child development as well as at least three years of experience and/or a masters degree.[6]

Some early childhood educators have suggested that a career ladder plan be established for early childhood teachers, with practitioners able to start at the entry level of professionalism and, through advanced training and experience, move on to higher levels. The CDA credential might be a rung in the ladder to higher levels of professionalism. Such a plan was the hope of the Head Start program when it began. This program, which was embedded in community action, was to serve adults as well as children by providing career opportunities for persons in the communities served.

While the proposal for establishing a career ladder is a worthy one, there are a number of difficulties involved and it has never been implemented on any scale. Often those who accept entry level positions in early childhood programs lack the academic qualifications for admission to colleges and universities. They also may be turned off by more formal educational programs, or have difficulty with college-level courses, and prefer the informality of workshops and conferences rather than classes. They also may be less willing to enroll in general education courses, an essential part of all teacher education programs leading to certification. In addition, there are often problems in transferring course credit from one institutional level to another level. While courses in vocational programs may cover the same topics as those offered in universities, the topics are addressed in different ways and at a different level.

The absence of real career ladders in early childhood education creates a dilemma for the field. It limits the possibilities for upward professional mobility for many persons, including women and minorities, who have worked effectively in the field of early childhood education as teaching assistants or aides.[7] In seeking ways to resolve the dilemma, it would perhaps be helpful to understand the content and nature of teacher education programs, the roles that theory and practice play in these programs, and how theory and practice are integrated.

Another view of levels of professionalism can be found in the work of Vander Ven.[8] She views early childhood teachers as becoming not only more proficient and sophisticated as they move through their careers, but also as functioning in a broader range of spheres within the profession. They may seek additional preparation, serve as mentors, administrators, teacher educators, or influencers of social policy. Practice becomes more complex at each successive professional stage.

The Content of Early Childhood Teacher Preparation Programs

In considering the content of programs that prepare teachers of very young children we need to differentiate between programs that prepare practitioners at different professional levels. At the higher two of the NAEYC levels of professionalism noted earlier, early childhood teacher preparation is offered at four-year colleges or universities. Preparation for practice at the lower two levels is provided at community colleges, vocational education centers, or secondary schools. For some entry level practitioners, unfortunately, the only preparation might be the in-service training activities provided at their job site.

As noted earlier, the nature and level of the preparation for teachers in early childhood programs is determined by public school regulations, state child care licensing regulations, or by the requirements of the employing agencies. Head Start programs, for example, will require that teachers have the Child Development Associate credential or its equivalent. Many preschool programs establish minimum requirements for teaching positions.

Because the requirements for teaching certificates are in fact criteria for employment, those requirements heavily influence the nature of teacher education programs. In fact, changes in certification requirements have been the single most important influence on changes in early childhood teacher education programs.[9]

The components of four-year teacher education programs and two-year associate degree programs in early childhood education are similar, consisting of four parts: general education, foundations, instructional knowledge, and practice.[10] The amount of study required within each component is different in these institutions, given the difference in their duration. Vocational programs may also have completely different components. Often these programs are only a small part of a high school program and will be truncated.

General education. The general education portion of the early childhood teacher education program is common to all higher education programs. In four-year teacher education programs, this typically constitutes from two-thirds to three-fourths of the degree program. Its content is determined by what knowledge is expected of any well educated person. In some programs the general education component is broadly conceived, with required courses widely distributed across scholarly disciplines. In other programs, a specialization is required which focuses a large proportion of the students' general education work in one discipline or core of subjects. Typically, general education courses are heavily concentrated in the first years of the program with professional courses constituting a greater proportion of the work in the upper division of the program.

The general education component should not be considered an add-on to the teacher education program for early childhood or elementary teachers. Because teachers at these levels are teachers of general education, it represents the core of the subject matter that teachers of younger children must master. Some of the content, however, has to be made specific to young children. Children's literature and music for children, for example, may need to become a part of the program along with adult literature and music.

In recent years there has been increased criticism of the nature of general education in higher education and controversy regarding its constitution. Some educators have argued that there is no single core of knowledge that all individuals in our society should master. Over the years this view has led to regarding an increasing number of courses as acceptable components of general education in colleges and universities. Sometimes elective courses within required areas of study have been accepted to meet general education requirements.

Among the spokespersons for an alternative view have been E. D. Hirsch, Jr. and Allan Bloom. In his *Cultural Literacy*, Hirsch argues that individuals need to share a common core of knowledge with others in a community to participate in the discourse and activities of a culture.[11] The argument that has raged over Hirsch's position is whether there is a clearly identifiable core of knowledge that should be required learning for all and whether this core is related to a broad range of cultural groups. Some even argue that the content of the core should be a matter of individual taste. Indeed, there have been serious controversies on many university campuses about the nature of general education and whether that core, which traditionally has reflected western culture as well as the products of male scholars from the majority cultural group, should be revised and expanded.

The general education component of community college programs typically is similar to that of four-year college programs. The

NAEYC guidelines for associate degree programs in early childhood education recommend that the general education component be no more than 50 percent of the entire program, and that it consist of work in English composition, mathematics, sciences, social sciences, and humanities.[12] Since associate degree programs are more limited than bachelor's degree programs, this would mean that early childhood education students at this level would have considerably less work in general education.

Educational foundations. The foundations component of the teacher education program is concerned with knowledge about education rather than with professional techniques. This component draws heavily on the disciplines of history, philosophy, psychology, sociology, economics, political science, and anthropology. It tends to be theory and policy oriented.

In early childhood education, child development makes up a large portion of the foundational knowledge that teachers are expected to learn. Often it is felt that child development knowledge is more necessary for early childhood teachers than for teachers of older children. Children at this younger age level are changing quickly and, more than at any other age, what children are capable of learning is heavily dependent on their level of development. Sometimes the justification of this is the view that early childhood education is the practical application of child development research and theory.[13] Thus, the greater the knowledge of child growth and development that teachers acquire, the better teachers of young children they will be. Typically, knowledge of child development is viewed as necessary for teachers to plan developmentally appropriate learning activities for children in their classes.

Other areas of foundational knowledge for early childhood practitioners include the other social sciences as well as philosophy of education. Since education is a moral activity reflecting the values of the community, these foundations would help teachers put their professional knowledge into a broader perspective in making classroom decisions.

Just as students in associate degree programs are offered more limited general education studies, they are also offered more limited foundations studies, often restricted to the area of child development alone.

Instructional knowledge. The instructional knowledge component of the teacher education program is related to the various professional roles of the teacher: curriculum designer, diagnostician, organizer of instruction, manager of learning, and counselor and adviser.[14] Teachers are helped to gain specific knowledge and skills to be used in planning and implementing educational programs. The work that students should take includes courses in early childhood curriculum and instruction. These courses are needed to plan programs and to teach music, art, language, and other subjects to them. Courses in classroom management, working with parents, and dealing with handicapped children in regular classrooms are also generally a part of such programs. Typically, these courses are offered in regular college classes; in some programs a practicum may be associated with each methods course. Similar courses are offered in community college programs, although neither the depth and breadth of study nor the time allotted to it is usually as extensive as in four-year programs.

The content of these courses is rooted in curriculum theory and instructional theory as well as developmental theory and learning theory. The courses are not completely theory-based, however, since no theory or set of theories can adequately justify classroom practice. Such courses are also rooted in the practical knowledge that teachers develop from working directly with children in classes. According to Elbaz, practical knowledge is related to teaching and learning. Practical knowledge is each teacher's integration of knowledge gained from accumulated teaching experience, from educational theories, and from individual values and beliefs. The importance of practical knowledge is attested to by the fact that most teacher education programs require that faculty who teach courses related to instructional knowledge have prior experience in teaching children.[15]

Practice. The practice component of a teacher education program, which includes field experiences prior to student teaching as well as student teaching, is generally the part in which instructors in teacher education institutions collaborate with practitioners in children's programs. Field experiences in early childhood schools or centers allow teachers-in-training to relate what they are learning in their college or university classes to actual classroom practice. Both observation and participation are important. This component typically culminates in the novice assuming total responsibility for teaching a group of children.

Observation helps the student become aware of all the elements of classroom teaching: the role of the teacher, the behaviors and interactions of students, the uses of materials and equipment, and the importance of scheduling and room arrangement. Observation is usually guided so that students focus on the critical elements in the teaching/learning process. This guidance might come from the specific assignments given, from observation guides used, or from directions offered by the course instructor.

Participation, including increased responsibility for classroom practice and for the decisions related to that practice, enables students to integrate the professional knowledge they have gained from their studies, along with their own values, understandings, and sensitivities, to create their own core of personal practical knowledge that will guide their teaching.

Four-year teacher education programs might require as many as 600 clock hours of student teaching in at least two different early childhood educational settings. They often also require 100 or more clock hours of pre-student-teaching field experiences. Over the years, the reduction in the number of laboratory schools on college and university campuses has shifted the placement of student teachers away from campus-controlled settings. Most of these student teaching experiences now take place in off-campus sites, including public schools and nonpublic preschools. Teacher education institutions attempt to select the best sites available for placement of observers, participants, and student teachers and the best teachers on these sites for cooperating personnel. In addition to selection as a form of quality control, many teacher education programs strive to improve their students' practice components by providing in-service work or tuition waivers to university courses for cooperating personnel enrolling.

Associate degree programs might limit their requirements for practice to half of that required of students in four-year college programs. Community colleges also use off-campus sites for field experiences.

The practice component of teacher education programs has long been considered an important part of teacher education programs. Among its positive outcomes, student teaching (1) improves teacher behavior and performance, (2) increases teachers' professional orientation, positive attitudes, and commitments to teaching, (3) increases preservice teachers' abilities to determine children's readiness levels, clarify program objectives, and motivate and evaluate students, (4) facilitates teachers' understandings and acceptance of disadvantaged children, (5) increases teachers' use of indirect teaching methods, and (6) increases teachers' orientation to democratic teaching styles.[16]

There may also be negative consequences of student teaching. Student teachers may project what they have observed in their practice situations as the only or proper way of dealing with classroom situations, even if inappropriate, and avoid seeking new knowledge and skills.[17] While such criticisms result from the negative impact of less than ideal student teaching placements, it is generally agreed that the practice component within teacher education is primarily a positive experience. It allows prospective teachers to apply the theoretical knowledge they receive from classes and textbooks to real classroom situations. It also allows them to construct and modify their own knowledge, skills, and personal-professional theories and understandings about teaching and learning.

While bachelors degree and associate degree programs have been described here, it should be noted that vocational programs, often at the high school level, also prepare early childhood practitioners. There are few descriptions of these programs in the literature. Typically, however, they consist of instruction in child growth and development and a laboratory experience with young children. Instructors in such programs are often certified vocational home economics teachers or persons with experience in the child care field.[18]

Reforms in the Preparation of Early Childhood Teachers

Currently there has been a call for the reform of teacher education programs, in general. The most widely publicized of these can be found in the reports of the Holmes Group and the Carnegie Forum on Education and the Economy.[19] These reforms, if carried out, have the potential for changing four- and five-year programs of early childhood teacher education. They will probably influence community college programs as well. Whether these reforms will positively or negatively influence the field of early childhood education is yet to be seen.

Cooper and Eisenhart have identified some of the suggested reforms that might affect early childhood teacher education programs.[20] They include: (1) abolishing undergraduate teacher education degrees, (2) creating programs of teacher education that extend beyond the bachelors degree, (3) placing a cap on the number of credit hours in education that would be allowed toward a university degree, (4) extending the field experiences in teacher education programs, (5) creating an induction period or internship for novice teachers, (6) creating alternative approaches to teacher certification, and (7) establishing more specific forms of teacher certification.

These recommendations, if implemented, will increase the length of preparation time required to become a teacher. This would increase cost of such preparation to students by adding an additional year of tuition, fees, food, and lodging to that already paid by the students. It would also defer the onset of a teaching career by one year, along with the income that would be generated. Thus, abolishing undergraduate teacher education degrees and creating programs of teacher education that extend beyond the bachelors degree would make access to the early childhood teaching profession less available to individuals from families with limited sources of financial support. It would seriously hamper the creation of career ladders that might allow persons from minority and low-income groups, who generally also have limited finances, to move through the stages of professionalism in early childhood education, especially since many of these individuals have greater difficulty with the general education component of teacher preparation programs than with the professional components.

Placing a cap on the number of credit hours in education that would be allowed toward a university degree might make for a better educated teacher, but not necessarily for a more professionally competent teacher. Teaching young children requires a greater amount of professional/technical knowledge. Limiting the number of education or child development courses that may be included in a program may also limit the amount of that knowledge that can be gained by the students. A proposal for a cap, which might make sense for teachers at the secondary level, could actually weaken the early childhood teaching profession.

Extending the field experiences offered within teacher education programs might have a positive influence on teacher education programs. It would probably lead to a greater proportion of the teacher education program taking place in children's schools or centers. It would probably also allow practitioners to have a greater and more important role in the preparation of early childhood teachers. This should lead to programs which provide greater support for teachers developing professional/practical knowledge. Whether it will weaken the theoretical component of early childhood teacher education programs might depend on how such a proposal is implemented.

Creating an induction period or internship for novice teachers could have a positive impact on the field. In the normal course of events, once teachers complete an approved program and are certified, they are hired by schools or school systems and immediately assume the same responsibilities as experienced teachers. Seldom is a support system available for a reasonable period of time to allow for a more gradual transition to professional responsibilities. Some school systems have instituted formal mentor programs to allow experienced teachers to offer help and guidance to novices. At other times, informal mentoring may occur among colleagues in a school. A more systematic approach to induction may lessen the trauma of beginning teaching and could lead to greater retention of teachers in the field.

Providing alternative approaches to teacher certification could help many practitioners in the field move from lower to higher levels of professionalism without completing a teacher education program for certification. It might also allow the CDA credential to become a stepping stone to certification. In addition, it could provide opportunities for individuals from allied fields, such as social work, home economics, or psychology, to become teachers of young children. This has been a part of the interdisciplinary tradition of early childhood education that has been limited as the field has become more bureaucratized.

Haberman, however, sees a possible conflict arising from alternative approaches to certification.[21] He predicts a situation where, on the one hand, teachers will be required to complete more rigorous and extensive programs of teacher education to be certified in the conventional manner. On the other hand, school systems would be able to hire individuals who have no pedagogical background to be teachers as well. If a proposal for alternative routes to certification is to be implemented, an effort needs to be made to avoid such a conflict.

Establishing more specific forms of teacher certification could improve the field of early childhood education. With broad certification now available, such as kindergarten through grade six or even grade nine, we now have a situation in which many persons teaching in early childhood programs were not actually prepared to teach in these programs, although their certificates allow them to do so and suggest that they have the necessary competence. A narrower teaching certificate might better insure that teachers teach the areas for which they have been prepared.

The suggestions noted above are designed to improve the quality of teachers in our schools. Yet, with the exception of the call for extended field experiences, they do not deal with improving the nature of the professional component of the teacher education programs. Few would say that we have achieved the ideal content in our preparation programs for early childhood teachers. It would seem that this is an area where early childhood professionals will need to identify problems or needs and design possible solutions. Otherwise, we could create a situation where, while teachers are better educated, they are not better qualified for their professional careers.

We need to identify the specific knowledge that is critical for one to have assimilated in order to become a professional early childhood teacher. What developmental theories should teachers know and what should be the extent of this knowledge? What other foundational areas must early childhood teachers know? We also need to identify other areas of requisite knowledge as well as the competencies expected. In addition, we need to test the effectiveness of our current programs to see how successful we are in preparing teachers who have the understandings and competencies we should expect. Perhaps we should be looking for alternative ways of preparing early childhood education professionals as well as alternative ways of certifying them.

Issues to Be Faced

The issues discussed in this chapter do not lend themselves to simple conclusions. More questions have been raised by the discussion than answers given. It seems more reasonable to end the chapter with a series of questions pertaining to issues related to professionalism and to the preparation of practitioners that the field needs to confront in the days and years to come.

ARE EARLY CHILDHOOD EDUCATORS PROFESSIONALS?

If one uses the sense of the word "profession" to describe someone who earns a living by following an occupation, then one must certainly say that early childhood educators are professionals. If, however, we use the term in the sense of the learned professions, such as doctors and lawyers, then early childhood educators are at best semiprofessionals. Early childhood practitioners are not as well educated as medical practitioners nor given as broad a range of discretion in their practice.

Additionally, we can raise the question of whether early childhood educators need to be as well qualified, or as highly skilled, or manifest the other aspects of professionalism found in doctors. We must question whether one needs to know as much to be an early childhood teacher, or any teacher for that matter. One might also question whether it would be desirable for early childhood practitioners to become professionals in that same sense. Professions are not only concerned with raising the standards of practice but with standardizing practice as well. Silin suggests that professionalism can be a conservative force used to promote docility and occupational control of practitioners.[22] It can also create greater social distance between practitioners and their clients.

Perhaps we are using the wrong analogy when we compare the professionalism of early childhood educators with that of doctors. Instead, we should compare fields. The health care field, which includes a number of different practitioners, is more like the early childhood education field than the field of medicine. Physicians, nurse practitioners, nurses, medical technicians, physical therapists, and a host of other occupations requiring different levels of preparation and representing different levels of professionalism, constitute health care professionals. Similarly, there are university professors, researchers, administrators, certified teachers, Child Development Associates, child care workers, teaching assistants, and others in the early childhood education field. Rather than representing a single level of professionalism, early childhood education includes many levels, probably more than the four identified by NAEYC.[23]

When one views the field as composed of practitioners manifesting different levels of professionalism, it is more possible to (1) identify the roles and responsibilities of different positions in the field, and (2) specify the qualifications for particular positions. Thus, in advocating the provision of half-day kindergarten coupled with half-day in-school child care, Olsen and Zigler suggest using certified child development aides to provide the child care services and certified public school teachers to offer the education portion.[24]

Given that the field of early childhood education is composed of practitioners at different levels of professionalism, one may question whether these levels are continuous or discontinuous. In a field composed of continuous levels of professionalism, one may move from one level to the next as the result of experience and increased training. In a discontinuous field, training for each level is not consistent with training for other higher levels. In the health care field, for example, one can move from being a nurse to being a nurse practitioner as the result of experience and additional preparation. But the preparation for becoming a nurse does not count toward preparation to become a physician. Similarly, the preparation for becoming a paralegal aide does not count toward the preparation in law school needed to become a lawyer, even though a number of individuals move from being a paralegal to becoming a lawyer.

Many early childhood educators view the field as composed of continuous levels of professionalism. There is a belief that one should be able to move from aide to assistant, to Child Development Associate, to certified teacher, to supervisor, teacher educator, administrator, or researcher. There is the expectation that additional courses or in-service work, coupled with practical experience, should enable the individual to move from one level to another. Yet, as noted earlier, this is not often the case in the real world, since technical courses at vocational schools and community colleges may not be considered the equivalent of upper division or graduate university courses and thus may not count toward teacher certification.

Perhaps there are valid discontinuities in the field, where some levels of practice are different in kind from other levels so that preparation for one level might not be reasonable preparation for the next. As we explore the nature of professionalism in early childhood education, and as we become a more professionalized field, these issues will take on increased importance. The standard setters, including state departments of education and children's services as well as professional associations, will have to come to grips with these issues in a realistic way in the years to come.

HOW CAN WE INCREASE THE LEVELS OF PROFESSIONALISM IN THE FIELD?

Certainly the most important way of increasing the level of professionalism is to improve the preparation of early childhood practitioners. The reforms reviewed by Cooper and Eisenhart are designed to improve certification-oriented teacher education programs.[25] The degree to which they will impact on the field of early childhood education is questionable. Many early childhood practitioners, especially those who practice in child care programs, are not professionally trained. In addition, we are not currently preparing enough early childhood teachers at the professional level to staff all the early childhood classrooms that presently exist and that will exist in the future.

WHAT ARE THE GREATEST PROBLEMS IN ACHIEVING HIGHER LEVELS OF PROFESSIONALISM?

Unfortunately, simply raising the standards for certified teachers will not affect the bulk of the early childhood practitioners, most of whom are employed in private preschools and child care centers. Child care centers and other preschool programs do not pay at a level comparable with public school systems. Nor do they require the same qualifications. In addition, many centers would prefer not to hire professionally trained personnel. Instead they prefer hiring individuals on an hourly basis, often at near minimum wage and sometimes on a less than full-time basis to staff their programs. In this way they can avoid the cost of employee benefits, such as sick leave, health insurance, and retirement. No improvement in the preparation of early childhood teacher education programs will solve this problem facing our field. Rather, we need to look at ways of increasing the salaries and benefits of early childhood practitioners, improving their working conditions, and making the field more attractive so that qualified practitioners will enter it and remain in it.

The fact that early childhood education is a women's field has been and will continue to be a barrier to higher levels of professionalism. Finkelstein, who has traced the historical traditions of professionalism in early childhood education, views early childhood education as an undeveloped profession.[26] She believes that problems result from the development and definition of early childhood education as women's work. She also believes that the field's concept of professionalism creates a problem in that it "promotes knowledge of child development as an indispensable professional ingredient but discourages efforts to raise the economic and occupational well-being of nursery school teachers, day-care workers, mothers, and the variety of guardians who oversee the development of the young" (p. 25).

It would appear that the field of early childhood education is a field that is moving toward higher levels of professionalism. This movement can be evidenced in the call for setting and raising standards of practice as well as for being and becoming a practitioner. Some of the advantages of becoming more professional are in the rewards for practitioners, both in salaries and in status. Some of the requirements for increasing the levels of professionalism include increasing the amount and quality of preparation required of beginning practitioners and improving the conditions of practice, that is, making the field of early childhood education a more attractive field for practice.

Among the requisites for increased professionalism are increased financial resources and more stringent standards of practice. These must come from outside the field, including government agencies. Other requisites must come from within the field, from practitioners themselves. A better understanding of the nature of high quality practice in early childhood education and how that practice can be achieved is needed. Also needed is a clearer self-definition of the field from practitioners and from the professional associations that represent practitioners.

FOOTNOTES

1. Robert B. Howsam, Dean C. Corrigan, George W. Denemark, and Robert J. Nash, *Educating a Profession* (Washington, DC: American Association of Colleges of Teacher Education, 1976).

2. Ibid.

3. National Association for the Education of Young Children, *Early Childhood Teacher Education Guidelines for Four- and Five-Year Programs* (Washington, DC: National Association for the Education of Young Children, 1982).

4. Child Development Associate Consortium, *Competency Standards* (Washington, DC: Child Development Associate Consortium, 1977).

5. Douglas R. Powell and Loraine Dunn, "Nonbaccalaureate Teacher Education Initiatives in the Early Childhood Field," in *Early Childhood Teacher Education: Yearbook in Early Childhood Education*, Vol. 1, ed. Bernard Spodek and Olivia N. Saracho (New York: Teachers College Press, 1990).

6. National Association for the Education of Young Children, *NAEYC Position Statement on Nomenclature, Salaries, Benefits, and the Status of the Early Childhood Profession* (Washington, DC: National Association for the Education of Young Children, 1984).

7. Martin Haberman, "Gatekeepers to the Profession," in *Professionalism and the Early Childhood Practitioner*, ed. Bernard Spodek, Olivia N. Saracho, and Donald L. Peters (New York: Teachers College Press, 1988), pp. 84-92.

8. Karen Vander Ven, "Pathways to Professional Effectiveness for Early Childhood Educators," in *Professionalism and the Early Childhood Practitioner*, ed. Spodek et al., pp.137-160.

9. Bernard Spodek, Michael D. Davis, and Olivia N. Saracho, "Early Childhood Teacher Education and Certification," *Journal of Teacher Education* 34, no. 5 (1983): 50-52.

10. Olivia N. Saracho and Bernard Spodek, "Preparing Teachers for Multicultural Settings," in *Understanding the Multicultural Experience in Early Childhood Education*, ed. Olivia N. Saracho and Bernard Spodek (Washington, DC: National Association for the Education of Young Children, 1983), pp. 125-146.

11. E. D. Hirsch, Jr., *Cultural Literacy: What Every American Needs to Know* (Boston: Houghton Mifflin, 1987).

12. National Association for the Education of Young Children, *Guidelines for Early Childhood Education in Associate Degree Granting Institutions* (Washington, DC: National Association for the Education of Young Children, 1985).

13. Bettye M. Caldwell, "Growth and Development," *Young Children* 39, no. 6 (1984): 53-56.

14. Saracho and Spodek, "Preparing Teachers for Multicultural Settings."

15. Freema Elbaz, *Teachers' Thinking: A Study of Practical Knowledge* (New York: Nicholas, 1983).

16. Rhoda M. Becher and William E. Ade, "The Relationship of Field Placement Characteristics and Students' Potential Field Performance Abilities to Clinical Experience Performance Ratings," *Journal of Teacher Education* 33, no. 2 (1982): 24-30.

17. Sharon Feiman-Nemser, "Learning to Teach," in *Handbook of Teaching and Policy*, ed. Lee S. Shulman and Gary Sykes (New York: Longman, 1983), pp. 150-170.

18. Powell and Dunn, "Nonbaccalaureate Teacher Education Initiatives in the Early Childhood Field."

19. Holmes Group, *Tomorrow's Teachers: A Report of the Holmes Group* (East Lansing, MI: Michigan State University, 1986); Carnegie Forum on Education and the

Economy, *A Nation Prepared: Teachers for the 21st Century* (New York: Carnegie Corporation, 1986).

20. James M. Cooper and Corinne E. Eisenhart, "The Influence of Recent Educational Reforms on Early Childhood Teacher Education Programs," in *Early Childhood Teacher Education*, ed. Spodek and Saracho.

21. Haberman, "Gatekeepers to the Profession."

22. Jonathan G. Silin, "On Becoming Knowledgeable Professionals," in *Professionalism and the Early Childhood Practitioner*, ed. Spodek et al., pp. 125-146.

23. National Association for the Education of Young Children, *NAEYC Position Statement on Nomenclature, Salaries, Benefits, and the Status of the Early Childhood Profession*.

24. Deborah Olsen and Edward Zigler, "An Assessment of the All-Day Kindergarten Movement," *Early Childhood Research Quarterly* 4 (1989): 167-186.

25. Cooper and Eisenhart, "The Influence of Recent Educational Reforms on Early Childhood Teacher Education Programs."

26. Barbara Finkelstein, "The Revolt against Selfishness: Women and the Dilemmas of Professionalism in Early Childhood Education," in *Professionalism and the Early Childhood Practitioner*, ed. Spodek et al., pp. 10-28.

CHAPTER VIII

The Private Sector as a Partner in Early Care and Education

ELLEN GALINSKY

At a recent Congressional hearing on Head Start, the expert testimony was markedly different than that of the past. As usual, the testifying party included a developmental psychologist lauding Head Start as a cost-effective investment, early childhood educators warning of the developmental consequences of ignoring the very young at-risk population, and an accomplished young Head Start graduate with his mother, both Head Start success stories. New to the proceedings, however, were several business chief executive officers discussing labor shortages and the lack of young people who are literate and sufficiently skilled for entry-level jobs. Their remedy, unexpectedly, was not to redouble their own training efforts but to urge the federal government to expand Head Start so that their future job applicants could have a sound educational foundation.

At a Forum on Education sponsored by the Ad Council, a company president urged all levels of government to improve their early childhood programs and called for other business leaders to invest in improving the educational system.

Within the past decade, business leaders have become new and on occasion powerful players among those concerned with early childhood care and education. This chapter will trace the development of this movement, describe the types of companies most likely to be involved, explore the impact of business involvement, evaluate incentives for continued collaborations, and posit the difficult issues that await resolution in the coming decade.

Corporate Involvement in Child Care and Early Education: Phase I

Although there have been business forays into employer-supported child care for over a century, these efforts have been the exception—fodder for the occasional newspaper feature story rather than components of a mainstream effort. In fact, the late 1960s and early 1970s saw as many corporate-sponsored child care centers close as open. In 1978, there were an estimated 110 companies nationwide that provided on-site child care, subsidies for the cost of child care through vouchers, and referral services to help employees locate child care.[1]

In the early 1980s, it became increasingly apparent that the Reagan administration planned to reduce government's role in the early childhood arena, to ignore national licensing standards (the Federal Interagency Day Care Requirements so carefully crafted by national experts) and to eliminate existing federal programs or turn them into block grants. The administration was intent on increasing the authority of the states while stimulating the business community to respond to social problems. Accordingly, leaders in the child care field turned to the business community, reasoning that business had a vested interest since its employees were negatively affected by the vagaries of the uneven, unstable child care system. Businesses had money and could perhaps create high-quality programs. Although some child care experts warned that the business sector could not be expected to rescue the child care field singlehandedly from federal cutbacks, a number of individuals (predominantly consultants) began to view corporate leaders as knights in shining armor.[2] The business community, for the most part, ignored these entreaties, closing their doors to the consultants who were primarily promoting on-site child care.

OBSTACLES TO CORPORATE INVOLVEMENT

There were obstacles to corporate involvement. First, almost all American business leaders were convinced that family needs were off-limits to the corporation and that becoming involved would constitute unnecessary infringement and unwelcome interference. Work and family were seen, as stated by Rosabeth Moss Kanter, as separate and nonoverlapping worlds.[3]

Concomitantly, however, a shift in attitude began. Women in the workforce were accepted as "here to stay." Although initially labeled a women's issue, the presence of mothers in the workplace was seen as leading to family stress.[4] This attitude is best illustrated by the Louis Harris General Mills national survey.[5] Although entitled *Families at Work: Strengths and Strains*, it focused on employed mothers. The survey found that a majority (52 percent) of the 1,503 family members felt that the effect on the family of both parents working was "generally negative," whereas only 28 percent thought it was "generally positive." Clearly, "both parents working" was a euphemism for "employed mothers," since no one thought "working fathers" were harmful. The negative image of mothers exchanging their aprons for briefcases served as a second obstacle to business involvement. Companies prefer projects considered socially beneficial. Moreover, the assumption that corporate work/family programs would predominantly serve employed mothers was a further disincentive—companies favor human resource programs and policies that serve their entire employer population "equitably."

Many business leaders assumed that if they became involved in assisting employees with child care, it would involve creating on-site centers. In the General Mills Survey, 77 percent of the human resource executives surveyed thought on-site child care would help employees and their families. Interestingly enough, only 38 percent of the parents surveyed agreed. The parents' preferred solution was part-time work with full benefits.[6] This focus on on-site child care served as yet a third disincentive to corporate involvement. At work/family conferences, company spokespeople said: "On-site child care is expensive"; "It only serves a few employees"; "There could be lawsuits and we have the deep pockets"; "Babies would be disruptive." In fact, some senior managers seemed to visualize young children running through the company halls and interrupting meetings in the boardroom.

TRAILBLAZERS AND THEIR COMMON CHARACTERISTICS

Despite these uncertainties and disincentives, a few pioneering corporations began to believe that it was appropriate to help employees with child care problems. Their justification was that since women were in the workforce to stay, child care problems affected their productivity as well as the productivity of their husbands.

At the same time, research evidence was mounting that this assumption was valid. A number of studies conducted throughout the 1980s have documented the on-the-job repercussions of child care problems. On average, one in two or three parents has trouble finding child care.[7] These difficulties correlate significantly with higher rates of absenteeism. Parents piece together a system of patchwork arrangements, often as many as three to four different child care arrangements per family.[8] Furthermore, there is a significant relationship between the number of child care arrangements and the number of times these arrangements fall apart.[9] Over a three-month period, 63 percent of the employed fathers and mothers in a nationally representative sample had at least one breakdown of their child care arrangement and 22 percent had three or more breakdowns.[10] Employees making last-minute child care arrangements because their usual arrangements had fallen apart were more likely to arrive at work late, leave early, or miss work altogether. They were more likely to spend unproductive time at work because they were worrying about their children. These parents had higher levels of stress, more stress-related health problems, more tension, less companionship in their marriages, and were less satisfied as parents.[11]

Although concerned with these problems, few companies regarded on-site child care as the solution. Because of its expense and its ability to serve only a small number of employees, most employers favored options that gave their employees information and financial resources to meet their *own* child care needs. These included:

1. *Child Care Resource and Referral (R&R)*, a counseling program to help parents find and evaluate child care. At best, these programs not only match parents with local child care but increase the supply by recruiting new child care providers and helping to start new centers. In addition, they improve the quality of care by training local providers.

2. *Flexible Spending Accounts (FSA)*, a salary reduction plan made possible by Section 125 of the IRS Code. It allows companies to offer employees a choice of benefits from a menu of taxable and nontaxable options. Employees can reduce their salaries by up to $5000 and be reimbursed for child care and certain other expenses with pretax dollars. FSAs have certain restrictions. Employees can use either an FSA or the Dependent Care Tax Credit (under Section 129), but not both. Since providers being reimbursed are required to give their Social Security numbers, employees cannot use the sizable underground child care market. Furthermore, if the funds in the account are not used up by the end of the first year, they must be forfeited.

3. *Parent seminars at the workplace.* These seminars, generally offered during lunch hours, frequently include discussions on how to find and evaluate high-quality child care.[12] Presumably, this consumer education affects the child care marketplace because parents choose stable, higher-quality arrangements.

A small number of companies developed on- or near-site child care. These programs are run directly by the corporation or are contracted out to a child care management firm. Very few centers are entirely employee-run, with negligible corporate involvement or financial support. In general, the companies most likely to create on-site centers have wanted to develop a showcase program, have had labor shortages and thus needed programs to recruit and retain employees, or have had nontraditional working hours (i.e., early morning, evening, and night shifts) so that employees had difficulty finding child care in the community.

A number of studies both quantitative and qualitative have identified the following characteristics of trailblazing companies that provided child care assistance in the 1980s.

1. *Company size.* In the 1988 survey of the American Society for Personnel Administration, the size of the company is associated with the level of company involvement.[13] Employers with 5000 or more employees are more likely to be informed about the importance of providing some form of child care service as well as more likely to be exploring employees' child care needs. The National Council of Jewish Women study, *Mothers in the Workplace*, found that 25 percent of the employees who work for large employers (over 500 employees) receive child care assistance, in comparison with only 7 percent of the employees working for companies with fewer than 100 employees.[14]

2. *Labor shortages.* A current or anticipated labor shortage seems to stimulate child care support aimed at recruiting and retaining employees.[15] Companies seem to feel these shortages most acutely with nurses, clerical workers, or highly skilled employees such as scientists.

3. *Business type.* Many of the companies most likely to provide child care assistance are businesses whose purpose is related to family needs. For example, Stride Rite, a children's shoe manufacturer, was one of the first to develop on-site care. Banks, insurance companies, pharmaceuticals, and computer companies are also likely to be involved.[16] According to *Mothers in the Workplace*, the workers most likely to receive assistance are professionals, technicians, and service workers employed by hospitals.[17]

4. *Competitive pressure.* Certain industries are more involved than others because providing child care becomes competitive. When companies perceived to be competitors offer child care assistance, those vying for that same labor pool or market share feel more compelled to offer similar or better programs.

5. *Location.* Friedman noted that corporate child care assistance has

developed in certain areas of the country, primarily along the eastern and western corridors and in some midwestern states like Minnesota.[18] Minnesota has a tradition of business providing for the community. There has been less activity in large cities such as New York and Chicago where space is expensive and employees commute by public transportation.

6. *Workforce characteristics.* A number of workforce characteristics appear significant: the age of the workforce (that is, the number of employees in the childbearing years), the proportion of female employees, and whether or not the company is unionized. Initially, nonunionized companies were more likely to develop family-responsive policies,[19] but that may change, especially following the historic agreement reached by AT&T and its unions to bargain for a "family-care" package.

7. *Economic health.* It is well known that the companies with the most outstanding child care policies have been among the most profitable: Merck, Johnson & Johnson, IBM. The extent to which the lack of monetary constraints enables companies to invest in work/ family initiatives or the extent to which progressive human resource policies lead to increased financial health is not known.[20] Companies undergoing downsizing, merger, acquisition, or deregulation are not expected to offer child care assistance, but AT&T and others disprove this assumption. Child care assistance can be used as a tool to improve morale or help contain the spiraling costs of health care.

8. *Presence of champions.* All companies with progressive child care policies have a champion or champions working hard to convince top management that these programs are viable. According to McDonald, these champions have enough perceived competence within the company to take on an issue perceived to be as eccentric or nonmainstream as child care.[21] These champions tend to be in mid- or upper-management and are not necessarily in human resources. Some have had personal experience with a child care problem while others believe that investing in human capital is essential to long-term profitability.[22]

The pioneering companies generally addressed the child care needs of their employees by appointing a task force or an individual to investigate employee needs, often through a survey or focus groups. Once the needs were identified, community resources were analyzed to determine if already existing programs could help solve problems of particular employees. Often, a competitive analysis was undertaken to see how other companies had treated similar issues.

When a solution was selected and enacted, management more often than not assumed that the child care problems were resolved and human resource management could move on to tackle other workplace problems. There was no systematic investigation of how other characteristics of the company (such as rigid time schedules or travel requirements) might also contribute to work/family problems. Without an integrated vision, the new programs and policies were a "single-issue approach."

Corporate Involvement in Child Care: Phase II

The late 1980s have seen the beginnings of change in the nature of corporate involvement. One characteristic of this change is a slowly emerging business interest in early childhood education. While the previous emphasis of employers was on the productivity of their current workforce, concern turned to the viability of their future workforce. The deliberations of the Committee for Economic Development, a think tank of business leaders, illustrate this trend. When charged with recommending ways to enhance American productivity in the twenty-first century, this group first sought technological answers, but upon further investigation concluded that one of the most important investments this country could make in its future productivity was in the early education of its "at-risk" young children. Their final report, *Children in Need*, calls for quality preschool programs for all disadvantaged three- and four-year-olds:

Quality education for *all children* is not an expense; it is an investment. Failure to educate is the true expense. In addition to improving our schools, investing in careful nurturing of children from before birth through age five will deliver a handsome profit to society, and to the individuals and families who have so much to gain.[23]

A decade of research confirms that comprehensive early childhood programs can be cost-effective because they reduce the likelihood that poor children will be sucked into school and life failure.[24] Despite the inexactitude of measuring cost/benefit, the U.S. House Select Committee of Children, Youth, and Families has priced the investment: $1 spent on early childhood education saves $4.75 in future costs for remedial education, welfare, and juvenile justice.[25] This interest in early childhood education, however, remains largely unconnected to corporate involvement in child care.

In the late 1980s, the number of corporations interested in child care and other work/family issues expanded. The trailblazers saw themselves as such, but many of the new companies becoming involved defined themselves not as "trendsetters," but as "fast followers." Developing child care initiatives was increasingly seen as "tried, tested, and safe." Statistics document the increased interest in child care. In a survey conducted by the American Society for Personnel Administration in the spring of 1988, half of nearly 1500 large and small companies said they were considering or actually planning child care initiatives in the next few years. Similarly, in a survey for *Fortune* magazine, we found that 86 percent of our 71 Fortune 500 respondents were planning new work/family programs. The most often cited inducements: the recruitment and retention of employees.[26]

Expected labor shortages are also fueling concern with work/family issues and productivity. The number of eighteen-to-twenty-four-year-olds is expected to decrease from thirty million in 1980 to twenty-five million in 1990 as the baby bust generation enters the labor force. Sixty percent of the human resource executives interviewed in our Fortune 500 survey predicted a diminished supply of employees in the future.[27]

Now that work/family concerns are more mainstream, more types of companies are becoming involved, and, unlike the pioneering companies, do not seem to share identifying characteristics.

NEW LEVELS OF CORPORATE INVOLVEMENT

As the new companies tackle work/family issues, they follow the same thoughtful but limited approach developed by the trailblazers in Phase I. By 1988, however, the pioneering companies had moved to the next stage by reframing their involvement in child care.[28]

1. *Expanded focus on work/family.* The exemplary companies in child care have broadened their vision to include the provision of care for elderly parents and policies that help employees balance work/family responsibilities no matter their age or life circumstances. The underlying assumption is that all employees feel some tension between their job and home responsibilities, whether they are single or married, parents or nonparents. This vision has been fueled by the growing awareness that the graying of America will have a serious impact on the workplace, and that elder care obligations may eclipse child care in number of employees affected. In one company study, we

found that 44 percent of those surveyed expect to be responsible for the care of an elderly relative within the next few years.[29]

2. *Executive-level commitment to work/family policies.* Most companies with work/family progams have a champion who is deeply committed to these programs but whose responsibilities for them are ad hoc, taken on in addition to regular work duties. In the exemplary companies, top leadership has begun to support work/family programs. The work/family area has been institutionalized with the appointment of an individual who has a legitimizing title such as "Director of Work/Family Programs," and is generally at the level of director, manager, or vice president.

3. *Commitment to work/family as a business issue.* Executives of exemplary companies are acutely aware of the shrinking labor pool and predictions of an increasingly diversified workforce. Thus, attracting, retaining, and managing their workforce have become priorities, and child care and work/family initiatives are seen as one means to this end.

4. *An integrated approach.* In most companies, work/family initiatives are developed as stand-alone efforts. Many of the exemplary companies, however, are reviewing a number of their human resource benefits and services. For example, they are examining time and leave policies, health benefits, training procedures, as well as their expectations vis-à-vis long hours, weekend work, travel, and relocation. In doing so, they assess the impact of these policies on the family or personal lives of employees and make changes accordingly. This process leads to a more holistic and integrated approach.

5. *Emphasis on time flexibility.* Child care assistance was the most common work/family initiative in Phase I. In Phase II, the exemplary companies are tackling the more complex work/family issue of flexible work schedules and exploring how to provide greater time flexibility. Previously, new time policies were developed for business reasons—to permit more extended use of equipment or to reduce the number of employees. Now such policies are being created for the express purpose of helping employees spend time with their children or other family members. Companies are looking into or developing more permanent part-time positions, extended flextime, longer and more flexible leave policies with part-time return-to-work provisions, legitimate days off to care for sick family members, and pooled time off.

6. *Company culture as key to work/family solutions.* The pioneering companies have realized that simply providing family-supportive

programs is not sufficient. For example, if flextime is instituted but first-line managers oppose it, employees cannot use it. Thus, these companies are now training managers to sensitize them to the changing nature of the workforce, to familiarize them with the company's programs, and to guide them in managing work/family problems that might arise.

A number of exemplary companies have also deliberately changed the company culture to make it more "family friendly." For example, Johnson & Johnson altered its Credo (the policy statement by which business decisions are made) to acknowledge the company's responsibility toward the well-being of its employees' families. The Credo is very important to Johnson & Johnson employees—the last time it was changed was many years ago. The Credo changes are intended to change employees' behavior. For example, at a business meeting consisting entirely of men, the agenda was not completed at 4:45 P.M. Previously, the chair would have forged ahead but now, aware that this might pose difficulties for some employees, he asked the group whether the meeting should go on or be postponed ("because some of you may have to pick up your children at day care"). After a stunned silence, one participant spoke up, acknowledging that he did have to pick up his child, and the meeting was postponed to the following day.

7. *Involvement in community partnerships.* In Phase I, companies tended to act alone in designing and implementing child care policies for their employees. In Phase II, certain companies are joining together to resolve problems and to develop joint services. For example, in Oregon's Linn and Benton counties, a consortium of companies led by Hewlett-Packard organized a multicompany needs assessment that indicated a need for child care resource and referral; with the support of local business and start-up funds from the state, a community college decided to run such a service. In New York City, several midtown employers have collaborated to provide emergency care for their employees in the case of last minute breakdowns of child care arrangements. In San Francisco, employers have created "One Small Step," asking all employer members to "take one small step" to improve local child care. A group of Maryland chief executive officers created a public/private partnership "to increase workforce productivity and promote economic development by strengthening the child care delivery system."[30]

In sum, the exemplary companies have moved away from a fragmented approach to a more holistic view, from an emphasis on child care to a broader concern for work/family issues involving employees in whatever stage their families are. The notion of corporate involvement in family issues has become more ingrained, integrated, and mainstream.

Business Contributions to Early Childhood

Business has played five roles in the early childhood field: (1) analyzer of the local early childhood marketplace; (2) provider of direct service; (3) contributor to local child care services; (4) legitimizer; and (5) change-agent.

ANALYZING THE LOCAL EARLY CHILDHOOD MARKETPLACE

While conducting their own needs assessments, companies often investigate community resources to ascertain whether or not employee problems can be met by local services. In other words, if employees are having difficulty finding infant care, companies will generally scan the community for available high-quality infant child care providers who are unknown to employees or who are filled to capacity but would expand if financial resources were available. This is the tack AT&T's Bell Laboratories took. They found that Summit Child Care, Inc., with its numerous facilities, was able to expand infant care to serve Bell Laboratories employees.

When companies conduct community assessments, they bring a fresh business perspective to the local child care system that for the most part has grown haphazardly. With the help of child care consultants or resource and referral agencies, companies look at demographic and census tract data, identifying the needs and gaps in services and projecting where services should be added. This overall analysis is novel to the largely unorganized child care community and provides an important and often legitimizing function as well.

It is expected that AT&T's historic settlement with its unions in the summer of 1989 will further expand this analytic role. As one feature of the agreement, AT&T has established a $10 million fund to help local sites meet their child care needs. As planned, employees at local sites will assess their child care needs, conduct community analyses, and propose solutions. AT&T further plans to help other companies create similar funds. Although such analysis generally takes place on a local level, a few employer-supported child care task forces (most notably the Maryland Employers Advisory Council on Child Care) have conducted state-wide analyses of the child care system. The state work/family clearinghouses established in several states could conceivably also perform this function.

Approximately 1200 employers (200 corporations, 200 government agencies, and 800 hospitals) now provide on- or near-site child care.[31] Some do so directly, others contract out the management function, while still others have no direct reporting relationship to the program, which is owned and operated by professionals or by a group of parent employees.

Many of the corporate-sponsored centers are renowned for their commitment to high quality. Perhaps due to fears about their liability exposure and the knowledge that the company name and reputation are on the line, most corporations have endeavored to create model centers. Some of these facilities have become or are becoming accredited by the National Association for the Education of Young Children, the industry-wide standard of quality assurance.

The standards of other corporate- and hospital-sponsored programs seem less satisfactory, as evidenced from the no-holds-barred discussions that take place at conferences on employer-supported child care. During these sessions or in private discussions, directors often complain about being pressured to make cost-cutting, quality-inhibiting decisions; to take more children, thus widening the staff/child ratio; to hire less qualified staff; to pay lower salaries, usually resulting in higher staff turnover rates.

Directors of the employee-run corporate centers face similar dilemmas. Without ongoing corporate support, breaking even financially is very difficult, and thus they may be pushed to cut corners on salaries and staffing. Furthermore, the parent fees that must be charged for the program to break even hinder the ability of these programs to serve the children of lower-earning employees. This fact is of grave concern to many directors who must make this kind of tough choice.

Most employer-supported child care facilities, no matter their sponsorship, have long waiting lists, especially for infant care. Thus, companies that want to serve more employees than can be accommodated by the center often provide other child care services such as FSAs or R&R.

On- or near-site centers have been provided far less frequently than other corporate work/family options.[32] There are 200 on-site centers, 2500 corporate FSA programs, and 1500 R&R programs.

However, it is clear that a modest increase in on-site care is likely. A number of companies that vowed never to consider on-site child care have recently changed course, Warner-Lambert and Metropolitan Life being two examples. The strong desire of their employees for on-site care is what changed the minds of executives at Warner-Lambert. Furthermore, there is growing interest in this option on the part of small companies that are joining consortium arrangements such as the one on Boston's Rte. 128 or the Harmony Early Learning Center in the Meadowlands area of New Jersey.

The most significant growth in the corporate sector, however, is likely to come from the real estate industry. Developers are beginning to view child care centers as an amenity, much like a restaurant or health spa, and are building them in office park complexes. In Miami Lakes, Florida, for example, television ads lure potential business tenants to an office park by featuring a child care center.

CONTRIBUTING TO LOCAL CHILD CARE SERVICES

By and large, company efforts to help their own employees have taken the form of buying into and enhancing the existing child care system within the community. This has been done through the supply-building, quality-enhancing aspect of child care resource and referral or through corporate contributions.

For many years, companies felt they had contributed to child care by donating funds to their local United Way. Other requests were generally met with "We've already given" or with in-kind contributions such as art supplies. Then, a few companies began to donate specific funds to local programs. Du Pont, for example, gave the seed money to establish Child Care Connection, an R&R agency in Wilmington, Delaware, and they have provided ongoing support and have enlisted other companies to join them in this venture. 3M's McKnight Foundation has given a sizable grant to attempt to raise child care providers' salaries in Minneapolis/St. Paul. AT&T's new fund may also spur other companies to follow suit.

How effective are these initiatives and contributions? The research evaluations reveal that the less direct the intervention, the more diffuse the effect.[33] On-site child care has more of an everyday impact on employees than resource and referral.[34] On the other hand, companies who begin by offering R&R tend to continue to develop other initiatives as the decision makers obtain a more realistic view of the magnitude of the child care problems employees face. A survey we conducted for *Fortune* magazine illustrates this shift in attitude. We asked company spokespeople to rate their company's involvement in assisting employees with work/family responsibilities. The spokespeople from companies with minimal programs tended to rate their companies as more highly involved than those who spoke for companies with more programs. The latter group often felt they were beginning to realize how much further they had to go to make a real dent in the child care problems afflicting their employees.

LEGITIMIZING THE FIELD OF EARLY CHILDHOOD CARE AND EDUCATION

The very fact that some prestigious members of the business community have become interested in early childhood care and education has enhanced the prestige and the clout of this field. It has been very meaningful to the teachers and aides in centers and to child care providers (many of whom feel the child care profession lacks sufficient respect) to have corporation presidents testify in Congress on their behalf. Likewise, it has been meaningful to members of Congress and state legislatures to have business leaders become participants in this field. One example is the testimony given by American Express during the 1988 hearings on the Act for Better Child Care in which the company called for national standards in child care. The different state-mandated staff/infant ratios (ranging from 1:4 to 1:7 and even 1:8) meant the quality of child care services available to their employees varied enormously and depended on the state in which they lived. American Express as a company had difficulty reconciling this inequity to itself. This testimony helped change the congressional debate about standards, lending the issue of national regulatory standards greater significance.

HELPING TO PROMOTE CHANGE

In several communities, corporate senior officers have participated in community task forces to address some of the problems in early childhood care and education that transcend their own company's concerns. Task forces are often initiated by the governor's office and operate on a state level. Virginia, for example, held a two-day conference and invited participants, including business leaders, to select from one of six tracks (such as "Quality Care" or "Accessibility" or "The Effects of State and Local Standards on Child Care"). In each track, participants were first briefed by experts on the subject, then asked to recommend changes to the governor, and, finally, to prioritize their recommendations. In other states, such as

Tennessee and Massachusetts, similar work was done in governor-
appointed task groups.

One of the purposes of the conference or task force is to increase
business involvement in child care. Numerous states (including New
York, Michigan, Virginia, South Carolina, and Indiana) have
convened such groups. Involvement by business leaders seems to
spiral after participation in task forces; many are inspired to look at
their own policies and to instigate new programs to serve their
employees. Such was the case for the chief executive officer of the
PHH Corporation, a Baltimore-based management services company, who, after serving on the Maryland Employers Advisory
Council on Child Care, began a dependent care needs assessment in
his own firm. Likewise, several business leaders on the Governor's
Corporate Advisory Commission (Virginia) have co-hosted "corporate leadership in child care" conferences in their localities with
the state Secretary of Health and Human Resources. Their
participation ranged from being keynoters to being moderators, but
in each case they inspired other business leaders to become informed
and involved. This led to numerous corporate requests for
additional information and technical assistance from the Virginia
Department for Children.

One of the most promising features of these state task forces is that
their members are generally averse to creating a report that will gather
dust on bookshelves. They see their end goals as bringing about actual
change, not merely producing a set of recommendations. The
responsibility for making change is sometimes spelled out in these
reports or the group opts to reconvene to evaluate how well they have
achieved their objectives.

Less common, but quite exciting, is the emergence of local task
forces. Sometimes the impetus for these groups comes from the
business community (e.g., the St. Paul Chamber of Commerce), the
child care field, the Junior League, the religious community, or the
social services community. Whatever the auspice, these groups bring
together local leaders (sometimes limited to the business sector,
sometimes more broadly constituted) to solve specific early childhood
care and education problems. Minneapolis's Success by Six is an
example of this kind of endeavor. Established by United Way and
chaired by the chief executive officer of Honeywell, it convened a
group of leaders in Minneapolis for the express purpose of
determining what prevented children from entering the school system
as successes. Another example is Charlotte Champions, convened by

a group of business leaders to raise substantial funds to improve child care in Charlotte, North Carolina.

Efforts to Increase Business Involvement

As awareness of the role the business community can play in early childhood care and education has spread, so too have efforts to increase the number of companies involved. Virtually all of the Governors' Task Forces on employer-supported child care have concluded that one obstacle to increased involvement is lack of information on the part of companies. The task forces have determined that most companies are unaware of the changing demographics of their workforces, of the increased work/family conflict that employees must bear, and of the negative impact on productivity. Finally, these groups have found, in the words of the Virginia Governor's Task Force, that

Virginia employers do not have sufficient knowledge of their options for child care involvement: flexible personnel policies, resource and referral services; financial assistance including reimbursements for child care; direct care services (on-site centers); and programs for unique child care needs (services for moderately ill or school age children).[35]

These task forces have further concluded that some of the anticipated obstacles are in fact far less inexorable than imagined. For example, liability insurance is often cited as a deterrent to company involvement.[36] This argument implies that the company is equating work/family initiatives with on-site child care; however, even if on-site care is selected, liability insurance has not been a problem for those companies with centers.[37] In sum, most task groups have decided that a first step in increasing corporate participation in early childhood care and education is to create means to disseminate information.

This recommendation generally results in the establishment of a state clearinghouse on employer-supported child care or on work/family. New York, for example, established such a clearinghouse within its Department of Economic Development. In Oregon, the clearinghouse resides in the Department of Human Resources. In New Jersey, the Governor appointed a liaison, located in the state licensing department, to convene breakfast forums for senior managers and to respond to requests for information from companies. The number of requests has multiplied dramatically since this office was established, testimony not only to the greater awareness of this issue in the public at large but also to the fact that every company requesting information is sent a packet, is called upon, and receives a follow-up call. Without such intensive efforts, providing information alone is likely to fall short of stimulating the amount of business participation that its proponents had envisioned.

Another way to increase corporate involvement is to offer tax relief or credits. Thirteen states currently provide tax credits toward the start-up costs of on- or near-site child care, employers' contributions to the center's operational expenses, purchased care (such as vouchers), and child care R&R. The credit ceiling ranges from $3,000 to $100,000 per employer.

However, an overall assessment of tax credits conducted by the Child Care Action Campaign indicates that they stimulate little employer activity, especially if communication about tax credits is haphazard,[38] if companies are insufficiently involved in framing these policies, or if the amount of tax relief is insignificant.

At this time, employers establish on- or near-site programs for their own business reasons; a tax credit is not a sufficient inducement to affect decisions. Larger companies that can afford to create centers are not concerned with tax breaks. Smaller companies that band together in consortiums may find tax credits more helpful. However, to claim this credit, companies must be large enough to pay corporate taxes.

An informal study of approximately 125 companies considering on-site centers asked two questions: 1. Should government assist you in establishing centers? 2. If so, what kind of assistance would be most useful?[39] All the companies felt assistance would make a difference in their ability to provide on-site care, and the form of assistance most frequently requested was grants. The Child Development and Education Act of 1989 proposes to "make grants, on a competitive basis, to businesses and eligible child care providers jointly, to establish innovative programs to provide child care services."

Florida has established a grant program for on-site or purchased care. The annual budget in 1989-90 was $333,000, with a $50,000 maximum per employer. The Child Care Action Campaign (1988) reports that because the Chamber of Commerce supported this bill, informing its 6000 members weekly about its progress, there was widespread enthusiasm in the business community upon the bill's passage.[40] Florida received 68 applications, totalling $1 million, in the first three days of accepting applications.

Noting that employer activity was most pronounced in areas with higher quality child care, New York State's Task Force on Work and Family commendably stated:

Notwithstanding the role we envision for employers and labor in assisting working families, primary responsibility for designing and assuring the adequacy of a system to meet the needs of all children and therefore our future labor force falls to the government.[41]

Thus, many of the recommendations of this group were related to governmental action to strengthen the system so that companies would be more likely to buy into it.

Corporate Involvement in Child Care: Concerns for the Future

Labor shortages suggest that businesses will remain involved in child care as a means to attract and retain employees. This involvement, however, is likely to be sensitive to external business conditions, particularly the threat of a recession. How would a downturn in the economy affect corporate initiatives? Although some suspect that work/family initiatives will be the first to go because they are seen as "soft" or extrinsic to the general business mandate, I think they will endure because they are increasingly regarded as strongly linked to current and future productivity.

How superficial or extensive will these initiatives be? Among the pioneering companies, there has been a progression from the "band-aid" approach to a more holistic view, in which a more comprehensive series of programs and policies is developed. Will this kind of progression be the norm for other companies, or will it be limited to the exemplary companies? Thus far, evidence indicates that progression does take place in many companies.

How will attempts to change the corporate culture fare? Can companies expect to train first-line supervisors to be more flexible and supportive of families while these same supervisors are simultaneously being urged to be more productive? The training model developed by Johnson & Johnson addresses this concern. At its core is a decision-making process between supervisor and employee in which both are expected to (a) get the work done and (b) provide work/family support for employees. Preliminary reports from supervisor trainees indicate that such an approach can work. It is my hope that work/family training will become more widespread.

Until now, the companies designing child care initiatives for their own employees have generally done so in a systematic, thoughtful way. As a result, most of these programs are aimed at specific problems their employees face and are custom designed. There is a concern that as these programs become more widespread they will be "mass-produced." That is, companies may skip the stage of conducting needs assessments and will slot in programs that may be less responsive to the specific needs of employees.

The gulf between the haves and the have-nots in American society extends to the area of corporate benefits as well. *Mothers in the Workplace* documents how very few women receive child care assistance.[42] The study listed possible employer child care supports, including (1) flexibility in scheduling work hours, (2) time off for family responsibilities without risk to one's job or reductions in pay, (3) a supervisor who is supportive when family needs arise, (4) on- or near-site child care, (5) help in paying for child care, and (6) assistance in finding child care. Most mothers of newborns (77 percent) had at least one of these supports, but only 3 percent had four or more.

In our research we have found that policies differ within a company for higher- and lower-ranked employees: (a) only the "valued" employee is offered substantial benefits (e.g., more time flexibility, more child care assistance); (b) only higher-paid employees gain from flexible benefits such as the FSA (one must be able to afford a salary reduction to use FSA).[43] The employees least likely to receive corporate child care assistance are those who need it most—the working poor. If, as anticipated, corporations provide more child care assistance, will these initiatives continue to serve the well-off employees and neglect the poorer ones?

It has become evident to leaders from the most progressive companies that their efforts pall beside the enormity of the need. As one said in a recent meeting, "Our efforts are really only adjustments. In themselves, they do little to help families in this country educate and care for their children." It has become cliché but is nonetheless true that considerable effort by every sector of society will be required to deal with the child care crisis. If such an effort is to occur on a local, state, and federal level, business leaders must participate fully. In the past, however, business leaders have tended to concentrate their civic efforts on higher education or social ills such as drugs and crime. The thrust of the Committee for Economic Development may help shift the focus of business leaders to early childhood issues.

It has been discouraging to participate in several Governor's Task

Forces and observe the pervasiveness of the assumed difference between education and care. Until now, most corporate efforts have targeted child care for their own employees and for their community. An entirely different and very small group of business leaders has been concerned about education. If change is to happen, and to happen constructively, this historic schism must be healed. Business leaders must be educated to understand that high quality early childhood programs, whatever their auspice and location, must provide a nurturing environment as well as learning opportunities.

One of the most disturbing issues before us is the role business will take in promoting quality. In the early years of business involvement, pioneering companies stood for quality improvement. Unfortunately, several states have recently attempted to reduce or eliminate standards in order to stimulate the growth of on-site corporate centers. The development of such proposals in Colorado and California has followed a similar pattern: high-powered employees (in law firms or in accounting firms) wanted to bring their babies to work; they found a conference room or other space to convert to a child care room, and then encountered what they considered bureaucratic licensing hassles.

Colorado's bill called for all licensing standards to be waived and a commission to be established to set new standards. The bill was passed but was vetoed by Governor Romer, who said: "We have an obligation both as parents and as responsible citizens to help our children receive the best, most affordable care available. I do not, however, believe we should be willing to compromise the quality of care in order to achieve this goal."[44] The following year, however, the bill was again passed and signed into law.

In some California firms, space has been found in high-rise buildings but licensing regulations require child care programs to be on the ground floor. Upset by these restrictions, the employees enlisted the support of their state representatives. Legislation, nicknamed the "High Rise Baby Bill" and calling for a severe reduction in standards, was soon introduced. This bill is now making its way through the California Assembly.

The research evidence is quite clear that licensing features can affect children's development for good or for ill.[45] The argument that parents are present and "know best" at on-site facilities does not excuse the proposed California law permitting up to six babies up to fifteen months old in thirty-five square feet per child with no outside space and a ratio of one-to-four or two-to-six adult caregivers per child. Furthermore, under this proposed bill, the caregiver is not required to have any early childhood training. Simplifying some unnecessary and bureaucratic standards may be a positive move in some states; eliminating basic requirements for group size, staff/child ratio, and training is a dangerous move.

The business community is the new player in the field of early childhood education and care. Within a few short years companies have become an important constituency. As business involvement grows and becomes more widespread, the impact of that involvement will become more evident. Will companies become a force for increasing the supply and improving quality? This is the question to be determined in the coming years.

FOOTNOTES

1. Dana E. Friedman, *Encouraging Employer Support to Working Parents* (New York: Carnegie Corporation of New York, 1983).

2. Ibid.

3. Rosabeth Moss Kanter, *Work and Family in the United States: A Critical Review and Agenda for Research and Policy* (New York: Russell Sage Foundation, 1977).

4. Mary J. Bane, *Here to Stay: American Families in the Twentieth Century* (New York: Basic Books, 1976).

5. Louis Harris and Associates, *Families at Work: Strengths and Strains*, The General Mills American Family Forum (Minneapolis, MN: General Mills, 1981).

6. Ibid.

7. Ellen Galinsky and Diane Hughes, "The *Fortune* Magazine Child Care Study" (Paper presented at the Annual Convention of the American Psychological Association, New York, August 1987); Ellen Galinsky, "Child Care and Productivity" (Paper prepared for the Child Care Action Campaign conference on "Child Care: The Bottom Line," New York, March 1988).

8. Robert Lurie, Ellen Galinsky, and Diane Hughes, unpublished data (New York: Bank Street College of Education, Resources for Child Care Management, 1988).

9. Marybeth Shinn, Blanca Ortiz-Torres, Anne Morris, Patricia Simko, and Nora Wong, "Child Care Patterns, Stress, and Job Behaviors among Working Parents" (Paper presented at the Annual Convention of the American Psychological Association, New York, August 1987); Diane Hughes, "Child Care and Working Parents" (Paper presented at the Annual Convention of the American Psychological Association, New York, August 1987); Galinsky, "Child Care and Productivity."

10. Galinsky and Hughes, "The *Fortune* Magazine Child Care Study."

11. Galinsky, "Child Care and Productivity."

12. Catalyst, *Work and Family Seminars: Corporations' Response to Employees' Needs* (New York: Catalyst, 1984).

13. American Society for Personnel Administration, *Employers and Child Care: The Human Resource Professional's View* (Alexandria, VA: American Society for Personnel Administration, 1988).

14. National Council of Jewish Women, *Mothers in the Workplace*, NCJW Center for the Child Report (New York: National Council of Jewish Women, March 1987).

15. Ellen Galinsky and Dana E. Friedman, *Corporate Reference Guide to Work/Family Programs* (New York: Families and Work Institute, forthcoming).

16. Ibid.

17. National Council of Jewish Women, *Mothers in the Workplace*.

18. Friedman, *Encouraging Employer Support to Working Parents*.

19. Ibid.

20. J. Douglas Phillips, unpublished paper, Rahway, NJ, Merck & Co., 1989.

21. Kathleen McDonald, personal communication with the author, 1986.

22. Ellen Galinsky, "Family Life and Corporate Policies," in *In Support of Families*, ed. Michael Yogman and T. Berry Brazelton (Cambridge, MA: Harvard University Press, 1986).

23. Committee for Economic Development, Research and Policy Committee, *Children in Need: Investment Strategies for the Educationally Disadvantaged*, Executive Summary (New York: Committee for Economic Development, 1987), p. 2.

24. John R. Berrueta-Clement, Lawrence J. Schweinhart, W. Steven Barnett, Ann S. Epstein, and David P. Weikart, "Changed Lives: The Effects of the Perry Preschool Program on Youths through Age Nineteen," *Monographs of the High/Scope Research Foundation*, no. 8 (Ypsilanti, MI: High/Scope Educational Research Foundation, 1984; J. Ronald Lally, Peter L. Mangione, and Alice S. Honig, *Long Range Impact of Early Intervention on Low-Income Children and Their Families* (Syracuse, NY: Syracuse University Family Research Program, 1987).

25. U. S. House Select Committee on Children, Youth, and Families, *Family and Child Care: Improving the Options* (Washington, DC: U. S. Government Printing Office, 1984).

26. Galinsky and Friedman, *Corporate Reference Guide to Work/Family Programs*.

27. Ibid.

28. Ellen Galinsky, Diane Hughes, and Judy David, "Trends in Corporate Family-Responsive Policies," *Marriage and Family Review*, in press.

29. Ellen Galinsky, Graham Staines, and Robert Lurie, unpublished data, Families and Work Institute, Resources for Child Care Management, New York, 1988.

30. Maryland Committee for Children, *Shareholders in the Future: Marylanders Invest in Child Care* (Annapolis, MD: Governor's Task Force Report, 1988).

31. Dana E. Friedman, "Estimates from National Monitors of Employer-Supported Child Care," unpublished memorandum, Families and Work Institute, New York, 1989.

32. Ibid.

33. Dana E. Friedman, "Perceptions and Realities of Child Care Liability Insurance" (Report prepared for the U. S. Department of Labor, July 1989).

34. Jules M. Marquart, "A Pattern Matching Approach to Link Program Theory and Evaluation Data: The Case of Employer-Supported Child Care" (Ph.D. diss., Cornell University, 1988).

35. Virginia Department of Children, *Report of the Governor's Corporate Advisory Commission on Employers' Initiatives for Child Day Care in Virginia* (Richmond, VA: Governor's Task Force, 1988).

36. American Society for Personnel Administration, *Employers and Child Care.*

37. Dana E. Friedman, "The Productivity Effects of Workplace Centers" (Paper presented at the Resources for Child Care Management Conference on "Child Care Centers at the Workplace," Chicago, June 1989).

38. Child Care Action Campaign, *Employer Tax Credits for Child Care: Asset or Liability?* (New York: State Financing Alternatives Project, Child Care Action Campaign, 1989).

39. Ellen Galinsky, informal study at the Resources for Child Care Management Conference on "Child Care Centers at the Workplace," Chicago, June, 1989.

40. Child Care Action Campaign, *Child Care ActioNews,* 5, no. 6 (1988): 5.

41. Governor's Task Force on Work and Family, "Final Report" (Albany, NY: Governor's Task Force, 1989).

42. National Council of Jewish Women, *Mothers in the Workplace.*

43. Galinsky and Friedman, *Corporate Reference Guide to Work/Family Programs.*

44. Governor's Veto Message of Senate Bill 118 (Colorado), Spring, 1989.

45. Richard Ruopp, Jeffrey Travers, Frederick Glantz, and Craig Coelen, *Children at the Center: Final Report of the National Day Care Study* (Cambridge, MA: Abt Associates, 1979).

Section Three
ISSUES OF POLICY

CHAPTER IX

Using Research to Inform Policy: The Case of Early Intervention

EDWARD ZIGLER

Although efforts to improve the lives and school performance of young children have a long history in the United States, they did not blossom into the circumscribed discipline of early childhood intervention until the birth of the antipoverty program, Project Head Start, in the mid-1960s. The early years of this young discipline were characterized by intense controversy and theoretical excesses that threatened its continued existence. The major controversy, of course, was whether early intervention did indeed have any long-term benefits for children.[1] Not until the publication of the Cornell Consortium data[2] and the reports by the High/Scope group[3] and the Department of Health and Human Services[4] was this question finally put to rest. In regard to economically disadvantaged children, a consensus now exists among behavioral scientists, policymakers, and taxpayers that early intervention is a cost-effective method for combating the effects of poverty experienced early in life. Further, it is viewed as being of value not only for poor children but for other high-risk groups. Evidence for the efficacy of early programming for a variety of at-risk populations was recently presented by the American Psychological Association under the title of *Fourteen Ounces of Prevention.*[5] Most recently, our nation has embarked on a major early intervention effort on behalf of developmentally disabled infants and toddlers under Public Law 99-457.

154

On the political scene, early intervention was first championed primarily by liberal policymakers. Today, programs for poor children are endorsed by more conservative elements such as the economic community.[6] During the 1988 political campaign, the moderate-conservative candidate George Bush voiced his enthusiasm for the Head Start program. His more conservative predecessor, Ronald Reagan, included Head Start in his safety net of programs which were kept in place during his term of office. In 1989, the nation's governors met with President Bush in Charlottesville, Virginia, and as a group endorsed early childhood intervention as a promising route toward solving a variety of problems. Thus, early intervention is now embraced by decision makers along all points of the political spectrum.

How did the field of early intervention gain this universal favor and support, when just twenty years ago the renowned scientist Arthur Jensen wrote, "Compensatory education has been tried and apparently it has failed."[7] Developments in both theory and research guided not only the field itself but public perceptions of it. Theories about how children develop have matured from simplistic views to complex explanatory edifices that strive to interrelate all facets of development. Research and evaluation have become much more sophisticated and are better able to assess a program's multiple effects on multiple human systems. Theorists and researchers alike have realized how seriously their work and words are taken and are learning how to communicate with the media and to deliver their interpretations responsibly. They have also developed a more productive relationship with policymakers, as both science and policy have increasingly come to depend on one another. The evolution of the field of early childhood intervention illustrates the interconnection between theory, research, and policy and the problems that occur when any one of these elements is out of step with the others.

Factors That Guided and Misguided the Formation of Early Intervention

Looking back over the past twenty-five years, several academic and popular viewpoints stand out as having had significant influence on the field of intervention and accompanying research. These perspectives have changed with the spirit of the times and with added knowledge, and the emphases and goals of current programs reflect these changes. In very general terms, the intervention efforts of the 1960s were based on a deficit model to explain the problems of poor children. There was a preoccupation with intelligence, to the exclusion of the social and emotional aspects of human development. The times were also characterized by a naive belief in the malleability of intelligence—that IQ scores could be raised to unrestricted heights through appropriate environmental intervention. The concept of critical periods of development was in vogue, and the preschool years were seen as the most critical—as the time when the entire course of the child's development could be shaped by the proper environment. By examining these points of view we can understand how they affected and were affected by experience with intervention programs. This discussion will focus largely on the development of the Head Start program not only because it is the nation's largest intervention effort but because it has been the most rigorously evaluated. Its dedication to evaluation and change have enabled us to learn many valuable lessons about early intervention.

DEFICIT MODEL

In the mid-1960s, President Lyndon Johnson initiated a massive attempt to eradicate social class inequities in the United States. One facet of this "War on Poverty" was the preschool intervention program, mounted in the hope of providing young children with a sort of inoculation against the ill effects of poverty.

The fact was that, compared to children of middle socioeconomic status (SES), lower SES children generally did less well in school and received lower scores on IQ tests. It was widely believed that a program of early environmental enrichment would give lower SES children the boost they needed to perform on a par with their middle SES peers. Intervention was supposed to impart immediate benefits so that class differences would be eliminated by the time of school entry. Furthermore, many expected that the brief preschool experience would be so potent a counteraction to the deficits in poor children's lives that it could prevent further attenuation in age-appropriate performance and a recurrence of the gap between social classes in later grades.

The deficit model embodied some paternalistic and erroneous notions that have had a long life in popular and practical forums. The notion of "cultural deprivation" or "cultural disadvantage" was a blatant assumption that the culture of the lower classes was inferior to that of the middle class. Since whatever was done in middle-class homes apparently worked, intervention programs were intended to provide poor children with the learning experiences supposedly lacking in their impoverished environments. The notion of middle-class supremacy was so strong that at the time few acknowledged that intelligence could be expressed in anything other than a middle-class milieu in any but middle-class ways.[8] As early critics asserted, the effect of this model was to blame the victim.

In contrast, the planners of Head Start were careful to avoid the deficit model. As a Community Action Program, funded by the 1964 Economic Opportunity Act, its mandate was to allow "maximum feasible participation" of economically disadvantaged populations in programs designed to serve them. One way Head Start did this was by emphasizing parental involvement—parents not only became involved in the daily activities of the program, but they exercised real decision-making power in all planning and administrative aspects of their neighborhood centers. This was a major break from past practices in which educated and paid professionals dictated the operation of poverty programs to passive recipients. Poor parents rose to the occasion and worked incredibly hard to assure the success and future existence of Head Start.

The inferiority-superiority basis of the deficit model has now given way to an approach emphasizing differences among children rather than deficiencies.[9] Studies in which profiles of characteristics rather than of a single trait have been assessed have shown that middle- and lower-SES children have both strong and weak points when compared with one another.[10] For example, in a study by Yando, Seitz, and Zigler,[11] lower-SES children demonstrated superior performance on tasks requiring creative thinking whereas middle-SES children performed better on several traditional academic tasks. These researchers concluded that many differences between SES groups, when they appear, reflect "stylistic patterns rather than capacity differences" (p. 107).

The difference model surely provides a more realistic view of group and individual differences in behavior. It also encourages a more productive approach to intervention in which we do not try to change children but instead try to build on the strengths that they bring to the program. In adopting a difference rather than a deficit model, optimal development is no longer sought by inculcating middle-class values but by discovering ways to allow various intellectual and personal potentials to emerge in a variety of settings.

FOCUS ON INTELLIGENCE

During the formative years of early intervention programs, there was an overemphasis on cognitive development in psychology, education, and popular forums. This was due to several factors and represented an important new area for scholars and practitioners. Until the mid-1950s, American behaviorism was the dominant theoretical view, and thought processes were generally considered to be a secondary phenomenon. While a small group of scientists developed an interest in cognition, the mainstream of research with children had to do with observable behavior, the learning of habits and response tendencies, and the role of external reinforcements in learning. Indeed, it was considered bad form even to ask children why they were doing what they were doing, since such subjective reports were considered highly suspect. Then thirty or so years ago, American researchers suddenly discovered the sizeable body of work on cognition by prominent European scholars, particularly Jean Piaget. They became so captivated with his classic efforts in charting the sequence of cognitive development that they quickly moved from too little emphasis on intellectual development to too much.

Not only was IQ the favored topic of interest, but there also developed a naive expectation that intervention had the power to accelerate cognitive growth markedly. In the 1960s, the favored theoretical position was what I have termed the "environmental mystique."[12] Essentially, this position held that young children are so malleable that rather minimal interventions in the early years will have major and lasting impact. The theorists whose work gave rise to this mystique were themselves rebelling against an earlier view of child development which emphasized hereditary or maturational factors.

Early in this century, the majority of scientists believed that biology was destiny. The maturational theories of Arnold Gesell and others emphasized that physical and cognitive growth were predetermined processes over which we could exert little control. Since the basic nature of children's development was thought to be biologically set, few efforts were made to shape the course of development. By the 1960s, a combination of social change and scientific research had radically altered this view of development. Environmentalism replaced predeterminism, and development was considered almost infinitely open to the manipulation of experts. In a nation as infatuated with intelligence scores as the United States, this viewpoint soon grew into a belief that IQs could be dramatically increased with minimal effort.

To a great extent, the enthusiasm with cognitive improvement was spurred by animal research on early deprivation. For example, the work of Riesen[13] and Hebb[14] suggested that early perceptual or environmental deprivation creates a permanent deficit in later problem-solving ability in laboratory animals. The concept of early enrichment programs to counter a lacking environment was a logical step, if one can equate the deprivation experienced by animals in laboratory research with the deprivation experienced by poor children. This analogy, however, is clearly open to question.

J. McV. Hunt's *Intelligence and Experience*[15] was another important influence in the 1960s. Hunt argued against the notion of genetically fixed intelligence by taking the opposite stance, that intelligence is essentially the product of environmental factors. He theorized (in part on the basis of the animal literature) that it is possible to promote a faster rate of intellectual development and higher level of adult intelligence by "governing the encounters that children have with their environments, especially during the early years of their development" (p. 363). Hunt continued into the 1970s to argue that IQ changes of 50 to 70 points could be obtained through one intervention effort or another.[16] By denying the importance of genetic and biological factors in human development, Hunt's position represented environmentalism gone astray.

The mass media were eagerly responsive to the notion of easy IQ changes through environmental manipulations. Reporters either misinterpreted or were misled by the early and still tentative results of various enrichment programs. Before these efforts could receive scholarly review, they were being publicized as though the secret of accelerated cognitive development had been uncovered. For example, the Deutsches' preliminary report[17] of a ten-point increase in IQ after their ten-month program was published in New York newspapers under the headline, "Program raises children's IQ scores a point a month." Books and articles in the popular press poured forth informing parents how to give their children a superior mind and how to teach them to read at the age of two, and "educational" toys flooded the market.

Although a few intervention programs were explicitly designed to raise IQ scores, Head Start was designed with the much broader goal of improving social competence—a concept that includes but is not limited to cognitive functioning. Yet this and other projects were widely regarded as educational efforts. As such, evaluators gauged their success in terms of IQ scores—the traditional measure and predictor of academic performance. Other reasons that the IQ score became the most popular measure for outcome evaluations include:

standard IQ tests are well-developed instruments with psychometric properties that are so well-documented that they allow the user to avoid difficult measurement problems; they are relatively easy to administer; they are related to a number of other behaviors that are of theoretical and practical significance; and finally, because of the lure of being able to demonstrate almost immediate results of a program in the form of increased IQ scores.

I take issue with the use of IQ as the ultimate outcome measure of intervention programs for a number of reasons. First, there is now considerable evidence that the reported increases in IQ reflect motivational changes that influence the children's test performance rather than changes in the actual quality of cognitive functioning. Consider for a moment the child who refuses to answer any questions on an IQ test. This surely does not mean an absolute lack of cognitive ability or knowledge. What is reflected here is an apprehensive, perhaps skeptical child who is minimizing all contact with the object of his or her apprehension, the tester. However, a child who has participated in an intervention effort, even a short six-week program, is likely to feel more self-confident and comfortable with an adult tester and therefore to score higher on the standardized test. This explains why Eisenberg and Conners[18] were able to find ten-point increases in IQ after only a short summer of intervention.

The difficulty of effecting true increases in IQ was recently noted by Herman Spitz.[19] (For a more complete discussion of this issue, see my review of Spitz's book.[20]) Interestingly, the long-term effects of intervention that have been found do not include permanently elevated IQ scores but rather everyday competence indicators such as being in the right grade for age and avoiding delinquency behaviors.[21] This brings me to my second objection to the use of the IQ scores as *the* standard for evaluating intervention programs. I do not believe IQ tests measure what intervention efforts are trying to achieve. The goal of intervention programs is to affect increased social competence, an aim much broader than measured intelligence. We must consider the child as more than a walking cognitive system, for cognitive ability alone will not dictate how well that child will function in our world. Even the most gifted child will not do well in school if he or she does not know how to interact with teachers or peers. Furthermore, we cannot even hope that children will achieve academically if they have not received the proper nutrition needed to function in their daily lives. A sick child will never be a competent child. The aim, therefore, of intervention efforts must be to affect positively all aspects of the child's development: social, emotional, physical, as well as intellectual. This is critical because all of these aspects are interrelated—one does not function independently of the others.

Looking at why various programs have failed at raising IQ scores but have succeeded in practical terms tells us much about the degree of malleability of various human systems. The developing child is a complex combination of emotional, physical, and cognitive subsystems, each differentially sensitive to environmental input. The brain appears to be the most buffered against external events and stressors, so we can expect intelligence to be the most stable of all behavioral traits. This does not at all mean that it is predetermined, but scholars today are suggesting that the practical reaction range for IQ is about twenty to twenty-five points; this is a defensible expectation of what intervention can in fact accomplish.[22]

IQ test performance reflects more than formal cognition, however, and involves factors that the environment can more easily shape and change. One factor is achievement, which is exclusively dependent upon experience with events, objects, and ideas. Thus it can certainly be enhanced by enrichment programs. Performance is also influenced by social and emotional factors, which I have already noted to have a high degree of plasticity. Many aspects of physical well-being, such as proper nutrition and inoculation against disease, are also substantially controlled by the environment. Experience with intervention has helped us to realize what areas of growth are most effectively targeted. By attending to the needs of the whole child, and to the more plastic aspects of development we know we can do something about, we can be confident that optimal cognitive development will follow.

CRITICAL PERIODS

Another guiding principle of the 1960s was that intervention is most effective if administered during some critical time frame, and, by conventional wisdom, the earlier the better. The critical period concept was popularized in Benjamin Bloom's influential work, *Stability and Change in Human Characteristics.*[23] Bloom argued that the human organism is most sensitive to environmental inputs during periods of rapid growth, which certainly occurs during the early years. From patterns of correlations between IQ test scores obtained at different ages, Bloom noted that IQ scores at about age four correlate a respectable .70 with later scores and account for half of the variance of adult IQ scores. Hence, there emerged what came to be a cliché of the 1960s: half of the child's learning is over by the age of four. Now just on the basis of logic, since we have no idea when all learning is over, how could we possibly know when half of it is over? Furthermore, we must heed the statistical dictum that correlations do not imply causation. Applying Bloom's logic to the fact that parents' and children's IQs also correlate about .70, we could make the assertion that half of learning is over before the child is born.

There were other champions of magic periods. Infancy became a very popular critical period after Burton White[24] professed that the solution to many problems in child development might lie in putting mobiles over infants' cribs, providing planned stimulation from the earliest days. He then declared that Head Start could not possibly be a success because it came too late in the life of the child. Soon there were signs of a new swing of the pendulum to the view that the critical period is later, not earlier, in development. Two outstanding English workers, Ann and A.D.B. Clarke, propounded this opinion,[25] but went a step further[26] to assert that Head Start is inefficacious because it is targeted too early in life. Other learned workers have heralded adolescence as yet another critical period.[27] What all of this fanfare will mean to the future of early childhood intervention is unknown.

The search for critical periods of development is by no means over. Yet when we examine the voluminous literature on magic periods, we see that the long rummage has gotten us nowhere. As reviewers have pointed out,[28] the notion of critical or sensitive periods was borrowed too directly from comparative and ethological studies. There is a long step from ducklings, which follow almost any model that is available within a narrowly specified time span, to children, whose behavioral development is a gradual and intricate process.

It is my belief that the critical period concept is not useful for directing intervention strategies. Development is a continuous process; experiences at any given age are affected by and built on experiences that have come before. Thus intervention at later stages of life can no more wipe out a history of disadvantage than can a brief early intervention inoculate a child against continuing disadvantage. As Victoria Seitz and I noted, the most instructive model for intervention efforts is the behavior of a secure family.[29] Parents do not give their children care only at a certain "critical" stage of development. Rather, a secure family (whatever its form) is permanently committed to children and flexible enough to support them appropriately at different ages.

Actually, it has been recognized for many years that intervention is most effective if it is continuous.[30] It is also well-known that the physical and psychological nutrients required for optimal development at each stage of life differ according to the needs of that age. Consequently, like a good family, the most successful intervention should comprise a series of dovetailed programs, independently available as the need requires, with each appropriate for a particular stage of development—prenatal, infancy and toddlerhood, preschool and the early elementary school years, middle childhood, and adolescence.

The principle of continuity applies not only from one stage of life to the next but from one aspect of daily life to another. Intervention must certainly be more effective, for example, when parents become involved in a program than when a child attends a center for a few hours and then returns to an unchanged home environment for the majority of the day. In fact, preschool programs appear to succeed best when parents participate in the education process.[31] In an immediate sense, parent involvement means that the child's environment is affected generally rather than in the one specific context of the preschool program. In terms of lasting program effects, involvement allows parents to perpetuate the benefits of the intervention even after it has formally ceased.

Today many intervention programs are starting earlier and lasting longer. The continuity principle can be seen in the implementation of Comprehensive Child Development Centers for children from the prenatal period to age five and the Follow Through program for school-age children. The services to be offered to disabled infants and toddlers and their families under PL 99–457, dovetailing with the educational programs provided for older children under the Education for All Handicapped Children Act, provide another example.

Lessons Learned and to Be Learned

As tests of the action-research cycle in the social sciences, early intervention programs have functioned as a productive, albeit tense, collaboration between researchers and politicians in an effort to add to scientific knowledge and simultaneously to solve social problems.[32] Head Start in particular has held a unique position as a national laboratory for the design of effective interventions, serving as a base from which to experiment with various theories and practical applications. The most general lesson learned is that early intervention does indeed have long-term benefits for children. Yet our current views of what intervention can realistically accomplish, and how, in no way resemble those of the early 1960s. Experience with intervention has shown us we do not have to raise children for poor families, raise their IQs, or find the perfect time to strike. Theorists have learned that intervention is most effective when the entire family is included, and they understand more about what systems of human development are most malleable to change. Researchers have vastly improved the methods and scope of their evaluations. Practitioners and policymakers have learned from the scientists and taught them as well. The evolution of social science and social intervention has led to today's more moderate theories of development and a much broader outlook of what is valuable in and to the child.

ECOLOGICAL APPROACH TO DEVELOPMENT

Since the theoretical foundations we had for early intervention in the 1960s clearly led us into many errors, the field could not have advanced had not a new theoretical paradigm been forthcoming. Thankfully, a new paradigm took firm hold in the 1970s. Arnold Sameroff provided us with his transactional model,[33] and perhaps of greatest importance, Urie Bronfenbrenner developed his ecological model.[34] As a result of these theoretical advances the entire approach to early intervention changed. Prior to this time early interventionists often viewed themselves as "child savers." We would take the child from the negative environment provided in the home and shape him or her into a more adequate person. Today successful programs see the unit of intervention not as the individual child, but the family itself. The early seeds of this type of thinking may be seen in Head Start's commitment to parental involvement and participation. This may well have been due to the important role that Urie Bronfenbrenner played in the conceptualization and implementation of the Head Start program.

The family systems approach provides us with a viable hypothesis to explain the long-term effects of early intervention. Ronald Lally and his colleagues, Victoria Seitz and I, and others have all advanced the view that the long-term effects are not due to the half-day program experienced by the child for one year during preschool, but are rather due to the parents.[35] As a result of their involvement with the intervention, parents become more optimal socializers of the child throughout the rest of the day and indeed, throughout the child's formative years.

With families viewed as having the most important and lasting influence on the child, it is naturally important for them to be as strong and secure as possible. Head Start began to move in the direction of general family support through programs to improve family functioning and interrelationships and to provide assistance in areas of need. For example, there were parent education and training programs to enable families to improve their parenting skills and financial status. In perhaps the first effort to provide total family support, the Child and Family Resource Program, a number of services were made available and each family could select those they thought would be of benefit. And in local Head Start centers across the nation, parents involved in planning could voice their needs and create services to address them. For instance, in many neighborhoods there was insufficient child care to enable parents to enter training or seek employment, so families instituted extended day programs in their Head Start centers. Such efforts to serve and strengthen families mark the beginnings of today's family support movement, an exciting grassroots movement which blossomed across America in the 1980s.[36]

Thanks to the ecological model, we are now aware that the child's development is not only influenced by the family system, but by other systems far removed from the family's control. The child is influenced by the family, which in turn is influenced by the nature and effectiveness of our major social systems such as the world of work, the school, the media, and available health services. Thus, any complete early intervention program would address the entire ecology of the child to make it more conducive to human development. Again, early seeds of this broad approach may be found in the history of Head Start. A unique study by Kirschner Associates indicated that the presence of Head Start in a community acted as a catalyst for improvements in two major systems affecting the child, the school and the health system.[37]

The ecological model has clear implications that we not oversell what we can realistically accomplish with current early intervention programs. In many instances these programs simply cannot change enough of the ecology or the larger environment to make a real difference in the lives of families. The problems of many families will not be solved by early intervention efforts, but only by changes in the basic features of the infrastructure of our society. No amount of counselling, early childhood curricula, or home visits will take the place of jobs that provide decent incomes, affordable housing, health care, optimal family configurations, or integrated neighborhoods where children encounter positive role models.

IMPROVED EVALUATION

Since the beginning of intervention efforts, both taxpayers and decision makers have been legitimately concerned with whether these programs succeed or fail. They have rightfully held the programs accountable for the public funds invested in them. By far the most commonly used outcome measure in the early years was the magnitude of the change in children's IQ scores, a near fatal mistake for the intervention movement. After years of experience and broader evaluations, we now know that the long-term effects of intervention do not include permanently elevated IQ scores. Rather, there are improvements in school performance, motivation, social behavior, and physical health. Yet evaluators had to learn how to recognize and assess such competence indicators, a task requiring patience because social capabilities do not become evident overnight. Over the past twenty-five years assessments of intervention have evolved from quickie pre- and posttreatment comparisons of IQ scores alone to more complete examinations of a variety of aspects of competence over substantial periods of time. Efforts to create a valid and agreeable tool to tap social competence have not yet succeeded,[38] but virtually all investigators today are looking beyond IQ scores in outcome studies.

Since the future of intervention hinges on evaluation, much more theoretical and practical work must be done in the design of appropriate assessment tools. Since the potential impact of comprehensive programs goes beyond the child, we must learn how to discover the effects on parents, siblings, and the community. Researchers must also address the concerns of decision makers and taxpayers and attempt to provide some indication of the cost effectiveness of intervention programs. This can be hard to do in the case of prevention programs such as Head Start, since it is difficult to estimate the amount saved when events such as juvenile delinquency and grade retention do not happen. It is also difficult to attach a monetary value to subjective benefits such as a child receiving dental care and parents gaining a sense of control over their own and their child's future. Some attempts at cost/benefit analysis have been tried with highly tentative but impressive results.

Such analyses might never have been envisioned if it were not for the vast improvements in the scope and detail of evaluation in both psychology and education. Yet this certainly does not mean that there is no room for refinement and further improvement. For example, while there is widespread acceptance of the value of early intervention, there is no agreement among workers as to exactly what processes mediate these benefits. The great empirical task of the future will be to identify these mediating processes. The future must also see a much more fine-grained approach to the efficacy issue. No early intervention program results in equal benefits to all those enrolled. We must strive to illuminate what factors determine which participants are aided by our interventions and which are not. Finally, by noting the errors of the past quarter of a century, we must realize how crucial it is to maintain an investigatory stance. Old data must continuously be reassessed and new data continuously collected if we are ever to understand the potential of early intervention in all its various forms.

INFORMING SOCIAL POLICY

Despite the differences in focus between policymakers and behavioral scientists, the two groups have developed an important working relationship. Researchers who study interventions have found themselves taken seriously by politicians and social planners. They have been forced to recognize that they possess an important, albeit incomplete, body of knowledge, some of which is of great immediate value to society. The 1960s and 1970s marked a coming-of-age for scientists in their ability to influence social policies in a substantial manner. In particular, Project Head Start was an educational experience for us, yielding firsthand information about the benefits and pitfalls of attempting to translate psychological knowledge into social action. From this and other involvements, psychologists have learned a great deal about designing and evaluating social programs and are far better prepared to bridge the gap between psychological theory and societal needs than they were only a decade or two ago. The time has come for us to take our responsibilities seriously, to assess what we have learned from our early forays into social policy, and to make recommendations for the future.

As Weiss has pointed out, there are many possible uses of psychological research in the construction of social policy.[39] Ideally, research could be used directly for solving societal problems. Yet many times the problem to be solved is not clearly delineated and there is no consensus among decision makers on the goals they wish to achieve. For example, "reducing poverty" is an amorphous goal that varies with time, place, and definition. Evaluation of antipoverty programs can be impossible because of the inevitable variability among programs implemented in very different communities and populations. Similarly, part of the difficulty in evaluating the Head

Start program has stemmed from the facts that its goals were initially presented rather vaguely and that the project varies widely at the local level.

Research can also be used as political ammunition. Even after policymakers have reached decisions and are unlikely to change their minds, they may use social science knowledge to bolster their arguments. This is a perfectly acceptable use of research, as long as the information is not distorted and is accessible to all sides. Sometimes, however, research is used in this way to advance self-interest. A politician may cite results that support his or her point of view and ignore those which do not. In other cases policymakers can delay taking an action they really do not favor by arguing that the needed evidence is not available. This was the case in the four-year moratorium on staffing regulations in the federal day care standards, pending the results from the Abt National Day Care Study and the "Appropriateness Report" from HEW to Congress.

Another use of social science research is the most amorphous, but perhaps the most important: "research as conceptualization."[40] This definition of use encompasses sensitizing policymakers to new issues, turning research problems into policy issues, clarifying alternatives, and supplying a common language. Although this is a "softer" use of research than is ideally desired, it can have far-reaching implications. Generalizations from the accumulation of research in an area can, over time, change the climate of ideas and become a part of the social consciousness. The negative aspect of this way of using research in policy is that not only hard facts, but myths and social fads, may be so publicized that they too become part of public "knowledge." Unfortunately, these myths often remain unquestioned and become the basis for new policy and further research. Examples of this problem include sentiments in favor of mainstreaming, deinstitution-alization, and the belief that "fade-out" is an inevitable fate of any positive effects of preschool intervention programs. A more positive use of generalities derived from social science research can be seen in the formation of Project Head Start. At the time of its birth, prevailing social science theories showed a revival of interest in the role of the environment in human development, and there were efforts to design educational interventions for disadvantaged children. On the political front, the nation was in the Civil Rights era and had waged the War on Poverty. These forces converged in the mid-1960s when a novel alliance between child development experts and social policymakers was created. From their combined efforts Head Start was born. Thus the use of broad principles based on social science knowledge can and does affect social policy.

The translation of knowledge into policy is obviously most difficult when the knowledge base is weak. If we had reason to believe that a few more years of research would yield definitive answers to pressing problems, we might counsel waiting for such research to be completed. However, it is unlikely that this will occur for such complex societal problems as school failure among poor children. We are unlikely soon to reach a consensus on defining it, on agreeing on its causes, or on prescribing efficacious remedies.

What the absence of a firm data base implies is the need for special expertise in examining existing data and for special care in making responsible recommendations. Researchers are in a better position than are nonresearchers to gauge the usefulness of incomplete psychological findings. However, the implications of research on intervention are often publicized even when the investigator would prefer to wait for additional data. Thus, like it or not, we have a difficult but ineluctable responsibility to draw the best conclusions trained scientists can draw from a complicated, imperfect data base.

Despite the gaps in our current knowledge, several recommendations can nevertheless be made with confidence. First, societal interventions should focus on improving social competence rather than on attempting to alter cognitive abilities directly. We know better how to increase social competence than how to influence intelligence. Thus our efforts will be most successful if we promote policies and programs that attempt to raise the level of functional intelligence, that is, the socially competent behavior that people emit, regardless of their formal intellectual capacities. Second, sound social policy should reflect an appreciation for the continuity of development. We have paid a high price for committing ourselves to a search for magic periods when we concentrate interventions at the expense of other periods in development. The third recommendation is related. Social policy must respect the fact of biological heterogeneity by recognizing that no single intervention will be best for all groups of individuals at risk. Fourth, we have learned the dangers of attempting to base social policy on extreme positions; future policies should reflect the moderate, defensible stances that can be justified by the actual state of knowledge. Finally, it now appears that effective interventions will be family support systems, not single programs designed to aid children alone or to remediate any one particular problem known to be correlated with low social competence.

These principles concerning the value of multiple services, the belief that all periods and processes of life are important, and the significance of the family certainly seem enlightened compared to the restricted views of the 1960s. Yet we have learned that what is modern today is old tomorrow, so we must commit ourselves to continuous re-evaluation and experimentation. With a wealth of intervention experience behind us, we can successfully build on the achievements of the past.

FOOTNOTES

1. For details of this controversy, see Edward Zigler and Winnie Berman, "Discerning the Future of Early Childhood Intervention," *American Psychologist* 38 (August 1983): 894-906.

2. Richard B. Darlington, Jacqueline M. Royce, Ann S. Snipper, Harry W. Murray, and Irving Lazar, "Preschool Programs and Later Competence of Children from Low-income Families," *Science* 208 (April 1980): 202-204.

3. John R. Berrueta-Clement, Lawrence J. Schweinhart, W. Steven Barnett, Ann S. Epstein, and David P. Weikart, "Changed Lives: The Effects of the Perry Preschool Program on Youths through Age 19," *Monographs of the High/Scope Educational Research Foundation*, No. 8 (Ypsilanti, MI: High/Scope Educational Research Foundation, 1984).

4. Carol E. Copple, Marvin G. Cline, and Allen N. Smith, *Path to the Future: Long-term Effects of Head Start in the Philadelphia School District* (Washington, DC: U.S. Department of Health and Human Services, 1987).

5. Richard H. Price, Emory L. Cowen, Raymond P. Lorion, and Julia Ramos-McKay, eds., *Fourteen Ounces of Prevention: A Casebook for Practitioners* (Washington, DC: American Psychological Association, 1988).

6. Committee for Economic Development, *Children in Need: Investment Strategies for the Educationally Disadvantaged* (Washington, DC: Committee for Economic Development, 1987).

7. Arthur Jensen, "How Much Can We Boost IQ and Scholastic Achievement?" *Harvard Educational Review* 39 (Winter 1969): 1-123.

8. Asa Hilliard, "Commentary," in "Young Children Grow Up: The Effects of the Perry Preschool Program on Youths through Age 15," *Monographs of the High/ Scope Educational Research Foundation*, No. 7 (Ypsilanti, MI: High/Scope Educational Research Foundation, 1980), pp. 105-106.

9. This issue was debated by Lloyd G. Humphreys, "The Orwellian Difference Model," *American Psychologist* 39 (August 1984): 916, and by Edward Zigler, "Meeting the Critics on Their Own Terms," *American Psychologist* 39 (August 1984): 916-917.

10. Mediax Associates, *Accept My Profile: Perspectives for Head Start Profiles of Program Effects on Children*, HEW Contract No. 105-77-1006 (Westport, CT: Mediax Associates, 1980).

11. Regina Yando, Victoria Seitz, and Edward Zigler, *Intellectual and Personality Characteristics of Children: Social-class and Ethnic Group Differences* (Hillsdale, NJ: Lawrence Erlbaum, 1979).

12. Edward Zigler, "The Environmental Mystique: Training the Intellect versus Development of the Child," *Childhood Education* 46 (May 1970): 402-412.

13. Austin H. Riesen, "The Development of Visual Perception in Man and Chimpanzee," *Science* 106 (1947): 107-108; "Plasticity of Behavior: Psychological Aspects," in *Biological and Biochemical Bases of Behavior*, ed. H. F. Harlow and C. N. Woolsey (Madison: University of Wisconsin Press, 1958).

14. Donald O. Hebb, *The Organization of Behavior* (New York: Wiley, 1949).

15. J. McV. Hunt, *Intelligence and Experience* (New York: Ronald Press, 1961).

16. J. McV. Hunt, "Parent and Child Centers: Their Basis in the Behavioral and Educational Sciences," *American Journal of Orthopsychiatry* 41 (January 1971): 13-38.

17. Martin Deutsch and Cynthia P. Deutsch, *Report to the Office of the Commission of Education*, Unpublished Manuscript (1963).

18. Leon Eisenberg and C. Keith Conners, "The Effect of Head Start on the Developmental Process" (Paper presented at the Joseph P. Kennedy, Jr. Foundation Scientific Symposium on Mental Retardation, Boston, April 11, 1966).

19. Herman Spitz, *The Raising of Intelligence: A Selected History of Attempts to Raise Retarded Intelligence* (Hillsdale, NJ: Lawrence Erlbaum, 1986).

20. Edward Zigler, "The IQ Pendulum," a review of Herman Spitz, *The Raising of Intelligence, Readings* 3 (June 1988): 4-9.

21. J. Ronald Lally, Peter L. Mangione, and Alice S. Honig, "The Syracuse University Family Development Research Program: Long-range Impact of Early Intervention with Low-income Children and Their Families," in *Parent Education as Early Childhood Intervention: Emerging Directions in Theory, Research, and Practice*, ed. Douglas Powell (Norwood, NJ: Ablex Publishing, 1988), pp. 79-104. See also, Darlington et al., "Preschool Programs and Later Competence of Children from Low-income Families," and Berrueta-Clement et al., "Changed Lives."

22. Edward Zigler and Victoria Seitz, "Social Policy and Intelligence," in *Handbook of Human Intelligence*, ed. Robert Sternberg (New York: Cambridge University Press, 1982), pp. 586-641.

23. Benjamin S. Bloom, *Stability and Change in Human Characteristics* (New York: John Wiley, 1964).

24. Burton L. White, *The First Three Years of Life* (Englewood Cliffs, NJ: Prentice-Hall, 1975).

25. Ann M. Clarke and A. D. B. Clarke, *Early Experience: Myth and Evidence* (London: Open Books, 1976).

26. A. D. B. Clarke and Ann M. Clarke, "Prospects for Prevention and Amelioration of Mental Retardation: A Guest Editorial," *American Journal of Mental Deficiency* 81 (May 1977): 523-533.

27. For example, see Reuven Feuerstein, *Instrumental Enrichment: An Intervention Program for Cognitive Modifiability* (Baltimore, MD: University Park Press, 1980).

28. H. Carl Haywood and Theodore D. Wachs, "Intelligence, Cognition, and Individual Differences," in *Psychosocial Influences in Retarded Performance: Issues and Theories in Development*, Vol. 1, ed. Michael J. Begab, H. Carl Haywood, and Howard L. Garber (Baltimore, MD: University Park Press, 1981); Frances D. Horowitz and Lucile Y. Paden, "The Effectiveness of Environmental Intervention Programs," in *Review of Child Development Research*, Vol. 3, ed. Bettye M. Caldwell and Henry N. Ricciuti (Chicago: University of Chicago Press, 1973), pp. 331-402.

29. Zigler and Seitz, "Social Policy and Intelligence."

30. Sally Ryan, ed., *Longitudinal Evaluations*, in *A Report on Longitudinal Evaluations of Preschool Programs*, Vol. 1, DHEW Publication No. (OHD) 74-24 (Washington, DC: Office of Human Development, 1974); Urie Bronfenbrenner, *Is Early Intervention Effective?*, in *A Report on Longitudinal Evaluations of Preschool Programs*, Vol. 2, DHEW

Publication No. (OHD) 74-25 (Washington, DC: Office of Human Development, 1974).

31. Urie Bronfenbrenner, "Is Early Intervention Effective?" in *Handbook of Evaluation Research*, ed. Marcia Guttentag and Elmer L. Struening (Beverly Hills, CA: Sage Publications, 1975); Jeanette Valentine and Evan Stark, "The Social Context of Parent Involvement in Head Start," in *Project Head Start: A Legacy of the War on Poverty*, ed. Edward Zigler and Jeanette Valentine (New York: Free Press, 1979), pp. 291-313. See also the references cited in footnote 30.

32. Robert Rapoport, "Research and Action," in *Children, Youth, and Families: The Action-research Relationship*, ed. Robert Rapoport (Cambridge, MA: Cambridge University Press, 1985), pp. 1-25.

33. Arnold J. Sameroff, "Early Influences on Development: Fact or Fancy?" *Merrill-Palmer Quarterly* 21 (1975): 267-294; Arnold J. Sameroff and Michael J. Chandler, "Reproductive Risk and the Continuum of Caretaking Casualty," in *Review of Child Development Research*, Vol. 4, ed. Frances D. Horowitz (Chicago: University of Chicago Press, 1975), pp. 187-244.

34. Urie Bronfenbrenner, "Developmental Research, Public Policy, and the Ecology of Childhood," *Child Development* 45 (March 1974): 1-5; idem, *The Ecology of Human Development* (Cambridge, MA: Harvard University Press, 1979).

35. See Lally et al., "The Syracuse University Family Development Research Program"; Zigler and Seitz, "Social Policy and Intelligence."

36. Sharon L. Kagan, Douglas R. Powell, Bernice Weissbourd, and Edward Zigler, eds., *America's Family Support Programs* (New Haven, CT: Yale University Press, 1987).

37. Kirschner Associates, *A National Survey of the Impacts of Head Start Centers on Community Institutions* (Washington, DC: Office of Economic Opportunity, May, 1970), ERIC ED 045 195.

38. Edward Zigler and Penelope K. Trickett, "IQ, Social Competence and Evaluation of Early Childhood Intervention Programs," *American Psychologist* 33 (September 1978): 789-798.

39. Carol H. Weiss, "Improving the Linkage Between Social Research and Public Policy," in *Knowledge and Policy: The Uncertain Connection*, ed. Laurence E. Lynn, Jr., Study Project on Social Research and Development (Washington, DC: National Academy of Sciences, 1978).

40. Carol H. Weiss, "Introduction," in *Using Social Research in Public Policy Making*, ed. Carol H. Weiss (Lexington, MA: Lexington Books, 1977).

CHAPTER X

Regulating Early Childhood Programs:
Five Policy Issues

GWEN MORGAN

As Congress considered child day care legislation in 1989, the issues of regulatory standards created a divisive controversy. Veterans of the ten-year struggle in the 1970s over federal interagency day care requirements experienced déjà vu. One more time, different perspectives on federal standards split the support of the child care field for federal legislation, weakened the possibility of strong public support, and created confusion that undermined commitment to the ongoing process of improving standards.

In this chapter I describe the contexts for child day care standards and give basic information about types of standards, focusing primarily on day care centers. Five key policy issues are then discussed:

1. Are there wide gaps in regulatory coverage?
2. How diverse are the standards for child day care? How can we achieve more uniformity?
3. Are federal standards the answer?
4. Do standards have a segregating effect?
5. Can licensing requirements for qualifications ever be reconciled with teacher certification in public education so that pay equity is possible?

In this discussion, I assume that the terms "child day care," "early childhood education," and "child development programs" are roughly synonymous. Some policymakers believe that it is possible for a program to provide care and custody without education, but child day care providers since before the turn of the century have been describing their programs as meeting all aspects of children's developmental needs. A visitor would have difficulty distinguishing a nursery school, preschool, or day care center.

173

A second assumption is that all programs for young children are educational, in the sense that they contribute to children's learning. The education may be good or bad, but the possibility of a program that is custodial but not educational does not exist, even for infants. The term "education," however, should be distinguished from "schooling," a narrower aspect of education.

The Contexts of Regulating Early Childhood Programs

The regulation of early childhood programs occurs in three contexts to be discussed here: a policy context, a program context, and a legal context.

THE POLICY CONTEXT

Policy analysts in the field of child day care have learned what every day care director knows: you cannot fix just one thing. The National Day Care Study[1] pointed out three factors in day care economics that are so inextricably connected that to improve one is to make the others worse. The agonizing trade-offs among wages, staff/child ratios, and affordability have come to be known as the "trilemma." In the last few years, the trilemma issues have sharpened. Because of a labor shortage in many geographic areas, it is no longer possible to trade off wages. Staff turnover in child day care centers rose from 15 percent in 1977 to 41 percent in 1988.[2]

The operators of quality child care centers are facing a crisis that may destroy them. Turnover itself reduces quality, and even basic safety. Some centers are operating with a constant change of staff, and possibly without enough staff as jobs go unfilled. The number of staff, however, is partly determined by regulation. In states with high required staff/child ratios, centers cannot choose to increase wages by altering those ratios. In states with low required staff/child ratios, it is difficult for centers to raise their sights to a standard higher than that required because of the effect on price.

If wages are raised, which is inevitable if centers expect to find and retain staff, the number of parents who can afford to pay the out-of-pocket cost of child care will be dramatically reduced. During the 1970s, the income level at which parents could afford child care was thought to be 115 percent of the median income for a family of four. As costs have increased, the affordability point has already risen, and in the next few years will be well above the median income—depending on the state, probably at least 135 percent of the median income.

Today, even more than in the past, advocacy for standards out of the context of the trilemma does serious harm. The basic question about quality is not just how to define it or who should require it, but who will pay what share of the cost.

The Vermont Department of Social Services estimates that the state pays 30 percent of the true cost of basic licensed care when it purchases subsidized care from a center. Unsubsidized parents paying the market rate are paying centers about 70 percent of their true cost. Neither the state nor unsubsidized parents pays 100 percent of the full cost. The remaining costs are borne by the day care staff and other in-kind subsidies. The cost of quality care, according to the Department, would be still higher, even if parents paid 100 percent of the cost of basic licensed care.

If national policy is to mandate quality in Vermont and elsewhere, the federal government will have to assume a significant share of the cost of quality. Under the Family Support Act of 1988, it will be possible for the first time for many states to "buy in" to the existing system of child care at the market rate. However, the market rate is already artificially low so that parents can afford the price. It does not reflect the cost of meeting even the licensing requirements.

The proposed Act for Better Child Care Services did not offer significant budget support for affordability. The bill created important infrastructure action that is essential in the long run to make the day care system work. But the level of federal dollars proposed to help parents pay for child care never came close to having a significant impact on affordability.

Zigler suggests the total cost of a national child care system could be $100 billion per year.[3] The combined amount currently being spent annually by the federal government in all ways is about $6 billion; original versions of the Act for Better Child Care Services proposed an additional $2.8 billion. Even if parents in the future pay half the cost, and even if Zigler's estimate is high, there is no way that a federal commitment of a few billion dollars can solve the trilemma.

In the trilemma context, the federal government could have the biggest impact on quality (a) if its *regulatory* approach offered states money to employ an adequate number of trained inspectors, to staff citizen committees for revision of standards, and to supply information for the guidance of such committees; and (b) if its *funding* approach offered dollars that leveraged other money from local and state government and private partners, with the understanding that

federal funding standards are to be applied whenever the federal dollar
is spent and that the states must pay a rate for child care that covers the
cost of meeting its standards.

None of these elements has been clearly present in the discussion of
national policy on standards. Instead, there has been the same
confusion over what standards are, the same inappropriate comparing
of licensing standards with funding and accreditation standards, the
same turf issues between federal and state advocates and between
differently regulated systems, and the same aloofness from the crisis
faced by providers of care that characterized the destructive effort to
achieve national standards in the 1970s.

THE PROGRAM CONTEXT: WHAT DO WE REGULATE?

Care/education of children falls into two broad categories: care
within the family, and care in the community. Care within the family
has been called care by kith and kin. It consists of (a) care by one
parent at home, either because only one parent works or because two
working parents stagger their work hours; (b) care by another family
member or relative, either in the child's home or the relative's home;
(c) care by someone very close to the family who is providing the care
because of strong attachment to the child or parents.

Kith and kin have an irrational commitment to a child, a
commitment that money cannot buy and standards cannot affect.
Society does not use police power to license care within the family. If
a child is abused or neglected, government will intervene in the family
on behalf of the child. When care for a child is purchased by
government from a family member, fiscal regulation is appropriate to
make sure adequate care is actually provided. Even then we do not set
standards for the quality of parenting or grandparenting.

Care in the community is a broad category that includes all the
types of care/development services that parents choose when they
turn outside family resources for supplemental care, either because
they are working or because they are looking for educational services
for their child or both. These types of care include: (a) in-home care
(nannies, babysitters, au pairs, etc.); (b) family day care (usually six or
fewer children in the home of the caregiver); (c) group day care homes
(usually seven to twelve children, with two adults, in the home of the
caregiver; (d) centers (which include, separately or combined, part-
day preschool, Head Start, nursery school, before- and after-school
programs, full-day centers). Centers and homes can include infants,
preschool children, school-age children, and children with special
needs, either in the same program or in specialized programs.

No states regulate unsubsidized parents' use of in-home care. The in-home provider is an employee of the parent, and not an autonomous facility. Some kind of occupational license or credential would be appropriate, but is rare. Two states have standards for in-home care, which they use for subsidized care. Family day care is defined and regulated differently by each state. Most states provide basic licensing for family day care, but the definitions of what is covered vary. Private full-day centers are usually licensed, but part-day nursery programs may not be. Coverage by standards will vary not only by licensing definition, but also by auspices.

Three major funded systems of child care. The three major funded systems providing child care/development programs are (a) Head Start (about $1.2 billion in federal money annually); (b) public school related care/development programs (about $100,000 in state money annually); and (c) state social service programs of purchasing care and education by contract with privately licensed programs (an unknown amount of state and federal money, at least $1 billion annually). Turf issues, biases, and administrative fragmentation have led to a different regulatory approach for each major system. Even though it is possible that a high-quality program for four-year-olds operated by any of the three major systems would not be recognizably different to a visitor, the regulatory systems applied to them are still quite different.

Years ago, some states made a distinction between programs they thought were primarily educational and those they thought were primarily care. In states that made this distinction, only the care programs were considered suitable for licensing. The educational programs were viewed as the responsibility of the state department of education or the locally elected school officials. Few states followed through with standards and inspection and the lack of attention deteriorated into an exemption from coverage by any agency.

Most states today view care and education as inseparable. By 1962, when a federal mandate for state licensing was made in the amendments to the Social Security Act, knowledge of child development as a necessary aspect of all programs for young children had become widespread, and many states were applying the same standards for staffing and program in both part-day and full-day child development programs. There are still a few states that define licensing as covering only programs that do not define themselves as "primarily educational." In most states, however, that self-definition has been recognized to be an enormous loophole through which full-day programs can escape coverage by any regulatory agency. The twenty-one states that still do not license private nursery schools and preschools now usually define a licensable program in terms of the number of hours per day for a child in the program. Almost all states require a developmental program in all licensed centers.

Head Start is covered by its own centralized performance standards, a contractual form of fiscal regulation by its funding source. Head Start is also licensed if operated by a private agency such as a community action program, but is not usually licensed when operated by a public school. Early childhood programs in public schools are seldom licensed by states. Organized private school systems are generally not licensed, even when they provide full-day early childhood programs. Most states consider public and private schools the responsibility of the state department of education or the local school board. In many states, no standards specific to young children may have been developed or applied to public or private schools.

Private centers, family day care, and group homes are usually licensed by the state. Parents purchase care/education from this diverse network, as do the states. When subsidized, the funding includes federal Social Service Block Grant (Title XX) funds, state tax dollars, Welfare Reform dollars, and some mainstreaming of special needs children by the schools. Although some states have set up segregated programs with these funds, most states use them to "buy in" to the private network of programs also used by nonsubsidized parents. This system can be called the "purchase-of-service" network.

THE LEGAL CONTEXT

The term "regulation" is used in this chapter in a general way to mean any uniform quality control applied across defined programs. Regulation consists of three parts: (a) the establishment of standards, (b) the application of standards to programs, and (c) the use of various sanctions to make sure that programs meet the standards.[4] There are many forms of regulation. Each has different sanctions, and there are different legal relationships between the regulator and the regulated. Because of these differences in the way they are used, the standards themselves will necessarily be different.

The term "standards" is a broad one and is used to cover both ideals and requirements. "Rules and regulations" are official standards that must be met, usually in licensing. (The term "requirements" is a better one to use when discussing licensing in order to make clear their mandatory nature.)

Table 1 describes four tiers of standards. Four forms of regulation (licensing, building and fire safety, health, and zoning) are applied at the basic first tier. Each of these forms of regulation is discussed briefly here, after which I turn to a discussion of other types of standards shown in table 1: fiscal standards, accreditation standards, and model standards. I conclude this section with a brief reference to the issuing of staff credentials, which is another type of regulation.

TABLE 1

Four Tiers of Standards

Type of Standard	Applicable to	Established by	Examples
Licensing requirements	All private child care programs	State or local agency	All states license centers; most license family day care; a few cities and counties have been delegated authority to license
Fiscal standards	All programs using fund from the agency contracting for or running the service	Funding or operating agency	Head Start's performance standards; military child care standards; state funding standards
Accreditation standards	All who voluntarily seek accreditation	Professional organization; agency membership organization; public agency	NAEYC[1] standards; Child Welfare League standards; Missouri accreditation standards
Model standards	All seeking help in the standard setting process	Experts	Building codes from NFPA[2]; APHA[3]/AAP[4] child care health and safety standards

[1] National Association for the Education of Young Children

[2] National Fire Protection Association

[3] American Public Health Association

[4] American Academy of Pediatrics

Licensing requirements. Licensing has been described as the "administrative lifting of a legislative prohibition."[5] A licensing law first prohibits the service from being provided at all, the legislative body declaring that it is illegal for anyone to care for children. Then the law will go on to say that certain people, after all, can care for children if they apply for and are given permission (a license) by the authorized agency of government. The permission must be based on their compliance with standards written by the agency.

Child day care licensing is a well-established consumer protection program dating back a hundred years, the first state licensing law having been passed in Pennsylvania in 1885. There is currently no federal licensing for child care, and it is not likely that the Congress would pass a national licensing law. All states, however, have passed such laws.

A licensing law is sweeping in its use of governmental police powers. It cannot be passed or enforced without massive public support. Providers have constitutional rights to be treated fairly when government exercises such broad powers. Standards must be written by a participatory process with interest representation and public hearings. Unless there is public consensus on the standards themselves, it will be impossible to achieve compliance. Once the agency gets its standards written by this democratic process, each standard has the force of law. They are law-like specifications of rights that children and parents have when they use child day care in that state.

On the face of it, licensing is a powerful legal protection for children, yet its powers are limited. There are no pure rights in society. All rights clash with other rights and all regulatory policy involves trade-offs. Children's rights to timely protection may lose priority to adult rights to fair treatment. Some states need to improve the enforceability of their licensing laws, and licensing staff need better training in law enforcement.

Because the licensing requirements are mandatory and intended to be enforced, they must be perceived as reasonable and fair by providers and the general public in the state where they are written. Government is conducted with the consent of the governed. Unless providers are able and willing to meet requirements, parents willing and able to pay for them, and the general public willing to support the closing down of programs that continually operate out of compliance, licensing standards cannot be implemented. The standards-development process itself is an important avenue to building the necessary consensus for implementation.

Licensing agencies can and do raise the level of the requirements as the field of practice improves, but they cannot put people in jail for failure to achieve ideals. Licensing standards are therefore minimum standards, in the sense that operators must "at least" meet them. Programs can go beyond the licensing level, but must not fall below it. Since licensing sets a base of acceptable practice, it should be expected that all programs will meet the standards and that many programs will exceed them. In the 1970s, centers in almost every state were operating at better standards than required,[6] as one would expect. It is not known whether this continues to be the case during the current crisis of underfunding and labor shortage.

Other base line codes. Child care regulation is complex because a number of different laws may apply. In addition to licensing, states and localities apply other sets of standards that are adopted under laws other than the licensing laws. To secure compliance with these standards, which include building and fire safety codes, health and sanitation codes, and zoning ordinances, inspection of child care facilities is carried out by agencies other than the licensing agency.

Building safety codes were adopted under state laws designed to prevent the loss of property and life in fires and other building disasters. Many states now have uniform statewide building codes, but others permit localities to adopt their own building codes. Either way, the inspection is done locally by a building inspector attached to municipal government. Fire safety codes in some localities are separate requirements enforced by the local fire department, over and above the building code. Health and sanitation codes were adopted under state laws designed to prevent the spread of epidemic disease and other health hazards. They typically are applied to hospitals and restaurants as well as to child care and other facilities.

Zoning is regulation of land use by localities under permissive state legislation. This form of regulation is often a barrier to child care, especially family day care. Zoning ordinances may include child care as a permitted use in certain residential or business zones. They may add other local requirements that are inconsistent with state licensing requirements. A few states have amended their state permissive law to prevent local zoning from outlawing child care. For example, New York State has been suing localities that restrict child care on the grounds that it is not legal under one state law to countervail other state laws that have a clear intention to increase the supply of child care.

Because so many different codes apply, a standard missing in licensing may be present in one of the other codes. In order to judge the adequacy of state regulation, it would be necessary to search all these codes and their statutes. The base line regulatory system is a complicated and time-consuming one. Day care providers report that the most frustrating issue arises when one code requires something that another code prohibits. In large municipalities, there may be intolerable red tape for new providers in negotiating these four different bureaucracies. The solution lies in careful problem definition and amendment of the laws and codes in question, not in adding more regulation.

Fiscal standards. The term "fiscal standards" is used for standards associated with funding. It includes operating standards when the government runs a program, and also funding standards that are conditions for receiving a grant or contract. When the government operates or pays for child care/development programs a very different relationship exists in the application of standards. Rather than using police powers, the government has a contractual relationship with the provider of the service. Fiscal standards, or funding standards, are the rules that accompany the funds. When a public agency operates its own program, and pays for it, the relationship is even more direct. The standards adopted by the different branches of the military service are examples of operating standards for a government-run program. Head Start's performance guidelines are fiscal standards, established as part of the contractual relationship between the funding source and the Head Start grantee. The grantees are monitored to see whether they are meeting the expectations of the funding source. In a fiscal relationship, police powers are not needed, and constitutional due process rights of providers are not central. The funding source can make any specifications it wishes; and the provider is free to negotiate for more palatable provisions or to decide not to enter into the agreement.

The now defunct Federal Interagency Day Care Requirements (FIDCR) were fiscal requirements. The long and unsuccessful effort to revise these federal funding standards and to get them applied at least to Title XX day care by social service agencies in the states is beyond the scope of this chapter. It is important to point out, however, the lack of clarity in the debate. There was confusion among the advocates over the difference between fiscal standards and licensing requirements. Programs without any federal funds were fearful that the proposed new federal standards would apply to them, potentially doubling the fees they charged parents. It was common then, and again now, to compare "federal standards" (fiscal standards) with "state standards" (licensing requirements). These standards, created for different purposes, are not comparable.

Some states have their own funding standards, especially after the demise of federal standards. For example, in Massachusetts the staff/

child ratio required for licensing programs for four-year-old children is 1/10, but for child care purchased under contract the ratio is 1/7. In California, the state "bought out" its child care program from Title XX because the state preferred not to apply the federal standards. However, the state did not operate its child care without funding standards of its own. The licensing agency inspects all programs, public and private, for compliance with basic licensing requirements. The state department of education, which is the funding agency for social service as well as education dollars, applies a higher level of standard to programs receiving its funds.[7] North Carolina developed an elaborate number of different levels of licensing and funding standards, and has recently tried to simplify them in order to avoid segregating funded children in high-quality programs not affordable to the public.[8]

Even though they may have fiscal standards, as well as licensing requirements, few states have provided adequate funds to cover the costs of meeting fiscal standards. In fact, they may not provide adequate funds to enable funded programs to meet basic licensing requirements.

Accreditation standards. A level of standard that is potentially higher than fiscal standards would be standards for accreditation. The best-known accreditation in the child day care field is the program established by the National Association for the Education of Young Children (NAEYC). The National Academy created by NAEYC accredited close to 1000 centers in its first three years. Centers wishing to be known as high-quality programs voluntarily apply for accreditation to the National Academy of Early Childhood Programs. A self-study process is conducted to make sure that the center meets the standards established for accreditation. At a time determined by the center, material is submitted to the national organization and a validator then visits the program to verify that it is ready to be accredited. Accreditation is granted by a national panel, based on information submitted by the center and by the validator. This process is regulatory, but it is completely private and voluntary. Since programs decide for themselves whether to participate, there is no coercion. If funding sources begin to require accreditation, their requirement may affect the voluntary aspects of accreditation in subtle ways, but accreditation will still remain quite different from the application of performance standards in a contract or from the use of police powers for licensing. Accreditation is valuable in identifying model high-quality programs. It helps the public to distinguish between programs that have met high standards and those programs that simply have a legal permission to exist. When accreditation is visible to parents and the community, programs that are merely licensed cannot wave their licenses as if they were banners of quality.

Model standards. Still a higher level of standard is possible in model standards developed by experts. These standards for good practice are based on the most recent knowledge available. Such standards affect the field of practice and in turn will affect the feasibility of what can be required through licensing. Such standards may also be used by groups that are writing regulatory standards.

Model standards have been written and discussed as guidance material at the national level for a century. A major role of the U. S. Children's Bureau when it was created in 1911 was to establish high standards to describe what programs should be like in order to contrast them with the reality of conditions that existed.[9] Model standards could be used for many purposes—as advice to practitioners, as technical assistance to state and local standard-setting bodies, or as conditions for funding.

Examples of one type of national model standard are the recommended building codes published by national organizations for the guidance of state building code writers and inspectors. These codes might be adopted in their entirety as a state or local building code, or might serve as a basis for a revised version of a code.

Another example of a model standard was *Guides for Day Care Licensing*, published in 1972 by the Department of Health, Education, and Welfare.[10] Experts were assembled to write material that included model building code provisions for child care, model health provisions for child care, model licensing codes, model zoning ordinances and policies, model administrative guidelines for licensing agencies, and a model licensing statute. This material, accompanied by small grants, was effective in improving regulatory practice in the states.

A final example of model standards has come from a joint project of the American Public Health Association and the American Academy of Pediatrics. Ten technical panels have written model health and safety standards, broadly defined, that will assist regulatory organizations, standards-writing groups, and the field of practice to access the most recent knowledge of importance to child care in a number of different technical fields. The standards were to be distributed for widespread public review in 1990.

Issuing of staff credentials. Distinguished from the above types of standards, staff credentials—a form of regulation—focus on individuals rather than on settings or facilities. The regulation of staff qualifications is very different in each of the three early childhood systems. In public schools, teachers are certified, most often by state authorities, after having acquired at least a B. A. degree. Head Start has been emphasizing the Child Development Associate credential, a competency-based credential that could be considered equivalent to about one year of college, assuming comparable quality. The purchase-of-service system's staffing qualifications are set within facility licensing. The term "facility" means the building and outdoor space, equipment and supplies, staff, and activities.

Five Major Regulatory Issues

I turn now to a discussion of the five policy questions regarding regulation that were posed at the beginning of this chapter.

ARE THERE GAPS IN REGULATORY COVERAGE?

Even though early childhood programs share the same concepts of high quality regardless of auspices, many of these programs are not covered by any regulatory standards, and those that are covered may not meet comparable standards.

Coverage by licensing. Twenty-one states do not license private part-day nursery schools/preschools. In four of these states (Arkansas, New York, Pennsylvania, and West Virginia), the state department of education does have standards and does offer some form of regulation to part-day programs, but the regulation is voluntary. Illinois exempts Montessori programs.

In 1987, twelve states exempted church-run child care programs from licensing. Ten states now have that exemption (Alabama, Florida, Illinois, Indiana, Maryland, Missouri, New Jersey, North Carolina, South Carolina, Virginia). New Jersey has already removed the exemption, which now applies only to centers started before 1984. South Carolina registers church-run programs and requires them to meet fire, building safety, and health codes even though they are exempt from licensing requirements. Illinois exempts only church-run programs that have no children under the age of three. In some of these states (e.g., North Carolina), most churches voluntarily apply for and receive licenses. There are fiscal incentives. If programs wish to serve subsidized children, then fiscal regulation would apply.

When private school systems offer child development/care programs as one level of a system that includes kindergarten and elementary grades, they are not usually regulated through licensing, the rationale being that they are the responsibility of local school boards or the state department of education. In practice, however, these programs may be virtually exempt from any standards, since no appropriate standards have been established and there is no inspection system. Private schools have been expanding early childhood programs rapidly and their de facto exemption from regulation is a large gap in regulatory coverage.

Coverage of funded programs. Centers subsidized by state social service agencies are also licensed. An unknown number of states apply additional funding standards, but it is clear that at least licensing standards apply.

Public schools are seldom covered by licensing. When public school early childhood programs are directly funded by the state department of education through grants or contracting, there are often fiscal standards. If, on the other hand, public schools pay for their child development/care programs through local tax dollars or are reimbursed by a formula allocation, there are no specific standards other than those of the general codes applied to schools.[11] These school codes were developed for school-age children and do not include provisions for younger children. For example, the school codes are not adequate with respect to group size, staff/child ratios, location of bathrooms, availability of fresh water in the classroom, and fire safety. In public schools, teachers may not have special credentials that qualify them for work in preschool child care programs. For example, they may not have had practice with the age group, or course work in child development.

Head Start has its own performance standards. This federally controlled system resists the application of other fiscal standards. When Head Start is run by a public school, no other standards apply. When run by private agencies, Head Start is also covered by state licensing.

Gaps in center coverage. Since public and private schools fall within the domain of the education bureaucracy rather than the health and social service agencies that usually license, it is important to look across both systems to get a picture of which programs are covered by any standards. In looking at both systems we find the following:

1. In twenty states, no standards other than school codes are applied to any public or private school systems that operate child development programs as part of their education system.

2. In twelve states, the licensing agency says it licenses public

school full-day programs, and eight of these also license part-day programs.

3. Fourteen states license full-day programs in private school systems, and eleven of these also license part-day programs in private schools.

4. Twenty-six states are funding early childhood programs in schools, usually through the state department of education. In eighteen of these states, the department of education applies standards but only to the funded programs. Some states have the flexibility to offer funds to nonschool agencies, in which case licensing standards would apply. State-funded programs in schools in four of the twenty-six states (Colorado, Maine, Minnesota, Vermont) may be covered by licensing.

At present, information about standards applied to schools is not completely reliable, since even the licensing offices are not clear about what they cover.[12]

HOW DIVERSE ARE THE STANDARDS FOR CHILD DAY CARE?

The most striking fact about state regulation of child day care is the variability of standards from one state to the next.[13] Staff/child ratios for infant care, for example, vary from 1/3 in Maryland to 1/8 in Louisiana and South Carolina and 1/12 in Idaho. The Idaho ratio was a legislative prohibition set in 1987 to prohibit any ratios greater than 1/12.

On the positive side, there is a trend toward improving staff/infant ratios. Most states do not like to find their names at the bottom of the list on an issue of such importance. As comparative information on what other states are doing becomes available, and as knowledge of the effects of ratios on infant development is increased, even the poorest states prefer to be somewhere in the middle. Mississippi, a state with very limited resources, valiantly maintains staff/infant ratios at 1/5. Thirty-one states now have ratios of 1/4 or better. Despite the overall improvement in staff/infant ratios, two states (Delaware and Tennessee) recently increased their ratios to 1/7.

There is also dramatic variability in the state qualifications for staff, ranging from no training to substantial college preparation. Five states (Idaho, Michigan, Missouri, Mississippi, and South Carolina) have no preservice or in-service training requirement for teachers. In 1987, that number was seven. Two of these states (Idaho and Mississippi) also have no training requirements for directors of child day programs. Fourteen states, including the above five, either have no training requirement or would permit experience to substitute for an educational requirement. In 1987, that number was sixteen.

Possibly because of increasing recognition of the problem of diversity in standards, states appear to be revising state requirements more frequently. Half of the states have center regulations dated more recently than January 1, 1987, and at least fifteen states have rewritten their center requirements since January 1, 1988.

It is not easy to change requirements. Operators of child care programs, faced with crisis, are fearful of any change. Their budgetary strategy is based on current standards. Changes in the requirements are a threat to survival. If standards were simply imposed on the field of practice, without a participatory process, the natural resistance would mobilize parents, the media, and the general public. The legislature would respond by weakening or abolishing the regulatory law.

Change is possible, however, and is taking place, always with the support of existing providers of all types. It does not work for one faction to try to win out over another in the regulatory process. The traditional process of interest representation means that committees are formed of parents, different types of providers, and experts. Initial disagreement is worked out within this group and consensus reached so that they will defend the adoption of new standards and their enforcement. The standards then come before the public for a hearing process. Real regulatory change is possible when consensus can be reached.

The success of state licensing is judged not just on how high the standards are, but on the effectiveness of their implementation. A state with high standards but with many programs that do not meet them is a failure. The goal for licensing is full implementation of standards, strong public support, and a dynamic process for raising the standards as the field of practice improves.

There is a chicken-and-egg aspect to the achievement of public support for standards. A state can write high standards when the quality of its programs is good and when the general public understands and supports quality. Why one state will have a strong climate of support and a neighboring state will not is a mystery. It probably relates to the degree of leadership coming from its academic institutions, to the resources available to parents and the state to pay the cost of quality, to the nonregulatory strategies used by the state to achieve quality, and to the history of its early childhood programs. Advocates and the licensing agency in Idaho obviously have a much more difficult task than they would have in Maryland.

ARE FEDERAL STANDARDS THE ANSWER?

Before discussing federal standards it is important to differentiate between types of standards the federal government might establish and to identify the federal interest in standards. During the debates over federal standards in connection with proposed legislation in 1989, two quite different rationales for federal interest were discussed. Because the rationales are different, the standards would be different. Whether the two rationales could result in a single set of federal standards is a further question.

The first rationale is a federal interest in how federal tax dollars are spent. A number of advocates have expressed the view that it is unthinkable to spend federal tax dollars on programs with a 12/1 staff/infant ratio, for example. That rationale points in the direction of funding standards, which the federal government could reestablish. Ideally, funding standards would cover any program using any direct federal dollars and would be accompanied by a requirement that the payment for the child care cover the cost of meeting the standards.

With this rationale, there would be no difficulty (other than political) in setting a standard well above the licensing level in the states. However, it would be undermining to the states with higher licensing and funding requirements if the federal government set its funding standard lower than the states' licensing requirements. If the federal government is going to set funding standards, it would be better to offer leadership to achieve high quality, and to insist that resources be committed to meet the cost. Federal funding standards, like state funding standards, are added on top of licensing. Progams would be required by state law to meet licensing requirements, and if federally funded, would also meet the higher standard.

A second rationale, however, reflects a national concern for all our children. Should not the federal government protect children against harmful conditions and establish more uniform quality of programs across all the states? This rationale points in the direction of federal intervention in all programs, regardless of federal financial participation. This suggests some intervention into the licensing of programs paid for by parents. One idea that has been promoted is for the federal government to set a level of quality that states must enforce in their licensing. The feasible level would probably be somewhere near the median of the states. One version of the Act for Better Child Care Services actually wrote in language requiring the adoption of the U. S. Army child care standards. Army standards are higher than those in the lowest-level states, but not as high as those in the higher-level states.

The problem with this strategy is that setting a median as a national standard is not likely to provide the leadership for improved quality that most advocates would like to see. It will not build consensus, since it will be opposed by advocates in states with lower standards as well as those in states with higher standards. This level of standard would be controversial as a licensing standard, and it would be inappropriate as a funding standard in many states. Even if the federal government attempted to set a floor for licensing requirements, there would probably be little effect on the primary target, i.e., the states with lowest requirements for licensing. Unless there is citizen support within the state for the enforcement of standards and unless providers are able and willing to comply, the strategy will not be effective. It could even undermine the potential for internal consensus building within the state because it would promote the idea among advocates, already poorly informed, that federal standards are superior and that state licensing processes are no longer important.

Another way to achieve the federal interest in greater uniformity would be to offer leadership to the states. For this strategy, the federal government would set high standards for the guidance of the states, rather than compromising its standards to some median level. The federal government would be inspiring the states to further improvements both in their funding and their licensing standards. It would be able to stay ahead of the dynamic of change that goes on in states, rather than lagging behind the timetable of change.

This strategy would entail the following elements: (a) federal model standards set every five years by a task force of experts, providers, and parents representing different geographic areas, economic levels, and ethnic groups; (b) federal technical assistance to states (data on what other states are doing; research findings on regulatable characteristics of child care); (c) federal funds to states for employing and training licensing inspectors; and (d) federal requirement of and funds for a citizen review of licensing requirements at least every five years, with specified composition of the review group. With this strategy, there would be federal standards that govern the composition of the review group and of the process for citizen review of standards. Federal standards for qualifications of licensors and for case loads would accompany federal funds for more effective licensing.

It is difficult to reach consensus on standards because everyone is highly influenced by the context of the state where he or she lives. Whenever national standards are suggested, initial support for them will emerge only if they are close to the standards each person knows best and feels comfortable with. In those states with a lower standard for licensing or for funding, providers will fear they will not survive since they are already facing a crisis at the lower standard. In states that have achieved a higher standard for licensing or for funding, providers will feel insulted that their national government is undermining the quality they worked so hard to achieve.

Consensus is impossible nationally unless there is clarity about what kind of standard is being discussed: licensing, funding, accreditation, or a model standard. If the goals are confused, and if the same standards are used for different purposes, the resulting controversy seriously weakens the standards-developing process already in place in the states.

DO STANDARDS HAVE A SEGREGATING EFFECT?

If our ultimate goal is to universalize quality child care/development programs, we do not want to prevent providers from accepting a socioeconomic mix of children. As currently structured, providers can accept poor children, who are subsidized, and middle-class children, whose parents can afford the price, but not children in blue collar families, who are caught in the middle where they are not eligible for public subsidy and not able to pay the cost of quality.

At present, poor families receive higher-quality child care services than working-class families because subsidized programs meet higher standards, but the programs are often segregated. Working-class families, not eligible for subsidy because of dual incomes but not able to pay the cost of quality, are receiving the lowest-quality service.[14] Upper middle-class parents receive higher-quality service and are empowered by wider choices because they can afford to pay the cost.

Equity and access are issues that cannot be solved without attention to all three aspects of the trilemma. However, it is important for these issues to be raised in any discussion of quality or standards. If the state's vendor/voucher subsidy for welfare reform meets only licensing requirements, while Title XX programs funded under contract with state or federal dollars meet funding standards, the different fiscal standard appears to be inequitable for the vendor/vouchered children. On the other hand, it may be inequitable to deny the poor access to programs that serve working-class families, thus forcing them into a segregated situation that may affect their self-esteem and will deny them the opportunity to increase their income.

CAN LICENSING REQUIREMENTS AND TEACHER CERTIFICATION BE RECONCILED TO MAKE PAY EQUITY POSSIBLE?

For the past twenty-five years, the public schools system and the network of early childhood programs have been like two rapid trains on a collision course on converging tracks. The public schools have been committed to preservice certification of teachers whose preparation might or might not include child development courses or experiences with preschool children, who are expected to take full responsibility for a much larger group of children than is the case in early childhood programs, and whose initial salary would be significantly greater than that of a teacher in an early childhood program. The early childhood field, on the other hand, has been committed to low staff/child ratios, small groups, specialized early childhood knowledge, and a team teaching approach.

The early childhood constituencies idealized that when the two trains converged, both the public schools and the child care programs would have developmentally appropriate education for children, small groups, low teacher/pupil ratios, and high salaries. However, as early childhood/care programs expand in public education, the public schools are encountering the same trilemma issues that directors struggle with in the purchase-of-service system. If standards assure high staff/child ratios, schools will have difficulty paying a dramatically higher per pupil rate for young children than is customary for kindergarten. There is also the problem of where to find the teachers in a tight labor market. All the colleges in the United States are not producing enough graduates to fill even a fraction of the current need, let alone any expansion.[15]

The professionalization of early childhood teaching has therefore been developing very differently in the three major systems delivering child care/development programs. The public education system emphasizes at least a B.A. degree for teachers, preemployment certification, and relatively static roles. Head Start has put major emphasis on the Child Development Associate as a static qualification. In the long run, Head Start may also have a commitment to a mix of staffing that includes some Associates in Arts (A.A.) and some professionals with the B.A. degree. The purchase-of-service network has emphasized a mix of staffing with emphasis on early childhood specialized education and experience.

There appear to be alternative strategies for dealing with the cost and labor issues. One strategy, more compatible with the public school model, would employ certified teachers for part of the day, during which they would teach but not care for children. The rest of the day (if covered) would employ less qualified staff who are permitted to care for children but not to teach. This model divides care from education, a division which the early childhood field considers false and educationally harmful. It could result in exploiting the child care staff at low wages. This model might be called a "static" model of professionalization because it does not encourage staff mobility, and holds teachers hostage to permanent tiered roles.

The model emerging in the purchase-of-service network might be called the "dynamic" or "career ladder" approach. This model envisions a number of different identified roles, such as teacher aide, assistant teacher, associate teacher, lead teacher, supervising teacher, program director, and executive director. Educational and experience qualifications would increase for each progressive role. As their professional qualifications increase through education, staff would have access to increased pay in the same role and to promotion to higher-paying roles.

The career ladder approach is finding its way into the field of practice through center personnel policies and union contracts. In regulation, an embryonic career ladder approach is emerging in certain states, where there are differentiated roles and qualifications as well as ongoing training requirements. All states have their own different names for the roles they identify. They often use the word "teacher" to describe the person in charge of a group of children, even though that term causes confusion because qualifications of teachers and staff/child ratios in early childhood programs differ from those in public schools.

Twelve states now have a concept in their licensing of two levels of teachers. At least one more qualified teacher is required in each center, and that teacher might be called a head teacher, lead teacher, chief caregiver, specialist, and the like. (These states are Connecticut, Massachusetts, North Dakota, New Hampshire, New Jersey, New York, Oregon, Pennsylvania, Rhode Island, South Dakota, Vermont, and Wisconsin.) This requirement for a more qualified teacher should not be confused with the requirements for the teacher in charge of a classroom. Often there are not rigid specifications for the role this more qualified person would play; the requirement simply assures that there is a role model of at least one more experienced and educated teacher in a center as an aspect of quality. Some states require centers to have a second of these more qualified teachers if their enrollment exceeds a certain number.

Other states have not yet developed the "career ladder" in their licensing. One older model in some states was to have a director qualified in early childhood education who would supervise and train all staff. The emphasis for directors was on programmatic competence rather than on administrative competence. Today, most states have added the programmatic competence to all staff qualifications and a few are beginning to require some additional training in administration for directors. The director's role is clearly distinguished from that of the lead teachers (by whatever name) and is part of the career ladder. Most states require directors to meet some educational requirements and to have substantial experience. Seven states require additional college courses in early childhood education and six others require additional courses in day care administration or management. Those states without specific director requirements usually have a requirement that directors meet the same educational qualifications as lead teachers or teachers, and/or they may require course work.

In Massachusetts, the licensing agency is now certifying staff as well as licensing facilities. Child care staff apply for their license, which is issued to the individual. The license specifies what role the individual is qualified to fill: teacher, lead teacher, director 1, or director 2. The development of a credential to the individual is likely to accompany more specific educational and experience requirements and ongoing training requirements in other states in the future. It becomes too cumbersome for the licensor to check staff qualifications on licensing visits to programs. It makes sense to centralize and computerize the licensing of staff, separating this work from the work of the inspector who licenses the facility. The granting of a credential to staff will also enhance the career ladder approach to professionalization. Required training can be used to document qualification to move to another level, and the license can be upgraded.

It will obviously be very confusing to try to make the system more coherent nationally if the states continue to use their own terminology. In the long run, the field needs a common terminology but it would be a mistake to develop it before there is full understanding of the issues across the different systems. Without necessarily changing the terminology, the states with two levels of teachers can begin to equate their "lead teacher" (by whatever name known) as the role most likely to be equivalent to a public school teacher.

Public schools are also beginning to adopt other roles, such as Associate Teachers. This may enable them to employ lead teachers from the purchase-of-service system who have the Associate in Arts degree, the Child Development Associate credential, or meet other state qualifications for lead teachers. However, the concept of ongoing training and upward mobility of role is important in this situation too, in order to avoid a static dead-ended pay and status differentiation.

Recommendations

From what has been said thus far, it appears that important improvements need to be made in our child care systems, and that regulatory policy is necessary, but not sufficient, to address these issues. Advocates need a broader perspective, in particular on the interrelation of regulatory issues and the affordability issue. They need sophistication on the different forms of regulation so that they do not inadvertently undermine licensing in their efforts to improve quality. And they need some skills in consensus building rather than dividing the constituency that must support regulatory change.

In that context, I propose the following recommendations for consideration.

Coverage. There should be state licensing of all full-day and part-day private centers without exemptions. The outmoded concept of exempting programs with a primarily educational purpose should be abandoned in the few remaining states that have it.

When they operate preschools of child care, public schools should be inspected and governed by standards that are no less stringent than those applied to private programs through licensing. In most states, the regulation of public schools will be the responsibility of the state department of education. They should develop their standards in cooperation with the licensing agency.

Part of the development of standards must be the revision of teacher certification requirements to provide for an appropriate certificate for teachers of nursery school through grade three.

States need to decide what staff is to inspect schools to determine compliance and to assure that the state department of education is adequately staffed to cover the increased work.

It is important to address the gap in coverage of private elementary school systems.

Facilitation. State zoning laws should permit child care centers and family day care in any zone, regardless of whether operated by schools or private agencies.

Coordination of inspections by health, building safety, and licensing agencies should be required, if necessary by amending all three statutes to require such coordination.

The federal government should offer technical assistance and technology transfer to help states make their regulatory systems more facilitative.

Federal role. The federal government should play a strong and continuous leadership role in the development of standards. Federally developed material should include: high model standards, technical assistance to states, comparative data on state licensing requirements, information on efforts to make standards consistent across schools and licensing, and research findings that connect regulatable characteristics with effects on children.

Federal funds should be distributed to states for improved licensing, inspection, and for development of standards.

Staffing. The licensing agency should identify differentiated roles or levels in the licensed system which could include aides, assistant teachers, associate teachers, teachers, lead teachers, program directors, and directors, and establish qualifications for the different levels of roles. Licensing of individuals as well as facilities should be considered.

State funding sources and private programs should establish the principle that a lead teacher (by whatever name) in the purchase-of-service system should be paid comparable salary to a teacher in the public school system when equally qualified.

The state department of education should identify roles in public education that could include aides, associate teachers, provisional teachers, teachers, mentor teachers, program directors, and principals (who should meet some child development educational requirements). These roles and qualifications will not be the same as those in the other two systems (Head Start and the purchase-of-service system), but the bridging roles should be identified, and in-service training opportunities should be available to help make transitions.

Head Start should add a second level of teacher qualifications to its performance standards, along with its requirement for a Child Development Associate in each classroom.

Colleges should train directors in administration, and include in the training the designing of reward systems in which increased salaries are based on role progression, longevity, and increased education.

Trilemma. States should pay the full cost of quality in parent-chosen programs under Welfare Reform, going beyond the market rate to allow salaries to increase.

When 25 percent or fewer children are subsidized, states should not apply funding standards over and above licensing.

States should establish a governmental rate-setting process that pays the cost of meeting standards.

Beyond regulation. States and the private sector should promote voluntary accreditation of centers to get some visible models of quality in schools, Head Start, and the purchase-of-service network.

States and the private sector should offer consumer education to parents through resource and referral services.

States should offer more staff training and relate it to qualifications for roles.

States and local groups should bring together the early childhood staff who work in schools, Head Start, and the purchase-of-service network for conferences, joint training, and work to improve transitions for children.

Concluding Statement

Standards are important for programs for young children, and advocates need to develop the sophistication to participate in the ongoing development of licensing, fiscal regulation, and accreditation. Standards, however, do not equal quality. Licensing requirements by themselves are necessary, but not sufficient to the quest for quality. Sometimes the effort to regulate can even reduce quality, as, for example, in the case where a state tries to regulate the curriculum in early childhood programs. The right question to ask is not "How high are the standards?" but rather "How effective is the implementation of the standards?" and "What is the appropriate mix of regulatory and nonregulatory actions to achieve quality?"

FOOTNOTES

1. Richard Ruopp, Jeffrey Travers, Fred Glantz, and Craig Coelen, *Children at the Center: Final Results of the National Day Care Study* (Cambridge, MA: Abt Associates, 1978).

2. Marcy Whitebook, Carollee Howes, and Deborah Phillips, *Who Cares? Child Care Teachers and the Quality of Care in America* (Oakland, CA: Child Care Employee Project, 1990).

3. Edward Zigler, *Schools of the Twenty-first Century* (New York: Yale University, Bush Center, 1988).

4. Norris E. Class, "Safeguarding Day Care through Regulating Programs: The Need for a Multiple Approach" (Paper presented at the Annual Meeting of NAEYC, Seattle, 1969).

5. Ernest Freund, as quoted in Class, "Safeguarding Day Care through Regulating Programs."

6. Craig Coelen, *Day Care Centers in the United States* (Cambridge, MA: Abt Associates, 1978).

7. Anne Mitchell, Michelle Seligson, and Fern Marx, *Early Childhood Programs and the Public Schools: Between Promise and Practice* (Dover, MA: Auburn House, 1989).

8. Gwen Morgan, *The National State of Child Care Regulation, 1986* (Watertown, MA: Work/Family Directions, 1987).

9. Katherine B. Oettinger, "Introduction" in *It's Your Children's Bureau*, Children's Bureau Publication #357, rev. ed. (Washington, DC: Children's Bureau, 1964).

10. U.S. Department of Health, Education, and Welfare, *Guides for Day Care Licensing* (Washington, DC: U.S. Department of Health, Education, and Welfare, 1972).

11. Mitchell, Seligson, and Marx, *Early Childhood Programs and the Public Schools*.

12. Gwen Morgan, *The National State of Child Care Regulation, 1989*, in preparation; Mitchell, Seligson, and Marx, *Early Childhood Programs and the Public Schools*.

13. Morgan, *The National State of Child Care Regulation, 1986*; idem, *The National State of Child Care Regulation, 1989*.

14. Whitebook, Howes, and Phillips, *Report of the National Child Care Staffing Study*.

15. Joan Costley, "Testimony for the National Association of State Boards of Education" (Boston, MA: Wheelock College, 1988).

CHAPTER XI

Equity, Access, and Segregation

ASA G. HILLIARD III

At a theoretical level few educators would argue against the idea that there should be equity of access to an excellent education for all children in the United States. But the history of education in America would lead us to another conclusion about the importance of the equity goal to public policymakers. In fact, no provision at all was made for the education of young children when the nation was founded; education was a private affair. Aside from the beginning of public schools in the northeastern United States, on a small scale, free public education for the masses of American children was something that did not happen until after the Civil War.[1] The education of young children takes place in a general social context and within actions and strategies in pursuit of the educational functions of that social order.

From that time (the Civil War) up to this very day, there has been a real struggle between those who wish to provide a free public education for all children and those who do not. Moreover, there has also been a struggle between those who wish to provide an education that is both free and excellent for all children and those who would be satisfied with an education that provides "minimum competency" training for the masses.[2] It is important to keep these things in mind since they help explain the slow pace of educational reform and the difficulty of obtaining results that would enable us to take our place as educational leaders of the industrial world, as well as economic and military leaders.

Even a cursory observation of American schools will reveal vast inequities in treatment among social and racial groups of children. While a good deal of publicity is given to differences in academic achievement by race and social class, little adequate publicity is given to the differential treatment that children receive. This omission is particularly troubling because, predictably, differences in treatment variables dramatically affect differences in outcome variables, helping to explain race and class differences.

Class segregation permeates American schools. At the outset, segregation exists between children who go to private schools and children who go to public schools. Once in school, children are grouped in semihomogeneous income categories, a practice which effectively separates children by both race and income. In addition, within public schools there are academic tracks that are associated with race and class.[3] Yet, there is still another level of segregation that occurs through the special education programs. Populations in the special education programs, whether gifted or retarded, appear to be divided by class and race as well.[4] Therefore, private schools, selective public schools, differentiated teaching within regular schools and even within regular classes,[5] and special education placement all are associated with both race and class, as are treatment differences that result in inequity between and among groups. Selective public schools, such as magnet schools for the gifted and talented, are like elite private schools. They are a form of segregation that is not justified by pedagogical necessity so much as by political demands of influential parents and communities.

Earlier in the nation's history the initial period of educational neglect of all children[6] was correlated with a type of informal miseducation associated with slavery and colonization, education associated with the exploitation of immigrant and migrant populations, and later legal segregation followed by racism in education. All these things had a major structuring impact on the initial informal education system and the later formal education system. For example, miseducation strategies included the explicit and implicit teaching of white supremacy and superiority in textbooks and in audio-visual media.[7] Some of these strategies were intentional and were developed systematically.[8] These practices were supported by a pseudoscience of mental measurement, and by sorting, placement, and treatment based upon that pseudoscience.[9] Miseducation also occurred due to omission of educational materials that would provide a racially and ethnically balanced view of the human experience. Texts, library holdings, and audiovisual media provided little if anything to illuminate the important part that minority cultural groups have played in all facets of human history, ancient and modern. In other words, for many years American education was designed systematically to be inequitable, to deny access to education to large segments of the population.[10] Legal challenges to inequitable education systems have resulted in the removal of the legal basis for inequitable treatment. Some examples of these are *Brown vs. Board of Education of Topeka* outlawing legal segregation of the races in schools, *Larry P. vs. Wilson Riles* on the misuse of IQ testing, and the Public Law 94-142 requirement that education be provided for all students in the least restricted environment. However, equity of access to educational opportunity is still very difficult to achieve.

The structures evolved during the long period of inequity still determine the direction of school practices. They rule our system. Indeed, they have the greatest impact on our very large systems, and certainly in the largest school systems that serve the greatest numbers of minority students.[11]

A structure may be an *idea* that drives practice such as thinking about "intelligence," "readiness," and "cultural deprivation." It may be an *organizational system*. It may be an "architectural form." It may be an "economic relationship." It may be a "political relationship." A structure may be "definitions" that are widely accepted and the "assumptions" that go with them. Structures produce a momentum. Structures sustain practice over time, even when the outcomes of such practice are not beneficial and may even be harmful. Therefore, we must look closely at structures to understand equity issues.

Structures of Inequity in the Education of Young Child

A precision analysis of the systems within which young children are educated will reveal many structures that are highly likely to lead to inequitable outcomes among classes and races in the nation.

BELIEF AND IDEOLOGY

Among the many beliefs and ideas held by educators and even by the general public are several that reinforce inequity. First, the question of the intellectual capacity of children has taken on central importance in American education. Educators and psychologists have operated as if one of the most important items of information needed for the design of effective education is information about children's intellectual capacities. An entire mental measurement movement and industry has arisen in response to this demand.[12] The way we have thought about the capacities of children in the United States has led us to design educational systems based upon the expectation that, if children can be divided into capacity groups, they are likely to remain in these capacity groups on a permanent basis, and that special types of pedagogical treatment are appropriate for each group. These ideas and remedies do *not* grow out of empirical work on problem solving in education. They are weak theories at best.[13]

The commitment of educators in this nation to the idea that the capacity question is a vital pedagogical question explaining low performance of many children is a clear example of a structural problem. Only in the last decade and a half have large numbers of educators come to verbalize a commitment to the idea that "all children can learn." It is interesting that the particular statement should become a cliché. It implies, of course, a challenge to a prior belief that many children could not learn. The very fact that it is repeated more frequently suggests that the view is not yet widespread or held with confidence. The interesting thing about the "all children can learn" cliché is that it really does not imply a belief that all children can learn well enough to meet certain *criterion levels of excellent performance*. In a way it is half a sentence. "All children can learn" does not tell us how much or what. It would be quite a different statement to say "all children can learn at demanding academic levels." Yet there is little in our practice or in professional writings to suggest that this latter belief is widely held. The consequence of holding any belief is that it will have a definite impact on practice.

Associated with beliefs about differential mental capacities among individuals and groups is the belief in certain ideas associated with culture and civilization. Until recently cultures and civilizations tended to be ranked in the minds of many people, including educators. In fact, one of the names or labels given to children of certain poor racial groups was "culturally deprived." If educators hold such ideas, once again we would expect that their practices would be influenced. For example, the ideology of IQ drives decisions about the structure of special education today.[14] The goals of public education, even in an era of "school reform," are mainly about "minimum competencies," reflecting a very low estimate of capabilities of the masses of Americans.[15]

Another example is the goal of acculturation and assimilation of Africans, Hispanics, Indians, Asians, and non-western Europeans into "American" culture. It reflects a failure to appreciate the value of diversity and the reality and the meaning of culture to groups. There can be one nation with cultural democracy. Culture is the creative product of a group that gives the group patterns for the interpretation of reality. Culture is testimony to the fact that all humans are participants as well as spectators in the human drama. To insist upon cultural uniformity is artificial and oppressive.[16]

The teacher education system itself mirrors the structure of the services in the public schools. It is hard to tell which came first. Teacher education institutions produce professionals to fill the slots in the school systems. However, it is not clear that filling the slots in so many special areas results in a meaningful contribution to students.[17] A final example of a belief or idea is one that is seldom expressed openly at this time. For the major part of the history of the nation, the idea of white superiority and supremacy was quite widespread.[18]

The point in citing these beliefs and ideas is to emphasize that, like other parts of social structures, they do not simply disappear when ignored. They must be systematically dismantled and replaced with other ideas more appropriate to a democratic education. One of the characteristics of large human systems is inertia. Because of this inertia it is very difficult to perceive and to change structures. We become comfortable with them. They feel natural. They require energy and service, occupying time that might be better spent on critical analysis of assumptions and the validity of practice. Not only does this identify a problem; it suggests one of the targets or activities to remedy the problem.

GOALS FOR STUDENTS

For the past few decades hundreds of reform reports have been issued. These reports are intended to analyze, critique, and stimulate change in the educational system. One of the striking things about virtually all of the reports is that they seem to be based upon the assumption that minimum competency attainment should be the goal for the nation. Few of the reports actually propose high-level academic and social goals, goals of excellence for the masses of America's children. Exceptions to this trend would be the Paideia Proposal by Mortimer Adler[19] and the report *Saving the African-American Child* by the National Alliance of Black School Educators.[20]

Adler's report is an exception since it states clearly that all children are expected to reach levels of achievement that many educators regard as accessible to only a few students. For example, Adler makes the use of the great literature of the Western World a central part of the curriculum. Except for the fact that the great literature of the rest of the world was not emphasized in the Paideia Proposal, Adler's standards were goals that would call for the best from educators. Similarly, the goals of education articulated in *Saving the African-American Child* reflected a high level of expectation for the masses of our children. The National Alliance of Black School Educators called for foreign language proficiency, mathematics through calculus, college preparatory English proficiency, science coursework equivalent to general chemistry, ethnic history, and other objectives to be met upon high school graduation.

We are constantly compared with Japan and with other industrialized nations of the world, especially in Europe. There are major differences between the educational system of the United States and those of other industrialized nations in the world. Certainly, *the differences have to do with the goals that we set for the masses of our people.* For example, the floor of educational goals for Japanese students is near the ceiling of educational goals for our own.[21] It makes all the difference in the world that *exit criteria for high schools be rigorous for the masses of students and that the masses of students attain the goals that are set.* In order for that to occur, education in the early years must be designed so that children learn prerequisites that will enable them to meet the standards they are fully capable of reaching.

Clearly we are likely to reach the goals that we set. The vast body of effective schools literature documents the fact that all children have the capability to achieve. One of the characteristics that sets high-achieving schools apart from low-achieving schools is the type of goals that are set. High-achieving schools set high goals.[22] Certainly, we will never reach excellent outcomes for students if the goals for excellent performance are not articulated, and if a commitment to reaching them is not made.

TEACHER TRAINING

We do not normally think of teacher training as a part of the structure of inequity. However, a close look at the historical practices in teacher training will reveal significant weaknesses in two places. On the one hand, the academic requirements for students in programs of teacher training have been notoriously low and narrow. For example, it is interesting that many, and perhaps most, of the elite private schools require an entirely different kind of teacher preparation than that required for the public schools. Most prefer a strong bachelor's degree or master's degree with a major and minor in academic subject areas, to programs heavy in pedagogy. Good teacher preparation, of course, would require *both* sound academic and pedagogical preparation.

Second, and perhaps most important, the deficiency in existing teacher training has to do with the pattern typically found in professional laboratory experiences, such as student teaching or in-service training for professional teachers. The Holmes Group, a group of major colleges and universities that seeks to reform teacher education, generally makes proposals concerning the number of years to be required for teacher preparation and the pattern of coursework to be required. However, they do not attack the problem at its core. The core of the problem is in the character of the laboratory experience. The root of the clinical problem is the fact that most teachers of teachers may not be required to be able to demonstrate they can be routinely successful with children, all children. As a result, *many teachers in training never actually have an opportunity to observe someone being successful with the types of students who are most likely to fail in school, such as the low-income children and racial minority groups.* As a result, they fail to learn strategies for success. In addition, negative beliefs about the low capacities of low-performing children may be reinforced because the teachers do not find that the traditional strategies they have been taught will work for them. If there is one thing that the effective schools research has shown, it is that quality of instruction can produce results independent of the income or race of the students.[23] The alternative to present practice in the field experience is a simple one. First, a "master teacher" must be defined as a teacher who is able to move low-performing students from the bottom to levels of excellence in academic performance, and not simply as a teacher with years of experience who may be available for a student teacher or intern. Second, the student teacher or intern must have the opportunity for a true apprenticeship with a master teacher. This is the pattern that is followed by teacher training programs that produce teachers who have dramatic results in raising the achievement of low-performing students.[24] This is the message that must be sent to those involved in pedagogical coursework for teachers in training and the lesson that must be learned in clinical practica. However, such will not be the case without a radical restructuring of teacher education programs.

THE GENERAL SCHOOL DESIGN

All rhetoric aside, most schools operate some type of tracking program. For example, students in the lower tracks in the secondary schools are not expected to master a college preparatory curriculum. So, the problem is not only that there is a tracking system, but that those in the lower track do not reach adequate criterion levels of performance. *Looking backwards, we would expect to find low-track students in low groups in the early years of school, for the pathway to failure begins in the early years.*[25] In other words, tracking is not beneficial for children. They do not get better and return to higher tracks after being served in lower tracks. The tracking system therefore reflects an acceptance of the notion that the actual present level of performance of a group of children is also the potential level of performance. Otherwise, we would expect to see major mobilization for change. American educators appear genuinely unable to imagine alternatives to tracking. Until this is done, millions of able children will fail to reach their full potential. Large numbers of these will be children of the poor and children of racial minority groups.

The design of systems that produce inequity includes the widespread practice of special education. At one point, special education services were offered to a small proportion of the schools population. At present more than four million school children have been assessed and placed in classes for special education. What is important is that children are distributed disproportionately by race and class into the three major categories of educable mentally retarded, learning disabled, and emotionally disturbed. In fact, together these categories account for nearly three quarters of the total special education population. These are soft diagnostic categories that are of highly questionable validity.[26] However, the tragic thing about special education is not only that so many children have been placed into it with the accompanying stigma, but research evidence does not support its effectiveness.[27] Given the vast amount of resources accorded through special education funding for assessment meetings and small class size, we would expect to see some evidence of *beneficial outcomes* for children. Such is not the case.

ASSESSMENT

The formal assessment through testing of children tends to yield global scores by which children are ranked in comparison to each other on IQ tests. The IQ test dominates decisions about what to do with children.[28] But given the requirement that services provided result in benefits to children, we must classify the assessment process as presently used for the masses of children as a mere ritual. IQ testing offers no meaningful help to educators in overcoming difficulties that children may have with schooling.

IQ scores are *outcome* measures. They tell us how many right answers a child gave to a somewhat arbitrary set of questions without telling us how a child arrived at the answers that were given. IQ tests in America were constructed based upon the assumption that a child's fixed ability could be measured precisely, that future academic performances could be predicted precisely from IQ scores, and that such predictions would be meaningful for the selection of instructional treatments.[29] There is no body of empirical literature showing that traditional uses of IQ scores yield diagnostic information that is useful in the design of instruction. In other words, IQ tests are in no way to be considered as diagnostic instruments. This is really a custodial paradigm. The IQ-based decision in traditional practice is really a decision about where to place the child in educational custody.

A powerful alternative to this bankrupt practice exists. It comes from a new paradigm, a remedial paradigm. There is already available an approach to instructionally related assessment that seeks to find and correct impediments to learning and problem solving. Based upon the seminal work of Binet and his "mental orthopedics"[30] and an applied Piagetian Reuven Feuerstein's "cognitive modifiability" system called Dynamic Assessment and Instrumental Enrichment,[31] a growing number of educators and psychologists[32] now know that many low-performing students can make profound progress, if given appropriate remediation. In this paradigm, manifest performance is not considered to be the same as potential performance. If this is not the paradigm that school people accept, then there is really no good reason for the use of mental measurement in education at all. Naturally, this does not apply to valid achievement tests.

In general, we may say that access to the type of teaching that is likely to produce excellent results is limited for many children mainly because of class and race due to the special way that tracking, testing, and special education are implemented.

CURRICULUM

The curriculum in schools, too, is a part of the structure of inequity. The open and hidden curriculum of any school paints pictures of the school's conception of reality. These pictures come to be viewed as legitimate by children. However, for many children the picture is one that is alien to their experience. We actually live in a culturally plural world. The school is populated by children from many cultural groups who bring their cultural reality to school with them, their languages, world-views, values, styles, and general experiential repertoires. Yet, the response of the school generally is to ignore this diversity. This is particularly acute where the general curriculum is concerned. It remains mainly Eurocentric and more specifically Western Eurocentric. *The problem with such a curriculum is that it is simply not a true rendition of the human experience.* It is a curriculum that must be changed, and it must be changed whether poor or minority children or racial minorities are present in schools or not. Every academic area needs to be reviewed by multidisciplinary, multiethnic teams of scholars to insure that the most truthful and beneficial picture is presented of the human experience as these courses are taught.

Most practices in education come to be regarded as legitimate as the result of many activities carried out by education professionals. This means that structures of inequity not only exist, but come to be regarded as valid. For example, the activities of thousands of educational researchers have provided support for the practices that we see in the public schools. Most of the educational literature will reveal a long-term preoccupation of researchers with such questions as the *differences* between black and white IQ or the *differences* between rich and poor children in academic achievement. In fact, the preoccupation of many researchers is with the *prediction* of academic outcome based on certain factors in a student's present experience. What is interesting about the thrust of much research in the United States is the *failure of researchers to document the differential pedagogical treatment* that children receive based upon income and race. Only recently have researchers applied the sophisticated methodologies of anthropology and sociology to accomplish this task. Educational research should provide insight so that we may find our way out of difficult situations rather than legitimation for practice as it presently exists.

We may also look at how funding patterns perpetuate educational inequity. Funding patterns tend to perpetuate the structures that exist even if the structures are illegitimate. A good case in point is the funding patterns that result in millions of dollars being poured into a special education system that has yet to demonstrate benefits for children. The requirement that 10 percent of the Head Start population at a center be made up of handicapped children is no doubt based on good intentions. Yet, if it results in a frantic search by center directors for very high numbers of "handicapped" children to meet quotas, especially in "soft diagnostic categories" such as language disorders, then the funding pattern may be driving the program.

Certification, licensing and accreditation are practices that tend to support the status quo. Teachers are certified or licensed and institutions are accredited for doing well the same things that have been done for years. Yet there may be no distinction between those institutions or educators who are certified, licensed, or accredited and those who are not. As a result, the certification, licensing, and accreditation systems may actually contribute to the maintenance of structures of inequity. The Child Development Associate Assessment System in early childhood education is a major departure from traditional practice. Professionals are assessed more on performance criteria than on paper and pencil tests.

Deconstructing Structures of Inequity and Constructing Powerful Systems to Serve Children

One thing that we now know is that there are hundreds of educators who manage to succeed quite well with children regardless of their income or racial background.[33] The acceptance of this principle is the first major step toward a solution of the national problem, a problem which is evident when we see the failure rate of so many children from low-income and racial minority groups. In the past, explanations for the low performance levels of many children were based largely on the belief that schools could do little to overcome the effects of poverty, limited cultural experiences, single-parent families, etc. Acceptance of these explanations leave school people in a position to do little. On the other hand, if school interventions can overcome the impact of outside forces, in whole or in part, then the obligation to do so is there.

The fact that many educators are successful provides us with the type of empirical data to challenge the basis for many of our structures of inequity. For example, if children can be taught to meet standards of excellence by the use of ordinary pedagogy regardless of race or class, then the belief system that has served as the foundation for much of our professional practice must be dismantled. If such children are capable of reaching maximum competency goals, then it is irresponsible of educators to work for anything less than that. However, if the teacher training that accounts for successful practice with children is different from the teacher training that we now conduct, then we are obligated to use these data for the reform of teacher education. In other words, we must begin to think of massive change in systems and structures if we intend to serve well the needs of all American children.

Certain clear steps must be taken in order to provide equity, access, and desegregation in our nation's system of education. First, it is absolutely imperative that many models of excellence be identified and fostered. Models of excellence are those models where children regardless of race or income complete schooling that is the equivalent of a college preparatory curriculum at the end of twelve years of schooling. Schools that produce these results do exist and have existed for many years. However, the attention of educational researchers has been upon the performance of schools in the *aggregate* rather than on the *outliers*. Other necessary resources should be allocated for the location of excellent schools.

Second, *excellent* schools must be studied systematically. *The "effective" schools movement was not an excellent schools movement.* It was an excellent movement. However, the criterion level of performance for children in the effective school was *minimum competency. It is probable that the character of an excellent school differs significantly from that of an adequate school. As a result, it is absolutely essential that the resources be made available to provide systematic study of excellent schools.*

Third, *provision must be made to duplicate excellent schools in many locations around the nation so that they may be used as training sites for educators.* Fourth, both preservice and in-service teachers in training must be provided *access to excellent schools* so that they may be able to use the models of excellent teaching and educational leadership for their own professional growth and for the training of preprofessionals they supervise. For example, to the best of my knowledge, the excellent work of Jaime Escalante and his associates at Garfield High School in East Los Angeles is well known by both the public and the profession. However, the next logical step has not been followed and that is to design a way that educators in training can have access to Garfield High School in order to learn the strategies that have been successful there. Then fifth, teacher education must be redesigned in imitation of teacher education systems that are consistent in producing teachers who do not fail to teach low-income racial minority groups effectively.

Conclusion

Equity, access, and desegregation require above all a new world view for educators. There is much more involved here than the mere matter of learning new skills. We need new beliefs and from that new practices will follow that will allow us to deconstruct the structures of inequity. Focusing on the successes that have already been achieved, we have the models now to provide for the design of an education for the future for all our children.

The National Black Child Development Institute has actually developed an action plan to guarantee more equitable treatment of young children.[34] The plan outlines ten "safeguards" as guidelines for establishing programs for four-year-olds. The ten safeguards are as follows:

1. Public school-based programs for black, preschool-age children should incorporate an effective parent education program.
2. Public school-based early childhood programs should involve parents in the decisions about the curriculum and policy.
3. The staff of early childhood education programs should include teachers who come from the community served by the program and who are racially and ethnically representative of the children served.
4. Teachers in public school-based programs should be required to have specific training in preschool education and/or ongoing, in-service training provided by qualified staff.
5. Curriculum for preschool-age children in the public schools should be culturally sensitive and appropriate to the child's age and level of development.
6. Public schools which house programs for very young children should meet the same health and safety standards which apply to independent preschools and center-based child care programs.
7. Public school-based early childhood programs should participate in federal and state programs which guarantee adequate nutrition to children.
8. Administrators of public school-based programs for preschoolers should ensure that children entering the programs have access to appropriate health care.
9. In assessing children of preschool age, the administrators of public school-based early childhood programs should not limit their assessment to, or base their program planning solely on, standardized tests.
10. Public school-based early childhood programs should be subject to a regular, external review by community members and early childhood development experts.

History shows us that while analysis of situations in education can be of some importance, the solution to our problem is less a matter of skill than a matter of will. Ronald Edmonds was right; we have always known how to educate all of the children whose education is of importance to us. Whether we do or not depends in the final analysis on how we feel about the fact that so far we have not done so.

FOOTNOTES

1. W. E. B. DuBois, *Black Reconstruction in America 1860-1880: An Essay toward a History of the Part Which Black Folks Played in the Attempt to Reconstruct Democracy in America* (New York: Athenum, 1973).

2. Asa Hilliard, "Democratizing the Common School in a Multicultural Society," *Education and Urban Society* 16, no. 3 (1984): 262-273; Meyer Weinberg, *A Chance to Learn: A History of Race and Education in the United States* (New York: Cambridge University Press, 1977).

3. Jeannie Oakes, *Keeping Track: How Schools Structure Inequality* (New Haven: Yale University Press, 1986).

4. Kirby A. Heller, Wayne H. Holtzman, and Samuel Messick, eds., *Placing Children in Special Education: A Strategy for Equity* (Washington, DC: National Academy Press, 1982).

5. Willy D. Smith and Eva W. Chunn, eds., *Black Education: A Quest for Equity and Excellence* (New Brunswick, NJ: Transaction Publishers, 1989).

6. Hilliard, "Democratizing the Common School in a Multicultural Society."

7. Donald Bogle, *The Devil Finds Work* (New York: Dial, 1974); Thomas Cripps, *Slow Fade to Black: The Negro in American Film 1900-1942* (New York: Oxford, 1977); Daniel J. Leab, *From Sambo to Superspade: The Black Experience in Motion Pictures* (Boston: Houghton Mifflin, 1976); Robert D. Toll, *Blacking Up: The Minstrel Show in Nineteenth-Century America* (New York: Oxford University Press, 1974).

8. Kenneth J. King, *Pan Africanism and Education: A Study of Race Philanthropy and Education in the Southern States of America and East Africa* (Oxford: Clarendon Press, 1971); Donald Spivey, *Schooling for the New Slavery: Black Industrial Education, 1868-1915* (Westport, CT: Greenwood Press, 1978).

9. Stephen J. Gould, *The Mismeasure of Man* (New York: W. W. Norton, 1981); Asa Hilliard, "IQ Thinking as the Emperor's New Clothes," in *Perspectives on Bias in Mental Testing*, ed. Cecil R. Reynolds and Robert T. Brown (New York: Plenum, 1984); Leon J. Kamin, *The Science and Politics of IQ* (Potomac, MD: Erlbaum, 1974).

10. Weinberg, *A Chance to Learn*.

11. Task Force on Black Academic and Cultural Excellence, *Saving the African-American Child: A Report of the National Alliance of Black School Educators* (Washington, DC: National Alliance of Black School Educators, 1984).

12. Reuven Feuerstein, Y'a acov Rand, and Mildred B. Hoffman, *The Dynamic Assessment of Retarded Performers: The Learning Potential Assessment Device, Theory, Instruments, and Techniques* (Baltimore, MD: University Park Press, 1979); Gould, *The Mismeasure of Man*; Kamin, *The Science and Politics of IQ*.

13. Asa Hilliard, ed., "Testing African-American Students," *Negro Educational Review* 38, nos. 2 and 3 (1987): Special Issue.

14. Paul L. Houts, ed., *The Myth of Measurability* (New York: Hart, 1977); Hilliard, "IQ Thinking as the Emperor's New Clothes."

15. Gene V Glass, "Effectiveness of Special Education," *Policy Studies Review* 2, no. 1 (1983): 65-78.

16. Martin Carnoy, *Educating the Powerless* (Belmont, CA: Wadsworth, 1974): Paulo Freire, *Education for Critical Consciousness* (New York: Seabury Press, 1973); Edward T. Hall, *Beyond Culture* (New York: Anchor Press, 1977); Manuel Ramirez and Alfredo Castenada, *Cultural Democracy, Bicognitive Development, and Education* (New York: Academic Press, 1974).

17. Glass, "Effectiveness of Special Education."

18. Robert Blauner, *Racial Oppression in America* (New York: Harper and Row, 1972); Barry N. Schwartz and Robert Disch, *White Racism: Its History, Pathology, and Practice* (New York: Dell, 1970).

19. Mortimer Adler, *The Paideia Proposal: An Educational Manifesto* (New York: Macmillan, 1982).

20. Task Force on Black Academic and Cultural Excellence, *Saving the African-American Child.*

21. Merry White, *The Japanese Educational Challenge: A Commitment to Children* (New York: Free Press, 1987).

22. Wilbur Brookover, Laurence Beamer, Helen Efthim, Douglas Hathaway, Lawrence Lezotte, Stephen Miller, Joseph Passalacqua, and Louis Tornatsky, *Creating Effective Schools* (Holmes Beach, FL: Learning Publications, 1983); Ronald R. Edmonds, "Effective Schools for the Urban Poor," *Educational Leadership* 36 (1979): 23.

23. Brookover et al., *Creating Effective Schools*; James Comer, *School Power: Implications of an Intervention Project*; Edmonds, "Effective Schools for the Urban Poor"; idem, "Improving the Effectiveness of New York City Public Schools," in Educational Testing Service, *The Minority Student and Public Schools: Fostering Academic Excellence* (Princeton, NJ: Educational Testing Service, 1981), pp. 23-30; Faustine C. Jones, *A Traditional Model of Education Excellence: Dunbar High School of Little Rock, Arkansas* (Washington, DC: Howard University Press, 1981).

24. Feuerstein et al., *The Dynamic Assessment of Retarded Performers.*

25. Shirley Brice Heath, *Ways with Words: Language, Life, and Work in Communities and Classrooms* (Cambridge, MA: Cambridge University Press, 1983); Oakes, *Keeping Track*; Ray C. Rist, *The Urban School: A Factory for Failure* (Cambridge, MA: MIT Press, 1973).

26. Alan Gartner and Dorothy K. Lipsky, "Beyond Special Education: Toward a Quality System for All Students," *Harvard Educational Review* 57, no. 4 (1987): 367-395; Heller et al., *Placing Children in Special Education.*

27. Glass, "Effectiveness of Special Education."

28. Heller et al., *Placing Children in Special Education.*

29. Gould, *The Mismeasure of Man*; Kamin, *The Science and Politics of IQ.*

30. Gould, *The Mismeasure of Man.*

31. Feuerstein et al., *The Dynamic Assessment of Retarded Performers.*

32. Carol S. Lidz, *Dynamic Assessment: An Interactional Approach in Evaluating Learning Potential* (New York: Guilford Press, 1987).

33. Council of Chief State School Officers, *School Success for Students at Risk: Analysis and Recommendations of the Council of Chief State School Officers* (Orlando, FL: Harcourt Brace Jovanovich, 1988).

34. National Black Child Development Institute, *Safeguards: Guidelines for Establishing Programs for Four-Year-Olds in the Public Schools* (Washington, DC: National Black Child Development Institute, 1987).

CHAPTER XII

Choosing Wisely for Children:
Policy Options for Early Childhood Programs

W. NORTON GRUBB

To the surprise of many, public interest in young children is growing. At the federal level, a campaign of child care advocates has succeeded in getting major legislation introduced. Sensing a hot topic, members of Congress have introduced over 100 bills related to early childhood programs. At least twenty-six states now provide funds for prekindergarten programs, almost all of them enacted in the past few years, and twelve add their own resources to Head Start programs; several others have convened commissions to consider their options.[1] The business community has also extended its support to programs for poor children and to early childhood programs in particular.[2] After the early 1980s, when nearly every program for children was the target of federal budget cutters, and the 1970s, when every major initiative for early childhood programs was defeated, the resurgence of interest in young children is gratifying. With all this attention, the 1990s might be the decade of the young child.

If the programs being contemplated in Washington and in state capitals are enacted, new institutional arrangements for early childhood programs will develop during the next decade. The current situation presents both promise and danger. The promise is that it will be easier, without an existing institution dominating early childhood programs, to develop a system *de novo*, considering alternative policies carefully and choosing those that best serve the interests of children. The danger is that, partly because the existing system on which future efforts must build is so chaotic and confusing, policymakers, especially at the state level, will be unable to grapple with the full range of options and to choose among them on the basis of clearly articulated goals, and will instead, under the pressure of "doing good," rush to adopt expedient but inappropriate policies.

The hallmark of current early childhood programs is their diversity. There are both private funding and a plethora of public funding sources. There is a bewildering variety of providers including churches, community-based organizations, schools and other public institutions, proprietary chains, mom-and-pop centers, laboratory schools, family day care providers, and nannies, and a variety of hours of operation, philosophies, and prices.[3] In our liberal society, this diversity ought to be positive, since it provides a range of options from which parents (at least, some parents) can choose. But the dismal side of diversity is the lack of common purpose, the absence of connections among programs, inconsistency in quality, bewilderment among parents, and confusion for policymakers. One challenge in the coming decade, then, is to preserve the positive aspects of diversity while developing an early childhood system that is more coherent, easier for parents and providers alike to negotiate, and more consistently beneficial to children.

One of the most important reasons for the chaos and lack of coordination in early childhood programs is inconsistency in conceptions of what they are about. In the first part of this chapter, I explore different strands of support, each with its own purpose, and each with its own distinctive form of financing. Reconciling these four strands, and developing policies that can accommodate all of them, is necessary to restructure the existing system.

A second source of fragmentation has been the process of legislating federal and state programs. The proliferation of federal categorical programs, and the enactment of state initiatives in addition, has created a situation where even paltry amounts of public funding create inconsistencies, divisions, and confusion. Even if it is impossible to reshape the way federal legislation is concocted, more coherent policy is possible if states are willing to take active roles. With this criterion in mind, it then is possible to consider a variety of policy options that structure the programs available to children in ways that preserve the beneficial aspects of diversity while imposing some coherence.

The "crisis" that many perceive in early childhood programs is first and last an issue of funding, and hopeful talk about "the decade of the young child" should not obscure how limited the gains in public funding have been. I conclude the chapter by suggesting a new justification for public funding—similar to the justifications for Social Security—that might help solidify support for young children.

The Strands of Support for Early Childhood Programs

One reason for confusion about early childhood programs is that so many different purposes coexist. Every generation seems to rediscover for itself the idea of programs for younger children, but with different motives that have in turn been educational, economic, and reformist, sometimes stressing the needs of children and sometimes forgetting the child in favor of social problems. Many of these models have died, but their legacies have included ways of thinking about young children and models of programs that continue to influence and confuse us.

The earliest of these models, which many call the *compensatory approach*, dates from the early nineteenth century, when philanthropists instituted infant schools to rescue poor children from their parents as early as possible.[4] The infant school movement died as the view spread that mothers should care for their own children. But its essential vision—that schools should take in children as young as possible to teach them and protect them from the evil influences of home—lives on in many forms. The most obvious current forms of the compensatory approach include Head Start and the many state-funded preschool programs for at-risk four-year-olds. The Perry Preschool, which has been the subject of voluminous publicity because of its much-trumpeted 7:1 benefit-cost ratio, is another example.[5] The compensatory approach also has a dominant funding mechanism (project grants to specific local providers) and a clear target group (low-income or "at risk" children who are three to four years old).

Somewhat later, in the 1880s, the movement for the kindergarten began as an extension of the ideal home, with teachers as mother surrogates emphasizing the value of play to the child's development and focusing on personal characteristics, which early childhood educators now call social and emotional development, rather than on cognitive development. An early form of what many refer to as the *developmental approach*, kindergartens began as part of urban reform, to teach poor urban children (including many immigrant children) industriousness, cleanliness, discipline, and cooperation, and to instruct their parents in the care of children.

Although the developmental conception of early childhood education was transformed, and in many ways undermined, when the kindergartens moved into the schools around 1900, the developmental model was revived in the nursery school movement of the 1920s. Nursery schools developed as complements to mothering, rather than "mother substitutes"; they were part-day rather than full-day programs, directed at the cognitive enrichment of middle-class children, and at educating parents "to a better understanding of their position in the scheme of education of their children's lives."[6] Because of their close links to parents and to middle-class children, the nursery schools avoided the stigma of programs associated with poor children. They provided a strong image of what early childhood programs should be, and with their success the split widened between self-consciously "developmental" programs and the more obviously "custodial" programs associated with poor children. The developmental model lives on most obviously in the child development profession, best represented by the National Association for the Education of Young Children (NAEYC), and in the demands by early childhood professionals and many parents alike for high-quality, developmentally appropriate programs.

Just as the kindergarten was being incorporated into the schools, a very different institution for young children began to develop, again in response to the poverty and wretched conditions of urban slums. The day nurseries established by settlement houses were, like the charity kindergartens, directed at low-income children, particularly at those whose mothers were forced to work. They had two purposes: "to provide a shelter for the children of mothers dependent on their own exertions for their daily bread; [but] also to rear useful citizens among the class represented by the children we reach."[7] While the day nurseries themselves declined under the stigma of working with the "unworthy poor," their legacy has been the *welfare model* of child care, providing "custodial" care so that mothers of poor children can work.[8] The most obvious current forms of this approach include the Social Services Block Grant (SSBG), which gives priority to low-income and welfare children, and funding for child care included in the Family Support Act of 1988 as part of the JOBS (Job Opportunities and Basic Skills) program requiring welfare mothers to work, with funds distributed through welfare departments rather than through education departments as is typical in compensatory programs.

A final strand of support for early childhood programs has come from steady increases in the number of women working. The numbers are by now quite familiar: in 1986, 54.4 percent of mothers with children under six were in the labor force, up from 46.8 percent

in 1980, 38.8 percent in 1975, and 25.3 percent in 1965.[9] The increase
in women working has both contributed to the demand for child care
and, just as important, made out-of-home care legitimate. This
approach to early childhood programs, which I shall call (for lack of
a better term) the *feminist* or *employment* rationale, stresses the need for
care during working hours, the importance of affordability since child
care costs are usually associated with mothers working, and the desir-
ability of parental choice. The feminist approach has been institutionalized in the single largest public subsidy for early childhood
programs, the Dependent Care Tax Credit available through the
personal income tax—a subsidy which maximizes parental choice, but
which fails to help low-income women since the credit is unavailable
to those who earn too little to pay taxes.

The legacy of this history, then, is one of fragmentation.
Compensatory, welfare-related, developmental, and feminist rationales for early childhood programs all endure, each with a different
emphasis, different institutional arrangements, and a different funding
mechanism; each has its own conception of quality and content.
Recent legislation has in many ways replicated these historic strands.
The Family Support Act of 1988 provides new federal funding for
welfare mothers, following the "welfare" model. In contemplating
new funding for early childhood programs, Congress cannot make up
its mind whether it prefers to expand tax credits, enlarge Head Start,
or institute a new program of direct funding, and the most recent
legislation compromises by doing a little bit of everything.[10] The
states have initiated a series of preschools in the compensatory
tradition,[11] though debates over "care" versus "education" persist.
Inconsistencies abound: supporters of early childhood programs cite
the benefits of the Perry Preschool, a program of very high cost and
quality, and then support low-quality programs; others mention the
increasing number of mothers working as justification for early
childhood programs, and then press for half-day preschools inappropriate for most working mothers.

But in many ways the divisions among different strands of support
are no longer appropriate. The reality of mothers working has
undermined the structure of the older compensatory and developmental models; nursery schools, which used to be half-day programs, have
generally evolved into full-day programs for working parents, and
many children can no longer attend half-day programs. Similarly, the
notion that child care should be merely "custodial," and that there is
a split between "care" and "education," is badly outdated. The view

that the early years are crucial to development has become convention. Most child care centers have some conscious policy about a developmental curriculum; many devote some time during the day to formal instruction, and most are clear on a variety of developmental goals for the children in their care. Most child care workers call themselves teachers and consider themselves professionals, resenting deeply the notion that they are merely "babysitters."

Above all, the idea that early childhood programs should be either "developmental" or "custodial," either "compensatory" or "employment-related," can only limit them. After all, the schools are rich, multipurpose institutions, with economic, political, moral, and avocational purposes coexisting. Early childhood programs at their best are similarly rich and multifaceted, providing cognitive, physical, social, and emotional development for children, security and full-time care for working parents, substantial cooperation between parents and caregivers, and parent education for parents seeking different ways of interacting with their children. The best programs provide children early, noncompetitive, and nonthreatening experiences with children of other races and class backgrounds, rather than segregating some children from others in classes for those "at-risk." To search for a single purpose for early childhood programs is to destroy this vision of what they could be.

One possible goal of both federal and state governments, therefore, would be to create policies that would eliminate rather than perpetuate the divisions among alternative conceptions of early childhood programs. The recent initiatives from Congress and from states have given little thought to this possibility, however, since they continue existing divisions rather than devising a structure which could support a variety of programs.[12] But the goal of integration is important, since the alternative is a limited vision of what programs for young children can be.

Policy Options for Early Childhood Programs: Federal, State, and Local Roles

A very different reason for the sense of chaos and confusion surrounding early childhood programs comes from the typical pattern of governmental support, which applies to several areas of social policy. The federal government typically enacts a series of categorical programs, each with a somewhat different target group or program philosophy; states then vary in their efforts to establish their own policies, rather than following the dictates of federal legislation. At the local level where services are finally delivered, the burden of devising a coherent "system" of programs falls on the shoulders of local providers, often goaded by state and federal coordination requirements but without the power to change the different federal programs—with their inconsistent purposes, regulations, and funding mechanisms—that create divisions in the first place. The result, at the local level where it most counts, is a sense of inconsistency among programs and incongruence between needs and programs, while federal policymakers fret about duplication and coordination and states often act relatively powerless.[13]

These patterns are already well established in early childhood programs. The major sources of federal support—the Social Services Block Grant, Head Start, the Child Care Food Program, and the Dependent Care Tax Credit—are inconsistent in their purposes and funding mechanisms; the funding for child care in the Family Support Act of 1988 is unconnected with any other federal programs, and the legislation now being proposed continues the tradition of establishing several small, categorical programs unconnected with one another. With only a few exceptions—perhaps California, New York, and Massachusetts—states have not established coherent early childhood policies and have spent little of their own resources. It then falls to local providers to try to make this chaotic "system" coherent, which some providers do by combining revenues from several programs and some local agencies (like resource and referral agencies or local Offices for Children) try to do. But by and large, coherence fails to happen.[14]

It is probably too late in the day to change the way the federal government enacts legislation.[15] The only alternative, then, is for *states* to play more active roles in creating coherent early childhood policies by combining all available federal funds and supplementary state revenues and using them to create coherent policies rather than acting merely as passive recipients of federal funds and passing them on to local providers. To some extent, a state role will be required by federal legislation, since certain parts of the bills now before Congress require state plans. However, establishing coherent state policies will require going beyond the requirements of federal legislation, encompassing *all* funding for early childhood programs including those federal programs (like Head Start and the Dependent Care Tax Credit) that do not require a state role.[16] Only this broad approach can hope to coordinate the variety of existing and proposed programs.

In this vision, then, states face two distinct challenges: (a) to devise policies that, as much as possible, narrow rather than perpetuate the differences among the compensatory, developmental, welfare, and feminist conceptions of early childhood programs; and (b) to draw together the strands of federal and state support into a coherent policy. In practice each state will develop a different approach, suited to its governing structure, the nature of local governments, existing early childhood programs, and the distribution of political power. But it is still possible to clarify the choices states must confront and to clarify the ways their options either further the goals of coherent policy or perpetuate the current dismal patterns of chaos and confusion.

ELIGIBILITY, PURPOSE, AND FUNDING

All governments face first a set of crucial decisions about the programs to be provided: Which children should be served, and which types of programs should be provided? (Table 1 presents an outline of the choices states face, paralleling the discussion here.) If "school readiness" is the principal goal, as part of the compensatory model, then four-year-olds may be the appropriate target; if states want to provide child care for working parents, then programs for two- to five-year-olds are necessary (and even this age range may be inadequate because of the serious shortage of infant and toddler care in most communities). The compensatory model may argue for the provision of half-day prekindergarten programs, but in an era when the majority of mothers with small children work (including many low-income mothers whose children are likely to be considered "at risk" of later educational problems), half-day programs are inadequate for most children.

Decisions about funding levels are similarly important. These choices—what cost per child to support from public sources—are simultaneously choices about quality, particularly through the effects of funding on adult-child ratios and on salary levels. The trade-off between costs and quality is inexorable.[17] However, if states are to recognize the importance of the developmental approach, rather than exacerbating the difference between "developmental" and "custodial" conceptions, it is crucial to recognize the higher costs of developmentally appropriate programs.[18] In addition, some decisions must be made about which ancillary services (including transportation, health screening, health care, counseling, and other social services) are to be

TABLE 1

POLICY CHOICES

1. *Who shall be served*

   Age groups: 4-year olds
                  3-4-year olds
                  toddlers and infants 0-2
   Target groups: Low-income children
                   Educationally "at-risk" children
                   Limited English-speaking children
                   All children

2. *Program type/hours of operation*

   Morning or half-day pre-school (2-3 hours)
   Full school day (5-6 hours)
   Full working-day (8-10 hours)
   Morning pre-school plus after-school program
   Parent education

3. *Funding level, services provided*

   Level Spending per child ranges between $1,000 and $6,000
   Services provided: Basic care/instruction only
                        Transportation
                        Health screening
                        Health care
                        Psychological screening
                        Counseling
                        Parent education
                        Social services/information to parents

4. *Funding mechanisms*

   Expand existing programs
   Voucher mechanisms:
        Vouchers to parents, unrestricted
        Vouchers to parents, restricted to programs of specified quality
        Vouchers administered by programs (vendor payments)
        Tax credits to individuals
        Tax credits to corporations
   Project funding via proposals:
        school districts only eligible
        school districts eligible, with subcontracts allowed
        districts and community-based organizations eligible
   Formula funding to school districts:
        existing school aid formula
        new aid formula specifically for early childhood
   Formula funding to towns, cities, counties, or special Service Delivery Areas
        (SDAs)
        matching grants
        nonmatching grants
   Extent of state restrictions on use of funds:
        local planning and priority setting
        "California model": categorical funding for specific types of early childhood
            programs

TABLE 1 (*Continued*)
POLICY CHOICES

5. *Mandates*

> Conventional licensing required
> Stricter licensing required for public programs
> Accreditation required for public programs
> Teacher certification and licensing
> Requirements for developers to provide space or funds
> Requirements for corporations to provide child care benefits

6. *Capacity-building mechanisms*

> Resource and referral agencies
> Technical assistance by state and local governmental agencies
> Improving teacher training through community colleges and four-year colleges, teacher certification and licensing

7. *State administrative agency*

> State department of education (perhaps with a new office of early childhood education)
> State department of education, with an interagency coordinating council
> State welfare agency
> State agency that licenses child care, or that currently administers Head Start
> State office for children
> New state agency
> Coordinating council to integrate policies from several agencies

funded, especially since the politically popular Head Start model has always included a wide array of ancillary services.

DELIVERY SYSTEMS

Once the target groups of children and types of programs have been decided, then more decisions about how to fund early childhood programs must be made. There are at least five alternatives to consider:

1. *Funding existing programs.* The simplest alternative is to expand existing programs, including Title XX/SSBG child care and Head Start, increasing funding in programs whose resources have been dwindling in real terms. Such an approach, however, would take the policies of the past as the blueprint for the future rather than investigating a wider range of alternatives. Title XX programs unfortunately have the stigma of welfare associated with them, and Head Start programs, for all their high visibility in Washington, are not well integrated with the rest of the early childhood community. Building on the existing system would do little to eliminate the deep

divisions among the different visions of early childhood, nor would it reduce fragmentation and inconsistency at the local level.

2. *Voucher mechanisms.* The primary appeal of voucher mechanisms, which include true vouchers, various kinds of constrained vouchers, and tax credits, is that consumers choose what to purchase, rather than having choices determined by government decisions. This is a particularly powerful argument in the area of child care, where parents should make crucial decisions. Vouchers would also facilitate funding family day care, and might help integrate child care facilities since both subsidized and unsubsidized children could attend the same facility. Finally, vouchers might reduce administrative costs by eliminating the need for additional bureaucracies to administer programs.

Despite their appeal, voucher mechanisms suffer from many drawbacks. They assume that consumers are well informed about choices available; but the information parents have about child care alternatives is often quite poor. This also makes it difficult to use vouchers for welfare-related programs, since welfare recipients are likely to be especially poorly informed. In California, which subsidizes a constrained voucher system, there is general consensus that voucher mechanisms cannot work without a resource and referral (R&R) agency to provide information to parents. Another drawback lies in the assumption of vouchers that increasing purchasing power will cause more child care to be provided. But in many areas this may not happen because the child care market is so imperfect, with many regulatory barriers to entry (including licensing requirements and local health and safety codes), poor information by providers about demand, a lack of suitable space, shortages of child care workers, and no one to help prospective providers through the complex process of starting a child care facility. The profit motive assumed to be so powerful in conventional markets is particularly weak among those who care for young children (happily so, many might add), and relying on market mechanisms to increase the amount of care may not work well.

In addition, since voucher mechanisms operate by increasing demand and therefore prices, the costs of child care will increase for all parents, including those who are not subsidized. Finally, it is not clear that voucher mechanisms—at least, true vouchers and vendor/voucher systems—are cheaper than direct spending programs. Both require administrative costs, potentially extensive if there is any effort to monitor quality.[19] There are no real efficiencies associated with voucher mechanisms, then, since the direct costs of child care must be paid in any event.

In addition to the general problems with voucher mechanisms, tax credits suffer other liabilities. Tax credit mechanisms are well-suited to the feminist or employment-related vision of early childhood, but they are very awkward (if not impossible) ways of getting subsidies to low-income parents. Because of the lack of control over programs funded through tax credits, governments cede the opportunity to establish clear goals and coherent policies to the vagaries of the market. The quality of programs is difficult to regulate, and the possibilities for promoting compensatory goals, or self-consciously developmental programs, would be lost. In addition, the amounts of government subsidy involved are often unknown; and it is easier for legislatures to ignore these financing mechanisms, continuing tax expenditures year after year without weighing the consequences.

Despite the flaws of voucher mechanisms, they may still have their place in a well-designed state system. In California, there is some agreement that vouchers are the best way of funding child care: (a) in rural areas, where there may not be enough children eligible for subsidy to establish a separate facility; (b) in support of family day care; (c) in cases of child care for children with special needs (handicapped children, for example, or those requiring care during unusual hours), where again there may not be enough children for a separate facility; and (d) in emergency situations, like cases of suspected abuse or neglect, where speed in placing children is crucial. Above all, in a system where there are also public subsidies to expand the supply of care and R&R agencies to provide information, a limited voucher system may increase the choices available to parents.

3. *Project grants.* The general alternative to voucher mechanisms is direct subsidy to programs. The most common are project grants, which solicit proposals from potential providers, and choose among proposals on the basis of criteria that may include geographic distribution, quality, and perhaps the variety of programs in a particular area (to facilitate choice). Project grants maximize government control over the content of programs because a state can choose among alternative applicants, potentially promoting goals like compensatory preparation and a variety of programs in any one area, and allowing the integration of different visions of early childhood programs.

However, project grants involve government in the continued selection of service providers, a situation of too much centralized authority for some tastes, especially in large and heterogeneous states. In addition, it may be difficult to achieve geographic equity with project grants, since the location of subsidized projects is partly due to the vagaries of who applies for grants; and project grants may give an advantage to organizations such as wealthy school districts, which are sophisticated at writing grant proposals.

4. *Formula funding.* An alternative to project funding is formula funding, in which a formula allocates state funds to local recipients. State aid to K-12 education is the best-known example, and in many ways is an obvious model for early childhood programs. Indeed, some states, including New Jersey, Pennsylvania, and Maine, have used their existing school aid formulas to direct funds for preschool programs to school districts; children in such programs are included in the average daily attendance counts that determine the state's aid.

This approach has the obvious advantage of building on familiar funding mechanisms. However, it restricts funds to school districts only. Furthermore, very few districts may take advantage of such revenue; in most states, state aid provides only a fraction of total costs, and districts may be reluctant to support novel or experimental programs from local revenues. In addition, the well-known problem of inequalities among rich and poor districts would be replicated in early childhood programs. A likely consequence would be that only wealthy districts aggressively committed to early childhood education would receive public funds, and these are unlikely to be districts where the children most in need of public support live.

An obvious alternative would be a distinctive formula for early childhood programs, with a higher level of support, and a greater inducement for poor districts, than existing school formulas. However, this would still restrict eligibility to school districts, and would be an implicit decision in favor of a public school monopoly over early childhood programs.

5. *Designating a local recipient.* A more elegant procedure would be to devise formula-based funding that directs state aid to some local government other than school districts. This local government would make decisions about which agencies would provide services, and could then subcontract with both schools and community-based organizations. In some states with strong county governments (like Maryland), counties could be the recipients of funds; in other states where towns and cities cover the state, they could be the recipients. Still another approach would be to designate local Service Delivery Areas (SDAs) that can be county or city governments, or consortia of

local governments, following the model of the Job Training
Partnership Act (JTPA).

The advantages of a state-local system are many. A local
government (or consortium of governments) could act as a planning
agency, making decisions locally about which types of early
childhood programs to provide. In most towns and cities, several
different organizations—existing child care programs, church-based
groups, social service agencies, neighborhood groups and minority
advocacy organizations, laboratory schools based in colleges—could
be expected to receive funding along with schools, and a mix of
different programs would emerge, allowing greater choice for parents.
Another advantage of relying on local governments is that they are
usually responsible for health and safety codes, and making them
responsible for funding would make it easier to coordinate different
funding and regulatory requirements.

CHILD CARE QUALITY AND REGULATION

Both the compensatory rationale and the developmental
perspective stress the importance of high quality (though sometimes
defined in different ways); and the evidence about the positive social
benefits of the Perry Preschool, a very high-quality (and high cost)
program, has also increased consciousness about the importance of
quality. In part, of course, decisions about funding are decisions about
quality. As already noted, in two areas in particular—the adult-child
ratio and the salaries of teachers—the trade-off between costs and
quality is inexorable. A political decision to provide prekindergarten
programs with an adult-child ratio of 1:22, as in Texas, is a decision
to offer programs of low quality; low funding and low salaries of child
care teachers guarantee low morale, high turnover, and constant
shortages.[20]

To be sure, some aspects of program quality may not cost more.
The National Day Care Study determined that smaller class sizes
enhance quality, regardless of the adult-child ratio, because smaller
groups reduce distractions and chaos and increase the interaction
between teachers and children; thus two classes of twenty are better
than one class of forty children, even with the same number of
teachers. In addition, the training of teachers that matters most is
specific preparation in early childhood development, rather than
formal years of schooling in general. This implies that teachers need
not have B.A. degrees, and teachers with community college
certificates in early childhood or with a Child Development Associate

credential would generally be preferable to those with elementary teaching certificates.

As in many areas of social policy, adequate funding is necessary for high-quality programs, though funding may not be sufficient. Governments also have regulatory mechanisms to improve quality, like licensing regulations that establish minimum adult-child ratios, teacher preparation, physical facilities, and other conditions of operation. But licensing is a mechanism for achieving minimal levels of health and safety, not for enhancing more subtle dimensions of quality. An alternative would be to rely on private accreditation of child care facilities, much as states do for higher education, private schools, hospitals, and nursing homes. The National Association for the Education of Young Children (NAEYC) has recently established a system of voluntary accreditation, involving an extensive set of guidelines for good practice, a self-study procedure, and, finally, a site visit by "validators" who then present their findings to the centers they visit.[21] The procedure emphasizes advice from peers, rather than the requirements and threats associated with licensing. The site visit is more thorough and informative than the typical licensing visit, since "validators" are looking for aspects of good practice far beyond the simple standards typical of licensing regulations. Finally, as a professional organization, NAEYC has a legitimacy among early childhood practitioners that would be hard to duplicate in any governmental body.

Another policy to improve quality is teacher certification and licensing. Since all early childhood educators believe that teachers of young children should have training in child development, this standard can be written into requirements for public programs. States can also improve teacher training by working with their community colleges and teacher training institutions, for example, by establishing comprehensive Associate degree or certificate programs to prepare early childhood teachers, or developing a sequence of training including both community colleges and public four-year colleges for child care aides, teachers, supervisors, and administrators. Policy about teacher training is one way of avoiding the dominance of the "custodial" approach on the one hand, with its indifference to the quality of care, and the "school-like" approach of elementary educators on the other.

Yet another influence over quality comes from technical assistance, provided by a state agency or a resource and referral agency. One implication is that a government's policy toward quality will take many different forms, some of them embedded in funding decisions, others in licensing or accreditation mechanisms, teacher certification, and capacity building. The different strands may be administered by different agencies, with varying levels of expertise in and commitment to early childhood programs, and then problems of coordination may arise. The only solution is to develop a coherent policy toward quality from the outset and to make that policy as consistent as possible.

CAPACITY-BUILDING MECHANISMS

States can also improve the capacities of early childhood programs to expand and develop and build competence in the community of providers, parents, and advocates. Capacity building does not directly provide services, and it may therefore be considered a frill; and its effects are sometimes uncertain and unmeasurable. However, capacity building can be viewed as an investment in future services.[22]

Resource and referral (R&R) agencies are perhaps the most powerful forms of capacity building. At their best, R&R agencies provide information to parents seeking child care, assistance to providers establishing new facilities, and advice to centers and family day care homes about good practice; they serve as advocates for children and children's programs, and can negotiate with government agencies to streamline regulatory barriers. They work simultaneously to increase capacity and improve quality, and they help the child care "market" operate more smoothly by providing the information that both parents and providers often lack. While many communities around the country have R&R agencies, public funding is still rare except in California and Massachusetts, which both support statewide systems of R&R agencies.[23]

R&R agencies could be governmental agencies, operated as part of school districts or city offices, but most of them are private organizations. As in the case of accreditation, there are advantages to private status; and because the roles of regulator and friend are hard to combine, there are benefits to a division of labor in which public agencies would provide funding and monitor compliance with regulations, and private organizations would give advice and technical assistance. One vision of a state-local system, then, would incorporate both local governments to allocate funds and regulate facilities, and private R&R agencies to plan, inform parents, and provide technical assistance.

Another form of capacity building is the technical assistance that public agencies can provide to early childhood programs, particularly to improve quality. Such efforts, however, require both sufficient staff and staff who have substantial expertise in operating programs and legitimacy with providers; efforts to economize on administrative costs and to select staff through a civil service procedure that ignores expertise can make such an effort useless.

States can also provide specific forms of technical assistance by grants to local private or public-private organizations. For example, the California Child Care Initiative provides assistance specifically for family day care in six communities, with local R&R agencies involved in recruiting, training, and providing continuing support to new family day care providers.[24] It provides an example of special-purpose assistance, initiated in this case by the BankAmerica Foundation but combining public and private funds.

Finally, state capacity-building mechanisms may arise in response to specific problems or crises. The inability of child care facilities to borrow in private capital markets has led some states and cities to set up loan pools, lending public funds at lower rates to improve physical facilities. The recent crisis in insurance, which left many child care providers unable to find liability insurance, led others to establish public insurance programs. These are essentially ways of clearing away barriers to expansion of the child care system.

ADMINISTRATIVE OPTIONS

Still another decision involves the choice of which state agency will administer early childhood programs. Administrative decisions are crucial because an aggressive and inclusive state policy should encompass *all* sources of funding, both federal and state, and an administrative structure that can accomplish this is then necessary. In addition, the dominant outlook of an agency and its personnel may partially determine the content of its programs, particularly because the divisions among "developmental," "welfare," and "compensatory" conceptions of early childhood programs are reflected in differences among government agencies. Reconciling the strands of support for early childhood programs therefore requires confronting these administrative divisions.

Currently, most federally funded child care is administered through welfare agencies, while most preschool programs recently enacted have been placed in state departments of education to emphasize their educational orientation. Neither alternative is completely satisfactory. Welfare agencies have an unavoidable stigma attached to them, and they have a greater concern with moving families off welfare and with abused and neglected children than with "normal" children and developmental goals. Education agencies are often unfamiliar with early childhood programs and unsympathetic to child care concerns and to the developmental orientation of many early childhood professionals.

To avoid these problems, states have sometimes considered administering early childhood programs in an independent state agency, like an Office for Children. The state of Washington decided to administer its new preschool programs through the Department of Community Affairs, which is also responsible for Head Start, partly because of feelings that the education department would be unsympathetic to programs for young children. Still another alternative is a model of interagency coordination, like that South Carolina has adopted. Although the South Carolina Department of Education is responsible for the preschool program, an interagency coordinating council, with members from all state agencies serving children, must approve all plans for the program. Similarly, Massachusetts has created a system that allocates different functions to different agencies and then coordinates all of them through the governor's Office of Human Resources.[25]

Given the current divisions over early childhood programs, developing a new and probably weak agency is not necessarily a good resolution of the administrative decision. An alternative would be to grant administrative responsibility to an existing agency, like the state's education agency, but then to ensure that it has the staff and the connections, including a strong advisory group, to ensure that programs adhere to good practice, and to bridge the different worlds of early childhood.

The policy options outlined in this chapter assume a particular division of labor among federal and local governments. The federal government is primarily responsible for funding. In addition, the federal government is the obvious level to sponsor data collection and research on early childhood programs and to provide some technical assistance to states. But given the enduring predilection of Congress for small, categorical programs, the federal government will not provide any coherent vision of early childhood policy. Instead, states are responsible for creating coherent policy out of the welter of federal programs and state supplements, with the additional goal of reconciling the different strands of support for early childhood programs. In some states, especially those that are large and heterogeneous, it may be desirable to establish a local government as an active partner, making decisions about local needs and providers but without providing very much funding lest poor communities be left with few resources. Such a federal-state-local partnership has the potential for creating coherent policy out of the bits and pieces that now exist. But to do so will require that states confront their options carefully, motivated by a clear vision of what early childhood programs can be.

Confronting the Limitations of Public Revenues

The sense of a "crisis" in child care and early childhood education among many advocates is first and last an issue of insufficient funding, which in turn prevents low- and middle-income children from gaining access to high-quality programs, limits the quality of care in many programs, results in low wages and high turnover among providers, and makes it difficult for welfare parents to work their way off welfare. The upsurge of interest in early childhood programs, and the political interest that has led to federal legislation and state programs, has been especially welcome for the resources it promises to generate.

But it is crucial to remember how limited the programs enacted and envisioned so far are. Current federal legislation contemplates annual funding of $1.75 billion, but this is sufficient to fund programs only for roughly 5 percent of low-income children age 0-5 in need of care.[26] By contrast, a recent National Research Council report recommended changes in federal policy that might cost $5 billion to $10 billion,[27] and the Committee for Economic Development estimated annual costs of $13.2 billion for their proposed child care program.[28] Funding for child care under the Family Support Act has so far been relatively low, even in those states that have been the first to implement welfare-to-work plans and whose funding of child care is relatively generous.[29] The recently enacted state prekindergarten programs have, with only a few exceptions (like Texas), trivial funding, providing a few million dollars for programs that are best interpreted as pilot projects.[30] Even in California, with the most generous early childhood program in the country and substantial state funding, only 8.7 percent of children age 0-5 eligible for public support (those below 84 percent of median income) and in need of care are in any kind of program, as well as 7 percent of children 6-10 in after-school programs. The most generous interpretation one can make of the recently enacted and proposed programs is that they constitute precedents and models for future funding rather than sources of substantial funding in their own right.

These numbers indicate that the arguments for public support of early childhood programs have been relatively weak. Despite the different strands of support for early childhood programs, a basic uncertainty persists about whether government should extend its support to young children rather than having parents remain entirely responsible. Especially for poor children, neither the compensatory rationale (with its associated benefit-cost argument) nor the welfare rationale have been able to generate the funding necessary. While the feminist rationale has justified the largest source of federal funding (the Dependent Care Tax Credit), it has done little for low-income children.

A different rationale for the public support of young children, one that is consistent with the changed realities of American families, depends on the timing of child care expenses. By definition, expenses for child care come when children are young. Their parents are also young, and most of them are at the lowest point in their earning capacities. Their incomes are further limited by the presence of children. But the earning capacity of most parents increases over their lifetimes, and when they are older they tend to have higher earnings without the drain of child care expenses. There are no mechanisms for borrowing against future earnings in order to support young children, but such an approach could be the basis for a Children's Fund, to be funded by a progressive tax on personal and corporate income and from which revenues for early childhood programs would come. Through this mechanism parents with young children would draw upon the fund, and those with children past the age where they need early childhood programs would be net supporters. In addition, those without children would be net contributors to the fund, reflecting the principle that children are in part a social responsibility, while those with children would be beneficiaries.

In many ways a Children's Fund is a children's analogue to the Social Security system, which has as its essential rationale evening out the flows of income and expenditures over an individual's lifetime. The Social Security system has been unique for its public support, unlike other income support programs. Evidently the logic of redistributing expenses over a lifetime is politically more potent than redistribution from rich to poor. Children's advocates should be able to use this logic on behalf of small children.

If we took John Dewey's precept seriously ("What the best and wisest parent wants for his own child, that must the community want for all its children"), then it would be relatively clear what to do.

Increasingly, parents need arrangements for children during working hours. They worry about the quality and the affordability of care, and, while parents disagree about the importance of cognitive and noncognitive goals in programs for young children, few of them would subordinate one to the other. Parents—all parents—have high aspirations for their young children; they want them to experience success and develop confidence outside their homes, to grow up competent and healthy, to get a good education, and not to be kept from the mainstream of American life because of poor schooling. To be sure, parents often don't know how to go about assuring these good things, especially if they are battered by the pressures of daily life, the strictures of poverty, and the daily insults of lower-class status. They may retreat in confusion or defer to professionals.

Still, it is not hard to see what is good for young children. The accumulated experiences of early childhood programs, the research on program effects and quality, the broad areas of consensus among parents and those professionals who have thought the hardest about young children, provide the materials for knitting together the divisions in the arena of early childhood programs. Then it will be possible to make good on our rhetoric about children as "our most precious natural resources," rather than leaving that rhetoric as evidence of broken promises.

FOOTNOTES

1. Anne Mitchell, Michelle Seligson, and Fern Marx, *Early Childhood Programs and the Public Schools* (Dover, MA: Auburn House, 1989).

2. Committee for Economic Development, *Children in Need: Investment Strategies for the Educationally Disadvantaged* (New York: Committee for Economic Development, 1987).

3. Panel on Child Care Policy, Committee on Child Development Policy Research and Public Policy, National Research Council, *Who Cares for America's Children? Child Care Policy for the 1990s* (Washington, DC: National Academy Press, 1990), Section III.

4. Carl Kaestle, *Pillars of the Republic: Common Schools and American Society* (New York: Hill and Wang, 1983).

5. John Berrueta-Clement, Lawrence J. Schweinhart, W. Steven Barnett, Ann P. Epstein, and David P. Weikart, "Changed Lives: The Effects of the Perry Preschool Program on Youth through Age 19," *Monographs of the High/Scope Educational Research Foundation*, no. 8 (Ypsilanti, MI: High/Scope Educational Research Foundation, 1984).

6. National Society for the Study of Education, "Survey of Programs in Parental Education," in *Preschool and Parental Education*, Twenty-eighth Yearbook of the National Society for the Study of Education, Part 1, ed. Guy M. Whipple (Bloomington, IL: Public School Publishing Co., 1929), p. 312.

7. Margaret Steinfels, *Who's Minding the Children? The History and Politics of Day Care in America* (New York: Simon and Schuster, 1973), p. 29.

8. W. Norton Grubb and Marvin Lazerson, *Broken Promises: How Americans Fail Their Children* (New York: Basic Books, 1982), chap. 8; Steinfels, *Who's Minding the Children?*, chap. 2.

9. Howard Hayghe, "Rise in Mothers' Labor Force Activity Includes Those with Infants," *Monthly Labor Review* 109 (1986): 43-45; U.S. Department of Labor, *Labor Force Statistics Derived from the Current Population Survey: A Databook*, vol. 1, Bureau of Labor Statistics Bulletin no. 2096 (Washington, DC: Bureau of Labor Statistics, 1982).

10. As of the writing of this chapter, H.R. 3 and S. 5 were the dominant bills in Congress, widely thought to be the basis of a reconciliation bill. They contained, in different proportions, funds for expansion of Head Start (a compensatory program), for the expansion of Social Service Block Grant (a welfare-oriented program), for the expansion of the Dependent Care Tax Credit (most appropriate to the feminist model), for early childhood programs specifically in the schools, and some funds for states to establish their own programs.

11. Mitchell, Seligson, and Marx, *Early Childhood Programs and the Public Schools*, chap. 2.

12. At the federal level, the practice of establishing small categorical programs has been continued in the Family Support Act and in H.R. 3 and S. 5. Most of the recent state initiatives have created half-day preschool programs for at-risk children, administered by state education agencies and local school districts without any connection to existing child care programs (public or private). At the same time, in different legislative committees and different agencies, states have been making decisions about Title XX/SSBG child care programs, with at least thirteen states making substantial increases in funds available for child care, but with no relation to schools or to compensatory preschools.

13. This description is based on research about vocational education and job training programs. For a summary of the research, see W. Norton Grubb and Lorraine McDonnell, *Work-related Education and Training: The System and the Policy Instruments* (Santa Monica: Rand Corporation, 1989), and idem, "Local 'Systems' of Work-related Education and Job Training: Interdependence, Diversity and the Quandaries of Effectiveness," Working draft (Berkeley, CA: National Center for Research in Vocational Education, University of California, 1990). But this is a more general pattern in areas of social policy dominated by federal legislation, especially policies for low-income individuals.

14. On the lack of coordination in the current "system," see especially Mitchell, Seligson, and Marx, *Early Childhood Programs and the Public Schools*, chap. 7. In the education and training world, many local "systems" prove to be remarkably coherent, but this is because the programs that make them up are often large and entrepreneurial, and have fiscal incentives to collaborate. (See Grubb and McDonnell, "Local 'Systems' of Work-related Education and Job Training.") In the early childhood world, providers are typically very small, not at all entrepreneurial, and usually face very weak fiscal incentives to collaborate, so the conditions necessary to establish coherent "systems" at the local level are absent.

15. The federal process is one of interest-group liberalism run amuck, with the federal government giving small amounts of money to each interest group rather than making hard decisions about which claims are most worthy. (I acknowledge my debt to Lorraine McDonnell's views and phrasing.) In my opinion the same process has taken place in recent federal legislation in early childhood, where a well-designed bill—the ABC (A Better Chance) bill, incorporating sound policies and developmental principles—has been replaced by a pastiche of small categorical grants, each placating a particular interest group.

16. For example, states could consider the location of Head Start programs in deciding where to locate programs funded with other funds, and devise afternoon programs to complement half-day Head Start programs. States should also devise sliding fee schedules, with fees calculated according to the tax credits parents receive, in order to incorporate the federal tax credit into state policy.

17. W. Norton Grubb, "Young Children Face the State: Issues and Options for Early Childhood Programs," *American Journal of Education* 97 (1989): 358-397.

18. U.S. General Accounting Office, *Early Childhood Education: What Are the Costs of High-Quality Programs?* GAO/HRD-90-43BR (Washington, DC: U.S. General Accounting Office, January, 1990).

19. In California, the vendor/voucher system appears to be slightly cheaper for preschool child care, but only because this system uses more family day care, less school-based care with high salaries, and is more extensively used in rural areas. In fact, the vendor/voucher program for school-age child care is relatively more expensive than other programs because of the administrative costs. See W. Norton Grubb, "The Conundrums of Early Childhood and Child Care Programs in California," in *The Conditions of Children in California*, ed. Michael Kirst (Berkeley, CA: Policy Analysis for California, University of California, 1989).

20. Marcy Whitebook, Carollee Howes, and Deborah Phillips, *Who Cares? Child Care Teachers and the Quality of Care in America* (Oakland, CA: Child Care Employee Project, 1990).

21. Sue Bredekamp, *Accreditation Criteria and Procedures of the National Academy of Early Childhood Programs* (Washington, DC: National Association for the Education of Young Children, 1984).

22. Lorraine McDonnell and Richard Elmore, *Alternative Policy Instruments* (New Brunswick, NJ: Center for Policy Research in Education, Rutgers University, 1987).

23. Alfred Kahn and Sheila Kamerman, *Child Care: Facing the Hard Choices* (Dover, MA: Auburn House, 1987), chap. 2.

24. California Child Care Resource and Referral Network, "Child Care Initiative Year-End Report, October 1, 1985-September 30, 1986," (San Francisco: California Child Care Resource and Referral Network, January, 1987).

25. Kahn and Kamerman, *Child Care: Facing the Hard Choices*, chap. 3.

26. To my knowledge there are no national estimates of the percent of eligible children who might be served under federal legislation, because the form of that legislation is still too unclear. However, one comparison is suggestive. If Congress appropriates $1.75 billion, California would receive roughly 10 percent, or $175 million. The state now spends about $320 million on early childhood and child care programs, and this sum provides various programs to almost 9 percent of children 0-5 (including 18 percent of those 3-5) who are eligible (under 84 percent of median income) *and* in need of care, and to 7 percent of those 6-10. See Grubb, "The Conundrums of Early Childhood and Child Care Programs in California." Roughly, then, new federal funds of $175 million would increase the proportion of eligible children served by about 55 percent, or would serve about 5 percent of eligible children age 0-5 as well as 4 percent of those 5-10.

27. Panel on Child Care Policy, *Who Cares for America's Children?*, chap. 10.

28. "C.E.D. Seeks $11.5 Billion for Reforms," *Education Week*, 25 May 1988.

29. Karin Martinson and James Riccio, *GAIN: Child Care in a Welfare Employment Initiative* (New York: Manpower Demonstration Research Corporation, 1989).

30. Mitchell, Seligson, and Marx, *Early Childhood Programs and the Public Schools*, Table 2-2.

CHAPTER XIII

Excellence in Early Childhood Education: Defining Characteristics and Next-Decade Strategies

SHARON L. KAGAN

In their recent volume, Tobin, Wu, and Davidson chronicle the nature of preschool education in three cultures and suggest that preschools have been more a force for cultural continuity than for cultural change.[1] They conclude that preschool education in China and Japan has been externally congruent with each country's overarching mission of education, and consequently, preschool education has remained fairly consistent over time. In contrast, preschool education in the United States has changed direction frequently, reflecting our national ambiguity regarding the purpose of education in general, and the disjunction of purpose between child care and early education, specifically. Concurring with the above thesis, in this chapter I suggest that American early childhood education (like education in general) is at the brink of a major shift in how it conceptualizes and defines its mission. Linking care and education, such redefinition affords promising options and opportunities. Following an analysis that delineates this change, I offer a new definition of excellence in early care and education and suggest strategies for achieving it.

The Changing Zeitgeist in Education and in Early Childhood Education

Alternately praised and criticized, the September 1989 presidential summit legitimated the groundswell for change that has been brewing

This paper was commissioned by the Office of Educational Research and Improvement, U.S. Department of Education. Since individuals undertaking such projects are encouraged to express freely their professional judgment, this paper does not necessarily represent positions or policies of the U.S. Department of Education, and no official endorsement should be inferred.

in educational circles for a good half decade. With its emphasis on setting national goals and a commitment to early intervention, the summit boldly reminded our nation of the inextricable link between societal and educational concerns. America was put on notice that "reading, 'riting, and 'rithmetic" are not the sole ends of education: a fourth "r" was added to the litany—namely, readying children to function optimally in an increasingly stressful and technologically sophisticated society. In so doing, the summit endorsed a place for social, emotional, and functional competence, alongside cognitive competence, as goals for education. Further, preventing problems before they begin, working with young children, supporting families in their complex roles, and collaborating with other community institutions were applauded as appropriate educational strategies. Such visions not only reflect an educational enterprise in flux, but changing attitudes toward the care and education of young children in our country.

With so much attention being accorded young children presently, it is interesting to recall that barely a half century ago, day care and early education were seen, first, as nonessentials, and, second, as distinct entities with very different functions. Day care, established as a social service for working or indigent parents, was essentially a child of the welfare system. Often considered custodial, day care was thought to be of inferior quality when compared with programs serving comparably aged children in the private sector. Private-sector programs, largely fee-for-service, were crafted to serve the needs of middle-class America; they were to rescue children and parents from suburbia by providing socialization opportunities for both. As our social conscience grew, federal- and state-supported preschool programs emerged to help children and families overcome the negative effects of poverty. Manifested in Head Start, Title I of the Elementary and Secondary Education Act, and a limited number of state initiatives, these efforts, largely part-day in length, attempted to meet children's cognitive, social, emotional, and physical needs, and often encouraged a significant role for parents.

Since the programs emerged from such different historical traditions, it is not at all surprising that they differed on nearly every major variable: staffing, funding, guidelines, and even the array of services offered. Less understandable is the degree to which even regulatable characteristics varied: ratios, group size, teacher or caregiver preparation. And most important, the troublesome legacies of such dramatic differences remain enigmatic.

Accounting for the situation, one interpretation suggests that lacking any overarching vision or policy, child care and early education grew like Topsy, yielding a nonsystem characterized by competition and fragmentation.[2] Without a unified vision, a single agency at the federal level, or any incentives to collaborate, individual programs bred and clung tenaciously to their own values and guidelines. A political climate in which funding was limited and program survival precarious exacerbated competition, forcing each program to focus on preserving its own existence. Consequently, programs were never seen as components of a broader whole. Rather they were independent entities, each fighting for its survival. And even when programs were linked for a particular project, they rarely coalesced in spirit or in duration. Thus, early care and education services evolved as little more than a polyglot array of disjointed programs.

In spite of this legacy, early care and education is on the verge of dramatic change for several important reasons. Widely cited demographics document changes in American family life that have propelled more women into the work force, creating the need for more early care and education services.[3] America's massive welfare reform effort, the Family Support Act of 1988, will also push low-income and unemployed women into training programs and work, and their children into child care. Escalating numbers of pregnant teenagers, "crack" infants, and single-parent families are increasing the need for parenting intervention and family support programs, two services closely aligned with early care and education. In short, social need is one potent force accelerating change in early care and education.

Beyond need, widely popularized research findings bespeak the effectiveness and cost-effectiveness of early intervention for low-income children, leaving little doubt of its personal and societal value.[4] Research has led those working in the field, regardless of auspices, to agree that quality for all children in nonfamilial care and education is most closely tied to (a) the nature of the relationship between the caregiver and the child, (b) the nature of the environment, and (c) the nature of the relationship between the caregiver and the parent. Led by the National Association for the Education of Young Children (NAEYC), the professional association representing the field, quality has been codified in a single volume, *Developmentally Appropriate Practice* (DAP).[5] Serving as a pedagogical and policy guide, DAP is being written into legislation at the state and federal levels, and is being adopted in foreign countries.

If rapidly accelerating need and the proven effectiveness of early intervention programs for low-income children have amplified the attention accorded early care and education, another force—business and political endorsement—has propelled it to unprecedented heights. Corporate America, concerned about its present and future work force, has broadened its interest not only in schools, but in child care and early education. Roughly 3,500 of the nation's six million employers offer their employees some form of child care assistance,[6] and many corporations are establishing foundations or corporate-giving strategies that accord priority to early care and education. In the political domain, elected representatives in most states and at the federal level have considered legislation to increase services to young children and their families. Thirty-two states have actually made commitments to some form of preschool service,[7] and the federal government is on the brink of passing the most comprehensive piece of early care and education legislation in history.

Just as a consensus is emerging regarding the mission and goals of education in general, such consensus is rapidly coalescing regarding early care and education programs. No longer seen as subordinate in purpose or importance to education in general or to each other, child care and early education programs, it is generally agreed, are pedagogically similar and should not be separated. While recognizing that most preschool aged youngsters are cared for in their homes, there is growing acceptance that those children in out-of-home settings, whether labeled care or education, must receive high-quality services that meet children's developmental, social, emotional, physical, and cognitive needs. Furthermore, because of the importance of family to healthy child development, young children receiving out-of-home services must be understood and served within the context of their family and community.

Despite rhetorical consensus regarding quality and pedagogy, there is little agreement over strategy—how best to accomplish these ends. Again, like education in general, early care and education are faced with the challenge of converting conceptual visions to concrete definitions and practical strategies.

Defining Excellence in Early Care and Education: The First Step

It is an odd paradox that though much energy has been expended on defining and implementing "excellence" in education, there has been comparatively little mention of "excellence" in early care and education. Early childhood educators are certainly familiar with *A Nation at Risk*, the 1983 report of the National Commission on Excellence in Education, as well as with the many scholarly treatises on excellence. Nevertheless, though they are well aware of the import of the excellence movement in education, they have not been engulfed by or enslaved to the concept of excellence.

In spite of this absence in early care and education, debates have revolved around defining and researching what may be an equivalent concept, "quality." Like excellence, quality embraces both the process and the outcome of education. For early educators, quality of process means devoting attention to strategies, curricula, and environmental elements. Quality of outcome means focusing multidimensionally on the impact of the intervention on youngsters' social, emotional, and cognitive competence, as well as on their families. Without doubt, quality has been and will remain a legitimate goal for early care and education programs, perhaps the most important goal.

But quality, as the early childhood profession has conventionally defined it, can not be the only goal. Certainly, early childhood programs must continue to serve individual children and their families. But given a changing national zeitgeist that demands expanded services, and the field's history of segregated services for children, inequitable compensation for providers, and programmatic inequities and fragmentation, current efforts must be directed to a higher standard of excellence, one that meets broader societal goals and transcends individual programs. Such a standard must embrace programmatic *quality* and commitments to *equality* and *integrity*. These three components of excellence in early care and education are like the legs of a tripod: no one can stand alone. Only the three together can bring the requisite stability and support. While recognizing their interdependence, I turn now to individual discussions of quality, equality, and integrity, concentrating on their unique dimensions and issues.

QUALITY: THE CRITICAL COMPONENT

Correlates of quality in early care and education have been well researched and documented. They fall, for purposes of this discussion, into three general categories: (a) findings associated with environmental variables, (b) findings associated with children's behaviors, and (c) findings associated with the interaction of environment and children's behaviors.

When discussing environmental variables in programs for young children, scholars are concerned with far more than the physical properties of the setting, though these are surely important. The nature, amount, and utilization of space and materials all affect the child's experience.[8] But environment is also shaped by ratios, group size, stability of caregivers, curriculum, and the involvement of parents. Studies indicate that keeping groups small so that there is ample opportunity for adult-child interactions leads to less aggressive behavior, greater involvement, and more cooperation among children.[9] Strong supportive child-adult interactions in turn contribute to children's social and intellectual competence.[10] We also know that a planned, sequenced, and developmentally appropriate program with a balance of child-initiated and teacher-directed activities enhances children's learning.[11] Active involvement of parents is related to lasting effects of high-quality programs.[12]

Findings associated with children's behavior repeatedly endorse the need for child play as the key to successful outcomes. Lieberman found correlations between play and the results of standardized intelligence test scores,[13] and Sylva, Bruner, and Genova pointed out improvements in problem-solving ability, academic skills, and attitudes.[14] Play leads to more complex and sophisticated behavior[15] and to improved memory[16] and language development.[17]

While quality is certainly not restricted to any singular curriculum model, recent research attests to the efficacy of developmentally appropriate practices that integrate environmental and child action variables. It appears that when curricula embrace developmentally appropriate practices (and many do), positive gains for children accrue. For example, when comparing children who had been in an academically enriched program with youngsters in developmentally appropriate programs, children in the former group were more anxious, less creative, and had less positive attitudes toward school than those in the latter group. Although youngsters in the academically enriched program had a slight advantage on ability tests when tested at age four, that advantage disappeared a year later when the children went on to kindergarten.[18]

Yet, despite these potent research findings and documented practices, teachers throughout the country report having great difficulty implementing high-quality, developmentally appropriate programs. In kindergartens, more structured programs are the norm. In a California study, for example, Smith reported that in over 400 kindergartens, workbooks and worksheets were used more frequently than any other activity.[19] And even though teachers were concerned about the negative consequences of such inefficient strategies, 62 percent indicated that they would continue these practices. In an Ohio study, Hatch and Freeman found that 66.7 percent of the teachers questioned felt that what they did each day was in conflict with their beliefs about what children need in kindergarten.[20] And a wide range of quality and appropriateness was found in a study of North Carolina kindergartens, with 60 percent of the observed classrooms falling well below the researchers' criterion of quality, 20 percent near it, and only 20 percent meeting it.[21]

The distance between what constitutes quality and what is implemented in classrooms throughout the nation is troublesome. While no single cause claims responsibility, there is little question that fast-track parents raising fast-track children (also known as gourmet babies or cornucopia kids) want results, as do low-income families who see educational success as one escape from poverty. Worried parents, concerned about the prevalence of child abuse, drug enticement, and television overdosing, overprogram their children, robbing them of the "leisure to think their own thoughts, an essential element in the development of creativity."[22] Such nonschool-based pressure is translated into demands for more structured curricula and activities within the classroom.

Beyond these external forces, others internal to the profession—the national mania for accountability, the drive for higher test results, and the readiness to retain young children—have accelerated more structured and academically oriented early childhood classes. Well-documented elsewhere, the consequences of such practices wreak havoc with young children.[23] Major professional organizations, including the National Association for the Education of Young Children and the National Association of Early Childhood Specialists in State Departments of Education, have adopted formal positions against such strategies, and the National Academy of Sciences Forum on the Future of Children and Families launched a panel to address the issue. Nevertheless, overtesting with its negative consequences for young children continues unabated in early childhood programs.

But parental pressures and selected school practices are not the only factors inhibiting the implementation of quality programs for young children. Two cost-based factors enter the picture also. First, because salaries and benefits for early childhood personnel are so low, current workers regularly seek employment options elsewhere and new people are not attracted to the field. Turnover is estimated to

average about 41 percent nationally,[24] and directors report the recruitment of qualified staff as their number one problem. High turnover and
its corollary, diminished staff quality, compromise program effectiveness on several dimensions. For young children who are the most
vulnerable and most dependent on consistent secure relationships,
short-term attachments, particularly among the all-important adults in
their lives, are difficult to comprehend and tolerate.

Challenging for children, turnover is also problematic in maintaining curricular and pedagogical quality. Heavy turnover means that
many more new child-care teachers are staffing classes. Inexperience
among neophytes naturally makes them insecure, fostering
dependence on prescribed activities and formal curricula. Couple these
insecurities with the press for institutional conformity encountered by
kindergarten teachers and it is not difficult to understand why
curricular spontaneity, individuality, and quality have been
compromised.

The second cost factor inhibiting quality is the discrepancy
between the amount of funding early care and education programs
require and what they actually receive. The highly successful and
widely touted Perry Preschool Program was estimated to cost $4,818
per child per year in 1981 dollars.[25] If one assumes that, given
inflation, costs double in eight to nine years, a comparable program
would cost about $9,600 in 1990. And though that amount of money
may not be needed for all preschool efforts, still it is a far cry from
current average expenditures of about $3,000 per child per year for
child care programs.[26] Further, it varies greatly from the recent U.S.
General Accounting Office study indicating average expenditures in
high-quality programs were about $4,660 including in-kind
services.[27] While parents, politicians, and the media predicate their
calls for more early intervention programs on the results achieved by
costly efforts, funding at commensurate levels is absent. America
*over*expects robust results from programs it consistently *under*funds.

The cost-quality dilemma permeates all debates regarding early
care and education policy and practice. Without sufficient funding,
staff turnover will escalate, and results for children and families are
sure to be compromised. Resolution of the cost-quality problem,
though apparently distant, centers on two questions: (a) Who should
be responsible for paying for early care and education services? and
(b) What should such services embrace? Once these herculean
questions are answered and services appropriately funded, the quality
component of excellence will be more readily achieved.

Predating America's recent commitment to young children, our national interest in equality of educational opportunity has a long history. Constitutional provisions, court decisions, legislative actions, and administrative mandates have all affirmed national commitments to equal access and equal justice in our society and in our schools. Concerned about assimilating "new immigrants"[28] and according opportunity to minorities,[29] generations of scholars and practitioners have looked to schools as societal equalizers. Liberal and progressive philosophers created a climate of concern for greater access and service.[30] And the Supreme Court sought to assure greater integration in the historic decision in *Brown* v. *Board of Education.*

While revisionist historians debate the effects of these efforts, Gordon and Yeakey suggest that such legal expressions have asserted the *right* to equality, but have not ensured it.[31] No description more aptly reflects the situation in early care and education. Rhetorically, practitioners in the field have loudly announced their commitment to early intervention as a means of reducing social alienation and enhancing opportunity among youngsters from low-income families. Head Start, the nation's premier program for young children, was grounded in just such a commitment to improve social competence and eradicate the deficits imposed on those beginning life in poverty.

But there were difficulties with the widely hailed deficit strategies that framed intervention efforts of the 1960s. By their very design, such programs were constructed to acculturate poor children to middle-class norms and values, thereby discrediting the strengths inherent in their own culture. Additionally, because the programs were targeted to those most in need and were open only to those who met specific financial eligibility requirements, a permanent two-tier system that segregated the poor was legitimized. Though presumably well intentioned, our social strategy effectively sanctioned economic segregation for preschoolers by sending youngsters from middle- and upper-income families to fee-for-service programs and children from low-income families to subsidized programs. Worse, this economic segregation often led to racial segregation, belying the law of the land and diminishing opportunities for equality and excellence for all children.

Beyond equality for the children themselves, early care and education is also plagued by a lack of programmatic equality. There are no consistent federal standards for child care, in spite of repeated attempts to establish them.[32] As a result, multiple standards have been established throughout the nation. Head Start has its performance standards, several national for-profit chains have developed their own means of "quality control," and NAEYC has established the Center Accreditation Program which serves as an index of quality across systems.

Standards exist at the state level, but they vary widely from state to state not only in the thresholds established but in the areas that are regulated. Even more problematic are the variations in regulations that take place within a single geographic locale. In some municipalities schools and churches are exempt from licensure while day care centers must meet burdensome and often costly regulatory standards. As a result, the more highly regulated child care centers often face more difficulty in launching and sustaining programs than do church- or school-based programs. Advocates argue that consistent regulations should apply in all settings: what is safeguarded for one child should be safeguarded for all. Nevertheless, in spite of pleas for regulatory equity among programs, little exists.

The complex problem of equity shared by early care and education, and education in general, relates to their joint task of defining what constitutes equality and then determining how to allocate finite resources to achieve it. The questions to be answered are twofold: Is equality a constant or may it vary so as to achieve equity? And given limited resources, should dollars be spent on children in targeted programs, thereby increasing segregation of the needy? Or should limited dollars be spent on universal services for all, thereby fostering integration and generating broader-based political appeal? Defining what we mean by equality—targeted or universal service delivery—and describing how best to achieve it are persistent issues that demand our attention.

INTEGRITY: THE UNCONSIDERED COMPONENT

It is not coincidence that the words *integrity* and *integrate* share a common Latin root: both refer to making whole or making sound, to linking disparate parts into an unimpaired condition. We speak of the "integrity of a ship's hull" or an "integrated plot" or an "integrated personality." The word *integrity* can also connote a qualitative dimension, suggesting adherence to moral and ethical principles.

While early care and education has been long on the latter definition of integrity (adherence to moral and ethical principles), it has been short on the former (linking disparate parts). The fragmented history discussed earlier set the course for the mix of programs and services embraced by the terms "early care" and "education." But this legacy of separation has been reinforced by our nation's episodic commitment and nonsystematic approach to children's policy.[33] Lacking an integrated scheme or vision, children's policy is an amalgam of separate children's programs that have been funded with little understanding or recognition of the whole. It is akin to strengthening an umbrella by randomly adding spokes without noticing that its linking mechanism, the fabric, is what makes the umbrella function. In short, early care and education has many spokes, but lacks the fabric of coordination.

Historically, such lack of coordination has mitigated against efficiencies of operation and economies of scale. For example, in spite of large numbers of eligible children not receiving services, Head Start and state preschool programs often compete for the youngsters.[34] Why? One frequently offered explanation is that the lack of comprehensive community-wide data and coordination in siting new services encourages different sponsors to locate programs in exactly the same pockets of high need. Because program sponsors do not communicate with each other before opening programs, services are "stacked" in high-need areas. The result is that program slots outnumber eligible children, providers compete for youngsters, and valuable slots often go unused.

But such inefficiency does not end with children; programs routinely compete for staff. Rather than coming together for joint recruitment or training, each program feels compelled to launch its own separate (and costly) efforts. Rather than coordinate to realize economies of bulk buying, hundreds of child care programs in a given community purchase goods and services independently. Not advocating the merging of programs or their consolidation under one auspice and fully respecting the need for program diversity, calls for coordination simply suggest that there are program functions that may be more effectively carried out collectively than individually. Such a strategy seeks to allow programs to maintain the benefits of independence while expediting those functions that overlap and/or cause inefficiencies among programs.

In spite of perceived benefits and the reduction of "systemic pain," such coordination is rare. The nonsystem survives. And within the subsidized sector, it has been perpetuated by government policy that has discouraged coordination. With funding threatened for violating regulations that prohibit "contamination" with other programs, federally supported early care and education programs, begun as separate entities, remained isolated for decades. A few innovative programs have "skirted" regulation to link funds so that services for children could be expedited. But this is the rare exception, not the accepted rule.

This ethos of separatism not only has affected routine functioning but has severely constrained the field's ability to think, vision, or act as a whole. When threats to Head Start surfaced, for example, the only practitioners who worked to counter them were from the Head Start community; they were not joined by school people or child care advocates. Similarly, when child care initiatives were debated, other service providers looked on at "arm's length." The legacy of programmatic fragmentation has left the profession bereft of policy integrity and policy capacity. Like the vicious cycle, uncoordinated advocacy has begotten more isolated programs which, in turn, have led to greater programmatic isolation.

And if matters weren't complicated enough, the advent of increased attention to early care and education has exacerbated the situation. Although it might seem that the prospect of more dollars would ease tensions, it has only intensified the historic acrimony and pitted program against program. Given that new programs could be housed in a variety of settings, including schools, child care centers, and Head Start sites, and given the lack of data attesting to the superiority of any one sponsor over another, policymakers are justifiably confused. At the federal and state levels, they debate the comparative merits of lodging new programs in human service or educational agencies. Advocates offer little solace, supporting their own individual choices.

Expansion of the sort now being considered poses tremendous operational challenges in such a fragmented system. Large numbers of new professionals are going to be needed. But in a field where programs already compete fiercely for qualified personnel and turnover is so high, the likelihood of expanded programs acquiring an adequate work force (much less doing so without causing pain to colleagues) is low. The need for highly specialized early childhood space will also increase. Programs that have been housed for decades in leased settings, particularly the schools, are being forced to relocate so that districts can make room for their "own" newly funded programs.

Beyond hurdling operational difficulties, competition for new programs is keen because the stakes are so very high. Not only will the "victorious" sponsor end up with sizable increases in financial support, but in all likelihood, the victor will set licensing requirements and professional standards that will influence salaries and practices for years. In effect, nothing less than the future direction of the field is at stake.

Like the other components of excellence—quality and equality—integrity presents its own conundrums. On the one hand, there is the long history of competition among providers that has rendered the field's policy structure impervious to integration. On the other, theoretical and practical paradigms have shifted: new commitments to serving the whole child in the context of family and community bespeak a need to integrate services and policies. How to reconcile current needs and thinking with an arcane but historically entrenched policy apparatus is the challenge.

Strategizing for Excellence: The Second Step

Three linked strategies address the above problems and offer hope that the profession can move from well-intentioned piecemeal programs to comprehensive services that reach new standards of excellence in early care and education. These include: (a) moving from "programs" to "systems" models; (b) moving from a particularistic to universalistic vision; and (c) moving from short- to long-term commitments.

MOVING FROM "PROGRAMS TO SYSTEMS" MODELS

Lacking sufficient support and resources to institute programs and services for all preschool-aged youngsters, the nation, supported by generous foundation efforts, sought to establish program models from which lessons could be deduced. In retrospect, this "program" models approach has been a mixed blessing.

On the positive side, it has allowed the field to experiment. In effect, Donald Campbell's concept of the experimenting society took root in early care and education. Because there was no single model or strategy, different programs with different goals emerged, enabling researchers to investigate what programs were most effective under what conditions. Certainly, our boldest experiment, Head Start and its related programs—Parent and Child Centers, Home Start, Health Start, Project Developmental Continuity—were subjected to rigorous analyses over the decades. In fact, the abundant experimentation and reconceptualization led Zigler to entitle his chapter in a definitive volume on Head Start "Head Start: Not a Program but an Evolving

Concept."[35] Besides experimenting with alternative program models, the nation supported a massive early childhood curriculum experiment, Planned Variation. The study was a large-scale attempt (involving 2,000 children in twenty-eight sites) to compare the effects of eleven curricular models.[36] All these efforts gave the field the opportunity to grow and to define and redefine itself through experimentation, a positive legacy of the program model strategy.

Further, we can not overlook the positive impact that such programs have had on those involved. While researchers garnered data to help the nation to craft policies, countless children and families were well served. Head Start alone has served 10,943,800 youngsters since the program's inception in 1965,[37] and experimental non-Head Start programs in large states like New York, California, and Texas boost that number significantly.

On the other hand, the program models approach has not lived up to all its glorious expectations. Program models, by definition, were designed to serve as a plan, an exemplar from which other efforts would flow. The inherent assumption of the "models" approach was that what worked well in one locale would work equally well in another. But the difficulties associated with transporting even effective programs from one locale to another soon became apparent.[38] Not only were problems encountered because different settings had their own unique cultures, but numerous challenges emerged as programs attempted to move from small to large scale. Golden points out that not the least of these include: accommodating differences in accountability and equity; maintaining consistency with the larger regulatory and financing systems; and dealing with the risk associated with dramatic and visible failure.[39] Similar concerns have been raised when consideration is given to using small community-based and often homogeneous models as the basis for large-system reform.[40] Perhaps the lessons have been best summed up by Edward Meade, former chief program officer for the Education and Culture Program of the Ford Foundation, who spearheaded many of this nation's most innovative educational efforts. In recalling the history of federal involvement in education, Meade said, "Don't think lighthouse programs travel. They don't. And they don't shed much light either!"

Beyond transportability, institutionalizing program models even in their own settings has been a challenge. Always seen as something special, the programs grow up apart from the mainstream and often are not fully incorporated into the life of the institution. Program staff, socialized into the doctrine of the model, retain a commitment to it, but not necessarily to the overarching goals of the host institution. In fact, the intent of the model program is typically to redress some deficiency in the host setting; hence commitment to the host setting often contradicts the mission of the model.

In addition to the psychosocial dimensions of institutionalization described elsewhere,[41] practical inhibitors plague the process. Often program models do not command consistent and sufficient funding to enable them to reach their full potency. Always worried about garnering the next dollar, those implementing the special efforts expend considerable time and energy sustaining rather than improving or disseminating information about their efforts. Unless buttressed by full financial or ideological commitments, most program models, by their very nature, remain limited in impact.

Learning from the difficulties associated with transporting and institutionalizing models, program planners have suggested several strategies. Converting model "adoption" to "adaption" has yielded some success. Rather than simply adopting the pure model as it was developed, potential implementors are encouraged to adapt it to local setting and need. A variant of this strategy suggests that aiming to transport programs or to adapt them is a mistaken approach. Rather, we should launch site-specific models with the goal of extracting operating principles or lessons to be shared. The goal is not to replicate a given pattern or even tailor it slightly, but to discern essential elements and principles and disseminate them.

However worthwhile these approaches appear, they fall short of addressing the real problem, particularly in early care and education. Simply creating another program model, no matter how effective, particularly given that the field already knows how to mount successful programs, is not the most efficacious strategy at present. While the program add-on approach (alternatively called muddling-through) was functional during a period of limited support, now with the ground swell of commitment to young children and families, a more pervasive and durable systemic strategy is in order. Consequently, we need to shift the focus from program development to system reform. We need to focus on making institutions receptive to the program models we have created. In short, we need to understand how to graft such efforts onto extant institutions so that model programs may be preserved. Moving from a programs to a systems strategy takes what we know and attempts to institutionalize it more widely and more permanently.

MOVING FROM A PARTICULARISTIC TO UNIVERSALISTIC VISION

For decades, early care and education has been largely a numbers game. That is, given the large numbers of underserved youngsters, advocates and politicians have focused on increasing the number of slots, or the number of children to be served. In some cases, this meant a watering down of quality, because dollar increases were rarely sufficient to cover both inflation and new slots. In no case, until recently, was anyone concerned with the effects of expansion in all sectors. Each sector operated on its own track, aiming toward what it considered to be a unique destination. But when train schedules and destination were compared, it soon became evident that programs were on the same track, from both ideological and service perspectives. The problem was that no one bothered to consider the whole system and synchronize services.

To stave off competition, to minimize expenditures and to maximize quality, equity, and integrity, strategists during the next decade must move from focusing on supporting any particular program to envisioning a whole system, one that includes profit and nonprofit providers, church and government programs, and one that acknowledges the importance of home-based programs and familial care. In short, we need to move from seeing federal programs in general, or any federal program in particular, as the totality of early care and education. We need to recognize it for what it is: a complex, highly fragile yet integrated system that involves parents at home with their own (and others') children, adults at home with others' children, home-based and center-based programs.

We also need to recognize that family day care and center care and education are expanding. And such expansion demands attention to coordination. Out-of-home providers are beginning to acknowledge the need to connect with one another. They recognize that what affects one sector dramatically influences others, making cooperation all the more necessary. Collaborative councils, interagency teams, or interagency working agreements are being established to foster cross-agency staff training, common planning for siting new programs, and information and resource sharing. Providers are coming to understand that such creative planning can yield innovative use of limited dollars so that more children have programs that better meet their needs and their parents' schedules. Collaborative efforts are helping to alleviate some of the field's tensions and inequities and reduce systemic inefficiencies. Schools are acknowledging their important, but not unique, role as a provider of service. In some communities, Head Start and child care are planning collaboratively for the implementation of the Family Support Act of 1988. Essentially, the by-word is cooperation—looking beyond individual programs or sectors to a more universal and integrated vision, one that affords options for diverse services to flourish.

Such vision is needed not only among programs that provide similar services to comparably aged youngsters but among early care and education programs and the schools. For decades, critics of early intervention have been concerned about the lack of collaboration between preschools, kindergartens, and elementary schools, and the effects of such discontinuity on young children. They have questioned the large investment of dollars in preschool services, given that many children will enter low-quality schools where there will be little continuity and where the advantages of early intervention programs will be diminished, if not quashed. Because it is a legitimate concern, continuity is being addressed by providers through collaborative entities. And with an additional impetus from major professional organizations that are calling for the establishment of primary units[42] and focusing attention on implementing high-quality programs,[43] a more integrated and appropriate array of educational practices should emerge.

Considering services to young children with a more universalistic vision also means integrating services more successfully than we have done in the past.[44] We know that one-dimensional programs are not likely to have the effect of multidimensional programs, and that meeting children's cognitive needs without attending to their social, emotional, physical, and nutritional needs is shortsighted. To help integrate services more effectively, agencies with entirely different goals are cooperating in planning and service delivery. For example, the Jewish Guild for the Blind has screened the vision of preschoolers in New York City. YMCAs and YWCAs are cooperating with schools to plan and implement before- and after-school programs.

But such worthwhile efforts need support, especially given a policy apparatus that discourages cross-agency, cross-system, and cross-disciplinary collaboration. Stringent regulations that prohibit creative and innovative programming must be removed and replaced with incentives for cooperation. Lessons from one sector must be transmitted to other sectors, so that the best of each may be shared. Such restructuring will not be easy; it will cause agencies that traditionally have been competitive to cooperate and those that have delivered one service for decades to change. Incorporating lessons from past change efforts will be essential if we are to alter the paradigm from particularistic to universalistic thinking.

MOVING FROM A SHORT-HAUL VIEW TO A LONG-TERM VISION

Beyond thinking more systemically and universally, we need to alter the zeitgeist to acknowledge that early care and education programs are now a permanent part of the social landscape. Unlike decades past, when such services met the needs of a limited segment of the population, programs for young children are needed by increasing numbers of families. With such varied needs and perspectives, we must alter our thinking; rather than devising one or two short-term add-ons or "quick-fix" programs, we must plan for more diverse and permanent efforts. This means we need to provide options for those who do not elect or need to have their youngsters in care. Opportunities for parenting education, now offered piecemeal throughout the country, should be made available to all families on a voluntary basis. Family leave should be considered an essential policy. Tax credits should be considered as a part of our policy strategy.

Equally important, we must consider the needs of youngsters in care and the needs of the early care and education system, today and tomorrow. We must shore up the infrastructure of early care and education (paralleling the infrastructure of any enduring entity). Long-haul thinking necessitates that we consider the quality of the facilities and transportation that we so often take for granted. It demands that we improve the recruitment and training of individuals entering the profession. Although barely able to keep pace with current turnover, caregiver and teacher preparation institutions must nevertheless plan for expansion in the field. But before asking teacher preparation institutions to invest in training, the field needs to establish competence levels and specify the essential balance of practical and theoretical elements needed at each level. More flexible in-service training and effective mentoring strategies need to be considered and appropriate compensation must be guaranteed.

Anticipating the inevitable and planning for it characterizes moving from short-term to long-haul thinking. But most communities lack integrated data bases that enable them to anticipate future needs for young children and their families. Securing funds and technical assistance to develop local planning capacities is critical to a codified long-haul vision. Engendering the need for comprehensive policy planning and adequate funding across multiple funding streams is necessary. At the national level, mechanisms for planning and funding that transcend agencies must be set in place. And finally, the recognition that children are important not only to their families but to the nation must be accompanied by a concomitant commitment to making appropriate investments in their lives.

Not easy, such calls for systemic, universal, and long-haul visioning demand collaboration. Through the 1980s, we have experienced the emergence of new and promising partnerships, the beginnings of a new ethos that stimulates inclusionary thinking. Next-decade strategies need to build on that footing, recognizing commitments to diverse and qualitatively improved systems of service delivery. Above all, next-decade strategies must be coordinated and weighed on a social scale that balances private rights with public responsibility.

Kierkegaard said, "We live our lives forward, but we understand them backward." From looking backward at the evolution of America's system of early care and education, a fragmented portrait of confusion and acrimony emerges. Let us use the knowledge and opportunities before us to paint a better forward picture, one where excellence, based on quality, equality, and integrity for all children thrives.

FOOTNOTES

1. J. J. Tobin, D. Y. Wu, and D. H. Davidson, *Preschool in Three Cultures: Japan, China, and the United States* (New Haven, CT: Yale University Press, 1989).

2. Sharon L. Kagan, "Early Care and Education: Tackling the Tough Issues," *Phi Delta Kappan* 70, no. 6 (1989): 441-445; Sandra Scarr and Richard A. Weinberg, "The Early Childhood Enterprise: Care and Education of the Young," *American Psychologist* 41, no. 10 (1986): 1140-1146.

3. Children's Defense Fund, *A Call for Action to Make Our Nation Safe for Children* (Washington, DC: Children's Defense Fund, 1988); Ann Rosewater, "Child and Family Trends: Beyond the Numbers," in *Caring for America's Children*, ed. Frank J. Macchiarola and Alan Gartner (New York: Academy of Political Science, 1989).

4. John R. Berrueta-Clement, Lawrence J. Schweinhart, W. Steven Barnett, Ann S. Epstein, and David P. Weikart, "Changed Lives: The Effects of the Perry Preschool Program on Youths through Age 19," *Monographs of the High/Scope Educational Research Foundation*, No. 8 (Ypsilanti, MI: High/Scope Educational Research Foundation, 1984); Irving Lazar, Richard Darlington, Henry Murray, Jacqueline Royce, and Ann Snipper, "Lasting Effects of Early Education: A Report from the Consortium for Longitudinal Studies," *Monographs of the Society for Research in Child Development* 48, Nos. 2-3 (1982): 1-151, Serial No. 195.

5. Sue Bredekamp, ed., *Developmentally Appropriate Practice in Early Childhood Programs Serving Children from Birth through Age 8* (Washington, DC: National Association for the Education of Young Children, 1987).

6. Child Care Action Campaign, *Child Care: The Bottom Line* (New York: Child Care Action Campaign, 1988).

7. Anne Mitchell, Michelle Seligson, and Fern Marx, *Early Childhood Programs and the Public Schools: Between Promise and Practice* (Dover, MA: Auburn House, 1989).

8. Elizabeth Prescott, "Relations between Physical Setting and Adult Child Behavior in Day Care," in *Advances in Early Education and Day Care*, vol. 2, ed. Sally Kilmer (Greenwich, CT: JAI Press, 1981); Peter K. Smith and Kevin J. Connolly, *The Behavioral Ecology of the Preschool* (Cambridge: Cambridge University Press, 1980).

9. Richard Ruopp, Jeffrey Travers, Frederic Glantz, and Craig Coelen, *Children at the Center: Final Report of the National Day Care Study* (Cambridge, MA: Abt Associates, 1979); Alison Clarke-Stewart and Christian P. Gruber, "Day Care Forms and Features," in *Quality Variations in Day Care*, ed. Ricardo C. Ainslie (New York: Praeger, 1984); Carollee Howes, "Caregiver Behavior in Center and Family Day Care," *Journal of Applied Developmental Psychology* 4 (1983): 99-107; Patricia L. Francis and Patricia A. Self, "Imitative Responsiveness of Young Children in Day Care and Home Settings: The Importance of the Child to Caregiver Ratio," *Child Study Journal* 12 (1982): 119-126.

10. Kathleen McCartney, "Effect of Quality Day Care Environment on Children's Language Development," *Developmental Psychology* 20 (1984): 244-260; Kathleen McCartney, Sandra Scarr, Deborah Phillips, Susan Grajek, and Conrad Schwartz, "Environmental Differences among Day Care Centers and Their Effects on Children's Development," in *Day Care: Scientific and Social Policy Issues*, ed. Edward Zigler and Edmund Gordon (Boston: Auburn House, 1982).

11. Merle Karnes, Allan M. Schwedel, and Mark B. Williams, "A Comparison of Five Approaches for Educating Young Children from Low-income Homes," in Consortium for Longitudinal Studies, *As the Twig Is Bent: Lasting Effects of Preschool Programs* (Hillsdale, NJ: Erlbaum, 1983); Lawrence J. Schweinhart, David Weikart, and Mary Larner, "Consequences of Three Preschool Curriculum Models through Age 15," *Early Childhood Research Quarterly* 1 (1986): 15-46; Bredekamp, *Developmentally Appropriate Practice in Early Childhood Programs*.

12. Ellen Galinsky and William H. Hooks, *The New Extended Family: Day Care That Works* (Boston: Houghton Mifflin, 1977); J. Ronald Lally "Syracuse University Longitudinal Study: Parents' and Students' Perceptions of School and Family Life" (Paper presented at the biennial conference of the Society for Research in Child Development, Baltimore, MD, April 1987); Craig Ramey and Ronald Haskins, "The Causes and Treatment of School Failure: Insights from the Carolina Abecedarian Project," in *Psychosocial Influences in Retarded Performance: Strategies for Improving Competence*, ed. Michael J. Begab, H. Carl Haywood, and Howard L. Garber (Baltimore, MD: University Park Press, 1981).

13. Josefa N. Lieberman, *Playfulness: Its Relationship to Imagination and Creativity* (New York: Academic Press, 1977).

14. Kathy Sylva, Jerome S. Bruner, and Paul Genova, "The Role of Play in the Problem Solving of Children 3-5 Years Old," in *Play: Its Role in Development and Evolution*, ed. Jerome Bruner, Alison Jolly, and Kathy Sylva (New York: Basic Books, 1976).

15. Olivia N. Saracho, "Play and Young Children's Learning," in *Today's Kindergartens: Exploring the Knowledge Base*, ed. Bernard Spodek (New York: Teachers College Press, 1986).

16. Eli Saltz, David Dixon, and James Johnson, "Training Disadvantaged Preschoolers on Various Fantasy Activities: Effects on Cognitive Functioning and Impulse Control," *Child Development* 48 (1977): 367-380.

17. Ann K. Levy, Lyn Schaefer, and Pamela Phelps, "Increasing Preschool Effectiveness: Enhancing the Language Abilities of 3- and 4-Year-Old Children through Planned Sociodramatic Play," *Early Childhood Research Quarterly* 1 (1986): 133-140.

18. Kathy Hirsh-Pasek and Jessica Cone, "Hurrying Children: How Does It Affect Their Academic, Social, Creative, and Emotional Development?" (Paper presented at the biennial conference of the Society for Research in Child Development, Kansas City, MO, April 1989).

19. Doris Smith, *California Kindergarten Practices 1986* (Fresno: School of Education and Human Development, California State University, 1987).

20. J. Amos Hatch and Evelyn B. Freeman, "Who's Pushing Whom? Stress and Kindergarten," *Phi Delta Kappan* 70, no. 2 (1988): 145-147.

21. Donna M. Bryant, Richard M. Clifford, and Ellen S. Peisner, *Best Practices for Beginners: Quality Programs for Kindergartners* (Chapel Hill, NC: Frank Porter Graham Child Development Center, 1989).

22. Bruno Bettelheim, as quoted in "For Many Kids, Playtime Isn't Free Time," *Wall Street Journal*, 20 September 1988, p. 41.

23. Samuel J. Meisels, "High-Stakes Testing in Kindergarten," *Educational Leadership* 46 (April 1989): 16-22; Mary Lee Smith and Lorrie A. Shepard, "What Doesn't Work: Explaining Policies of Retention in Early Grades," *Phi Delta Kappan* 69 (October 1987): 129-134.

24. Marcy Whitebook, Carollee Howes, and Deborah Phillips, *National Child Care Staffing Study* (Oakland, CA: Child Care Employee Project, 1989).

25. Berrueta-Clement et al., *Changed Lives.*

26. Child Care Action Campaign, *Child Care: The Bottom Line.*

27. U.S. General Accounting Office, *Early Childhood Education: What Are the Costs of High-Quality Programs?* GAO/HRD-90-43BR (Washington, DC: U.S. General Accounting Office, July 1989).

28. Ellwood P. Cubberley, *Changing Conceptions of American Education* (New York: Educational Mimeographs, 1909).

29. Edmund Gordon, "Assimilation in America: Theory and Reality," *Daedalus* 90 (1961): 263-285.

30. Lawrence Cremin, *The Transformation of the School* (New York: Vintage, 1961).

31. Edmund Gordon and Carol Camp Yeakey, "Social Policy and Schools: The Case for Educational Equity," in *Children, Families, and Government: Perspectives on American Social Policy*, ed. Edward Zigler, Sharon L. Kagan, and Edgar Klugman (New York: Cambridge University Press, 1983).

32. J. R. Nelson, "The Federal Interagency Day Care Requirements," in *Making Policies for Children: A Study of the Federal Process*, ed. Cheryl D. Hayes (Washington, DC: National Academy Press, 1982).

33. Gilbert Y. Steiner, *The Futility of Family Policy* (Washington, DC: Brookings Institution, 1981).

34. Irene F. Goodman and Joanne P. Brady, *The Challenge of Coordination: Head Start's Relationships to State-Funded Preschool Initiatives* (Newton, MA: Educational Development Center, 1988).

35. Edward F. Zigler, "Head Start: Not a Program but an Evolving Concept," in *Project Head Start: A Legacy of the War on Poverty*, ed. Edward F. Zigler and Jeannette Valentine (New York: Free Press, 1979).

36. L. B. Miller, "Development of Curriculum Models in Head Start," in *Project Head Start: A Legacy of the War on Poverty*, ed. Zigler and Valentine.

37. Project Head Start, *Statistical Fact Sheet* (Washington, DC: Project Head Start, January, 1989).

38. John I. Goodlad, *The Dynamics of Educational Change* (New York: McGraw-Hill, 1975); Seymour B. Sarason, *The Culture of the School and the Problem of Change* (Boston: Allyn and Bacon, 1971).

39. Olivia Golden, *Strategies for Large-Scale Program Operations: Avoiding the "Hot-House" Dilemma*, Innovations Working Paper, Program on State and Local Innovations (Cambridge, MA: Kennedy School of Government, Harvard University, 1989).

40. J. L. Evans, "Developing an Early Childhood Care and Development Strategy for the '90s" (Paper presented at the Childhood in the 21st Century Conference, Hong Kong, August, 1989).

41. Louis M. Smith and Pat M. Keith, *Anatomy of Educational Innovation: An Organizational Analysis of an Elementary School* (New York: John Wiley, 1971).

42. National Association of State Boards of Education, *Right from the Start* (Alexandria, VA: National Association of State Boards of Education, 1988).

43. Cynthia Warger, *A Resource Guide to Public School Early Childhood Programs* (Alexandria, VA: Association for Supervision and Curriculum Development, 1988).

44. Robert Slavin, "Students at Risk of School Failure: The Problem and Its Dimensions," in *Effective Programs for Students at Risk*, ed. Robert Slavin, Nancy Karweit, and Nancy Madden (Boston: Allyn and Bacon, 1989).

Name Index

Subject Index

Abcedarian Project (Chapel Hill, NC), 78-79

Ability grouping, as strategy for avoiding developmentally appropriate practice, 4

Accreditation, of early childhood programs, 183-84

Act for Better Child Care Services, 144, 175, 189

Aims of education, concept of, in developmental and psychometric philosophies of education, 8

American Society for Personnel Administration, 1988 survey of, 135, 138

Assimilation, inappropriateness of, as goal of American education, 202

Assessment, contrasting views of, in developmental and psychometric philosophies, 13-14

Bilingual education: controversies over, 34-35; early immersion in English, as alternative to, 35-36; research on, 34-35

Brookline Early Education Project, 75

Brown vs. Board of Education, 201, 245

Capacity building, mechanisms for, to improve early childhood education, 229-30

Carnegie Forum on Education and the Economy, 122

Child and Family Resource Program, 95, 96

Child care: alternate arrangements for (table), 73; categories of, 176; confusion on standards for, 176; corporate involvement in, 134-51; costs of, to parents, 174; licensing of programs for, 177-78; major funded systems of, 177; national costs of, 175; parents' difficulties in securing, 133-34; potential impact of federal government, on quality of, 175; problem of access to, in corporate programs, 149; regulation of programs for, 174-85; Resource and Referral (R & R) programs for counseling parents regarding, 134

Child development: emphasis on, in preparation of early childhood teachers, 119; field of, as specialization for early childhood teachers, 10; principles of, as basis for curricular and pedagogical practices, 52

Child Development and Education Act (1989), 147

Child Development Associate credential: 112, 114-15, 116, 117, 124, 126, 185, 192, 195, 209, 227

Children's Fund, proposal for, to support early childhood education, 233-34

Committee for Economic Development, report of, on children in need, 137, 149, 232

Continuity, in early childhood programs: barriers to, 84-86; efforts to strengthen, 76-83; lack of, 69-70, 73-74

Corporate involvement, in child care: characteristics of companies leading the way in, 135-38; concern for future of, 148-51; efforts to increase, 146-48; expanded interest in, in 1980s, 138, 240; levels of, 138-41; obstacles to, 132-33; phases of development of, 131-41

Curriculum: experimental approach to, in early childhood education, 11-12; local vs. national emphasis in, 11-12; need for revision of, 207; use of principles of child development in planning of, 54-66

Development, ecological model of, 164-65

Day care centers: costs of, 175; economic factors affecting, 174; staff/child ratios in, 174, 187; staff turnover in, 174

Deficit model, for early childhood programs: avoidance of, in Head Start, 157, 159-60; predominance of, 156-57; replacement of, by model emphasizing differences, 157

Dependent Care Tax Credit, 134, 220, 233

Developmental characteristics of children, normative and dynamic dimensions of, 56-60

"Developmental" philosophy of education: concepts of, in contrast to those of

265

INFORMATION ABOUT MEMBERSHIP IN THE SOCIETY

Membership in the National Society for the Study of Education is open to all who desire to receive its publications.

There are two categories of membership, Regular and Comprehensive. The Regular Membership (annual dues in 1991, $25) entitles the member to receive both volumes of the yearbook. The Comprehensive Membership (annual dues in 1991, $45) entitles the member to receive the two-volume yearbook and the two current volumes in the Series on Contemporary Educational Issues. For their first year of membership, full-time graduate students pay reduced dues in 1991 as follows: Regular, $20; Comprehensive, $40.

Membership in the Society is for the calendar year. Dues are payable on or before January 1 of each year.

New members are required to pay an entrance fee of $1, in addition to annual dues for the year in which they join.

Members of the Society include professors, researchers, graduate students, and administrators in colleges and universities; teachers, supervisors, curriculum specialists, and administrators in elementary and secondary schools; and a considerable number of persons not formally connected with educational institutions.

All members participate in the nomination and election of the six-member Board of Directors, which is responsible for managing the affairs of the Society, including the authorization of volumes to appear in the yearbook series. All members whose dues are paid for the current year are eligible for election to the Board of Directors.

Each year the Society arranges for meetings to be held in conjunction with the annual conferences of one or more of the major national educational organizations. All members are urged to attend these sessions. Members are also encouraged to submit proposals for future yearbooks or for volumes in the series on Contemporary Educational Issues.

Further information about the Society may be secured by writing to the Secretary-Treasurer, NSSE, 5835 Kimbark Avenue, Chicago, IL 60637.

RECENT PUBLICATIONS OF THE NATIONAL SOCIETY FOR THE STUDY OF EDUCATION

1. The Yearbooks

Ninetieth Yearbook (1991)
Part 1. *The Care and Education of America's Young Children: Obstacles and Opportunities.* Sharon L. Kagan, editor. Cloth.
Part 2. *Evaluation and Education: At Quarter Century.* Milbrey W. McLaughlin and D. C. Phillips, editors. Cloth.

Eighty-ninth Yearbook (1990)
Part 1. *Textbooks and Schooling in the United States.* David L. Elliott and Arthur Woodward, editors. Cloth.
Part 2. *Educational Leadership and Changing Contexts of Families, Communities, and Schools.* Brad Mitchell and Luvern L. Cunningham, editors. Cloth.

Eighty-eighth Yearbook (1989)
Part 1. *From Socrates to Software: The Teacher as Text and the Text as Teacher.* Philip W. Jackson and Sophie Haroutunian-Gordon, editors. Cloth.
Part 2. *Schooling and Disability.* Douglas Biklen, Dianne Ferguson, and Alison Ford, editors. Cloth.

Eighty-seventh Yearbook (1988)
Part 1. *Critical Issues in Curriculum.* Laurel N. Tanner, editor. Cloth.
Part 2. *Cultural Literacy and the Idea of General Education.* Ian Westbury and Alan C. Purves, editors. Cloth.

Eighty-sixth Yearbook (1987)
Part 1. *The Ecology of School Renewal.* John I. Goodlad, editor. Cloth.
Part 2. *Society as Educator in an Age of Transition.* Kenneth D. Benne and Steven Tozer, editors. Cloth.

Eighty-fifth Yearbook (1986)
Part 1. *Microcomputers and Education.* Jack A. Culbertson and Luvern L. Cunningham, editors. Cloth.
Part 2. *The Teaching of Writing.* Anthony R. Petrosky and David Bartholomae, editors. Paper.

Eighty-fourth Yearbook (1985)
Part 1. *Education in School and Nonschool Settings.* Mario D. Fantini and Robert Sinclair, editors. Cloth.
Part 2. *Learning and Teaching the Ways of Knowing.* Elliot Eisner, editor. Paper.

Eighty-third Yearbook (1984)
Part 1. *Becoming Readers in a Complex Society.* Alan C. Purves and Olive S. Niles, editors. Cloth.
Part 2. *The Humanities in Precollegiate Education.* Benjamin Ladner, editor. Paper.

Eighty-second Yearbook (1983)
Part 1. *Individual Differences and the Common Curriculum.* Gary D Fenstermacher and John I. Goodlad, editors. Paper.

Eighty-first Yearbook (1982)
Part 1. *Policy Making in Education.* Ann Lieberman and Milbrey W. McLaughlin, editors. Cloth.
Part 2. *Education and Work.* Harry F. Silberman, editor. Cloth.

Eightieth Yearbook (1981)
Part 1. *Philosophy and Education.* Jonas P. Soltis, editor. Cloth.
Part 2. *The Social Studies.* Howard D. Mehlinger and O. L. Davis, Jr., editors. Cloth.

Seventy-ninth Yearbook (1980)
Part 1. *Toward Adolescence: The Middle School Years.* Mauritz Johnson, editor. Paper.

Seventy-eighth Yearbook (1979)
Part 1. *The Gifted and the Talented: Their Education and Development.* A. Harry Passow, editor. Paper.
Part 2. *Classroom Management.* Daniel L. Duke, editor. Paper.

Seventy-seventh Yearbook (1978)
Part 1. *The Courts and Education.* Clifford B. Hooker, editor. Cloth.

Seventy-sixth Yearbook (1977)
Part 1. *The Teaching of English.* James R. Squire, editor. Cloth.

The above titles in the Society's Yearbook series may be ordered from the University of Chicago Press, Book Order Department, 11030 Langley Ave., Chicago, IL 60628. For a list of earlier titles in the yearbook series still available, write to the Secretary, NSSE, 5835 Kimbark Ave., Chicago, IL 60637.

272 PUBLICATIONS

2. The Series on Contemporary Educational Issues

The following volumes in the Society's Series on Contemporary Educational Issues may be ordered from the McCutchan Publishing Corporation, P.O. Box 774, Berkeley, CA 94702.

Boyd, William Lowe, and Walberg, Herbert J., editors. *Choice in Education: Potential and Problems.* 1990.

Case, Charles W., and Matthes, William A., editors. *Colleges of Education: Perspectives on Their Future.* 1985.

Eisner, Elliot, and Vallance, Elizabeth, editors. *Conflicting Conceptions of Curriculum.* 1974.

Erickson, Donald A., and Reller, Theodore L., editors. *The Principal in Metropolitan Schools.* 1979.

Farley, Frank H., and Gordon, Neal J., editors. *Psychology and Education: The State of the Union.* 1981.

Fennema, Elizabeth, and Ayer, M. Jane, editors. *Women and Education: Equity or Equality.* 1984.

Griffiths, Daniel E., Stout, Robert T., and Forsyth, Patrick, editors. *Leaders for America's Schools: The Report and Papers of the National Commission on Excellence in Educational Administration.* 1988.

Jackson, Philip W., editor. *Contributing to Educational Change: Perspectives on Research and Practice.* 1988.

Lane, John J., and Walberg, Herbert J., editors. *Effective School Leadership: Policy and Process.* 1987.

Levine, Daniel U., and Havighurst, Robert J., editors. *The Future of Big City Schools: Desegregation Policies and Magnet Alternatives.* 1977.

Lindquist, Mary M., editor. *Selected Issues in Mathematics Education.* 1981.

Murphy, Joseph, editor. *The Educational Reform Movement of the 1980s: Perspectives and Cases.* 1990.

Nucci, Larry P., editor. *Moral Development and Character Education.* 1989.

Peterson, Penelope L., and Walberg, Herbert J., editors. *Research on Teaching: Concepts, Findings, and Implications.* 1979.

Pflaum-Connor, Susanna, editor. *Aspects of Reading Education.* 1978.

Purves, Alan, and Levine, Daniel U., editors. *Educational Policy and International Assessment: Implications of the IEA Assessment of Achievement.* 1975.

Sinclair, Robert L., and Ghory, Ward. *Reaching Marginal Students: A Prime Concern for School Renewal.* 1987.

Spodek, Bernard, and Walberg, Herbert J., editors. *Early Childhood Education: Issues and Insights.* 1977.

Talmage, Harriet, editor. *Systems of Individualized Education.* 1975.

Tomlinson, Tommy M., and Walberg, Herbert J., editors. *Academic Work and Educational Excellence: Raising Student Productivity.* 1986.

Tyler, Ralph W., editor. *From Youth to Constructive Adult Life: The Role of the Public School.* 1978.

Tyler, Ralph W., and Wolf, Richard M., editors. *Crucial Issues in Testing.* 1974.

Walberg, Herbert J., editor. *Educational Environments and Effects: Evaluation, Policy, and Productivity.* 1979.

Walberg, Herbert J., editor. *Improving Educational Standards and Productivity: The Research Basis for Policy.* 1982.

Wang, Margaret C., and Walberg, Herbert J., editors. *Adapting Instruction to Student Differences.* 1985.

Warren, Donald R., editor. *History, Education, and Public Policy: Recovering the American Educational Past.* 1978.

Waxman, Hersholt C., and Walberg, Herbert J., editors. *Effective Teaching: Current Research.* 1991.